Street Signs

American Society of Missiology Monograph Series

The ASM Monograph Series provides a forum for publishing quality dissertations and studies in the field of missiology. Collaborating with Pickwick Publications—a division of Wipf and Stock Publishers of Eugene, Oregon—the American Society of Missiology selects high quality dissertations and other monographic studies that offer research materials in mission studies for scholars, mission and church leaders, and the academic community at large. The ASM seeks scholarly work for publication in the Series that throws light on issues confronting Christian world mission in its cultural, social, historical, biblical, and theological dimensions.

Missiology is an academic field that brings together scholars whose professional training ranges from doctoral-level preparation in areas such as scripture, history and sociology of religions, anthropology, theology, international relations, interreligious interchange, mission history, inculturation, and church law. The American Society of Missiology, which sponsors this series, is an ecumenical body drawing members from Independent and Ecumenical Protestant, Catholic, Orthodox, and other traditions. Members of the ASM are united by their commitment to reflect on and do scholarly work relating to both mission history and the present-day mission of the church. The ASM Monograph Series aims to publish works of exceptional merit on specialized topics, with particular attention given to work by younger scholars, the dissemination and publication of which is difficult under the economic pressures of standard publishing models.

Persons seeking information about the ASM or the guidelines for having their dissertations considered for publication in the ASM Monograph Series should consult the Society's website—www.asmweb.org.

Members of the ASM Monograph Committee who approved this book are:

James R. Krabill, Mennonite Mission
Judith Lingenfelter, retired from Biola University
Roger Schroeder, SVD, Catholic Theological Union

Previously Published in the ASM Monograph Series

David J. Endres, *American Crusade: Catholic Youth in the World Mission Movement from World War l through Vatican ll*

W. Jay Moon, *African Proverbs Reveal Christianity in Culture: A Narrative Portrayal of Builsa Proverbs Contextualizing Christianity in Ghana*

E. Paul Balisky, *Wolaitta Evangelists: A Study of Religious Innovation in Southern Ethiopia, 1937–1975*

Auli Vähäkangas, *Christian Couples Coping with Childlessness: Narratives from Machame, Kilimanjaro*

Street Signs

*Toward a Missional Theology
of Urban Cultural Engagement*

DAVID P. LEONG

American Society of Missiology
Monograph Series

VOL. 12

☞PICKWICK *Publications* · Eugene, Oregon

STREET SIGNS
Toward a Missional Theology of Urban Cultural Engagement

American Society of Missiology Monograph Series 12

Pickwick Publications
An Imprint of Wipf and Stock Publishers
199 W. 8th Ave., Suite 3
Eugene, OR 97401

www.wipfandstock.com

ISBN 13: 978-1-61097-452-3

Cataloguing-in-Publication data:

Leong, David P.

  Street signs : toward a missional theology of urban cultural engagement /
David P. Leong.

  American Society of Missiology Monograph Series 12

  xx + 250 pp. ; 23 cm. Includes bibliographical references and indexes.

  ISBN 13: 978-1-61097-452-3

  1. Christianity and culture. 2. Cities and towns—Religious aspects—Christianity. 3. City churches. 4. City missions. 5. Missions—Theory. I. Title. II. Series.

BV601.8 L5 2012

Manufactured in the U.S.A.

To Chris and Jonas:
You have supported and inspired every step of this journey.

To the urban church:
May this work strengthen and further your mission.

And to the urban community:
May your character cultivate the shalom of the city.

Contents

Conclusion: The Church Engaging the City / 221

Foreword

A s ONE WRITING OR teaching in books or courses that attempt the bringing of theology and city together in the same sentence, over a thirty-year period, my discovery of David Leong has been one of delight and surprise; delight as he engaged so much that was new and far reaching in the literature, but also surprise that he is now a neighbor in the same city so we may continue our collaboration in a classroom that moves around our city for the sake of our students.

Following my own graduation in 1965 from Seattle Pacific University, where David is now a professor, I plunged into Chicago for study and ministry for thirty-five years. As I was entering Chicago, much of Protestant Christendom seemed to be evacuating Chicago and most major cities. Amid the twin revolutions protesting racial injustice, on the one hand, and the Vietnam War on the other, much of my church was engaged in "white flight" and "white fright." The good side of revolution is when it forces one to become informed, and also set priorities. Both happened for me, and I've written out of those years of study for a generation.

Part of my own doctoral experience involved setting up and chairing the Seminary Consortium for Urban Pastoral Education in 1976, beginning with five theological seminaries that came together as partners. We shaped the SCUPE curriculum to be the second year of MDiv programs for Calvin and Western Seminaries in Michigan, Associated Biblical Seminaries in Indiana, Wartburg in Iowa, and Acadia Divinity School in Nova Scotia, Canada. Other seminaries joined us in the second year. All of these schools, including North Park of Chicago and Bethel of Minnesota, came from the second wave of ex-ethnic Americans of European background. Each of those seminaries and their denominations maintained strong legacies and ethnic commitments to their traditions. And, like Trinity and my own MDiv program, all these were traditionally requiring students to take sequences of Hebrew and Greek.

Students came to us with rather strong backgrounds in biblical exegesis, and with tools to match.

That is when I began to use the term "community exegesis" as well, and for perfectly logical reasons when it came to communication. So much of what the theological scholarship some of these evangelical schools feared—and it was reflected in the churches I knew in the Chicago area—was that somehow "urban ministry" was a "social gospel" approach that might be cutting corners on biblical truth. I needed a way to remind people who trusted the tools and disciplines of biblical exegesis that to gain the tools to understand the intersections of the biblical word and the urban world up close, both personally and congregationally, was totally sound and consistent. So many of our evangelical friends had world-class knowledge of first-century cities, and almost no exposure or understanding of the modern industrial cities—the urban worlds of their students. Our task was to bridge this gap.

Shortly thereafter, in 1979, I was asked by the Lausanne Committee for World Evangelization to head the urban track for this international consortium of evangelicals. I began to take that language into the global urban ministry and mission dialogue, and people found it helpful. Billy Graham, John Stott, and others from many Protestant and Evangelical traditions articulated in the Lausanne Covenant of 1974 a balance of biblical proclamation and demonstration of the gospel in word and deed. My task was to help explain this task in an urban world, and where all agree that "mission is to, in and from, all six continents."

Lausanne Movement participants came largely in four quadrants. On the one hand, almost half of the participants came from within church bodies identified with the World Council of Churches around the world, and the other half came from standalone evangelical free churches, or charismatic denominations. And among both of these groups, there seemed to be a good balance between missiologists on the one hand and evangelists on the other. Because I taught both evangelism and missiology (i.e., the study of, and strategy for, the world mission of the church) at the seminary level, I knew full well some of the robust debates between these groups. Evangelists were reapers and intensely practical, often with little appreciation of the culturally nuanced theological discussions.

By contrast, most missiologists I knew had very wide-angle lenses in which to reflect on history, culture, and ministry. They worked often from contextual studies that integrated wide varieties of disciplines. Self consciously, I put myself in this latter group, where no one discipline or perspective controlled the conversation. Missiology needs evangelism to have integrity, and I believe also the reverse to be true, but much of what passed for theological tension in the Lausanne Movement came from these divergent starting points. I recognize in David Leong one who would have joined the missiologists' side in the discussions of world evangelization.

Also obvious to me back in 1980, while I was discovering a "theology of the city" for my own speaking, writing, and teaching, was that an "urban fault line" was developing with those who argued what I call a "missiology for the city." This is a key distinction, and I discovered that in this book David Leong has moved the ball far down the field from where I first began my own studies.

I was beginning to see that cities were what John Calvin would later call a "gift of common grace," because they have caring institutions from water systems, transit systems, health care systems, police and protection systems, justice systems, and even the lowly sewer systems. These benefit all people, and whereas the immediate concerns of churches are the more "saving grace"-oriented urban programs that reach out to people, I was seeing that cities, as gifts to care for peoples from pediatrics to geriatrics, are like sinking ships. More than mercy ministries are required, and more than relational ministries are expected. Some are called to fix that "sinking ship."

Unfortunately, and some say inevitably, corruption to city systems arrives to bend the public services to reward communities that reward the politicians, and punish communities where "peoples of lesser value," i.e., people of color, perhaps, have come into majorities. Services shift in predictable ways. The sins of leaders find their way into public policies and institutions, so the evil is systemic. Evangelicals who were quite good at mercy ministries to wounded persons or families, had less understanding of power politics, and few sensed a biblical mandate to access power or confront power to demand justice.

For me, it led to three years service on a public task force called the "Future of Chicago Planning Committee." There some of us began to reflect on our city as a custodian of 20 percent of the world's surface fresh water, which is the Great Lakes, and ask how Chicago, Cleveland, or other cities can steward God's water system in a world facing ultimate water shortages someday. In my understanding of Paul's Colossian perspective of "Christ above us," Christian leaders will address all the tools possible and what happens is part of urban ministry.

By contrast, many mission friends were anthropologists, or linguists, and many with tribal or single-culture experiences abroad. They focused on people. I began to see the validity of these I identified and called "Philippian" because of their "Christ in me" perspective that one finds from Wesley to Pentecostals. Theirs is the "high-touch faith" for a high-tech culture, but the people focus can limit any appreciation for systemic sin that roots in layers of unjust urban policy formation.

Fortunately in my case, Chicago was the repository of great studies and great schools for all things urban, and I drank deeply at the studies coming from Chicago, Loyola, Northwestern, and Notre Dame. But for three years, while trying to be the pastor of a poor inner-city congregation, I also taught Pentateuch and Prophets at Trinity College, partly to keep my biblical languages alive. I was discovering afresh the corporate solidarity and community studies in ancient Israel from their oppression, migrant and exile days, biblical community studies from H. Wheeler Robinson, H. H. Rowley, and E. F. Moore among others. I was finding parallels to those most urban of Jewish institutions, the synagogue tradition from Babylon and the Septuagint biblical tradition from Alexandria, to the way Israel was defining its own theology of place, and how communities are extensions of persons and families.

I came to appreciate why three-fourths of Holy Scripture, our First or "Old" Testament, provided a missing piece in the evangelical discussions of why our churches could so easily detach and abandon urban places. We had become somewhat gnostic. We had reduced theology from a full and operating Trinitarianism, which left us (and I include me at that point) with a theology of persons and programs, and a purely pragmatic approach to urban places.

Simultaneously, from 1969 to 1977, I was teaching church history at McCormick Seminary and engaging the Orthodox churches from the Middle East to Alaska in serious ways. Going back even before the AD 787 filioque creedal discussions, the Orthodox argued since the missionary theology of Cyril and Methodius that the Holy Spirit is always in a culture before we get there with our gospel of Christ. So we must approach communities to look for those signs of the Spirit, which may or may not be acknowledged, but we begin our work by identifying and naming what God has been doing in that culture or that place.

John McKnight at Northwestern and Mary Nelson from Bethel Lutheran joined us and others in the Chicago dialogue around SCUPE that emerged as ABCD, or Asset-Based Community Development, but my own piece of the discussion, as a pastor and teacher, was that integration I found in some very old biblical and theological wells that were ignored in the two most widely read streams of books in that very yeasty era. From the literature of Black Rage to the reasoned pen of Martin Luther King on the one hand, to the pragmatic church growth theories emerging from Fuller Seminary on the other, I read but struggled with both. By then my two oldest sons were in an inner-city public high school in my neighborhood, and had 63 nations in the student body of some 2200 students. In Chicago, and around the world, I knew cities were more than discussions of black and white conflict, for the largest cities of the world were neither black nor white. The research showing that homogeneous churches grow fastest reminded me that this is also why gangs in my area grow fast also. And, theologically, it suggested that we exit the city and resegregate the church in communities where we can design congregations in the images of pastors.

While I was out on the streets with our local gang, or with the Twelve-Step ministries, or designing worship for migrant members who reminded me of Moses desert pilgrims in ways that kept me rooted, I was discovering some new ancient wells in biblical and historical places. My own mentors, like Bill Webber and the East Harlem Protestant Parish in New York, Gordon Cosby in DC, Bill Leslie of LaSalle Street Church Chicago, Harvey Conn at Westminster, Roger Greenway from Calvin, and David Shepherd and others in London, were speaking and writing before I got to the city. They all contributed richly to my own journey, motivation, and information. Most of us found reasons to meet; some in each other's writings as time went on.

My own role sought to bridge biblical, historical, congregational (with a contextual understanding in the river wards of Chicago) communities silted by the overflow of cultures from the Rhine, Rhone, Po, Danube, historically, and the Mississippi since WWII. As a generalist, I was trying to get my head around very disparate sources of information in order to make sense of it as an urban pastor.

So this perspective, or baggage, is what I brought to my reading of David Leong. He is in the "doing theology" genre in the shadow of a great church in the heart of the most ethnically diverse community of

Seattle, and perhaps the nation. It is a city and community where I had a ministry fifty years ago, and now struggle to re-engage. His dissertation proposal enabled him to probe to great depths theological writings and categories I hardly touched, and the Asian lenses on his American journey enable him to see what I could not, and better that which I could. It is a Pacific Rim world, and Seattle is a Pacific Rim lab for David.

David will remember that as soon as I read his text, I got in touch to see if I could be with his Seattle class, which he graciously approved. There were no courses in urban mission or ministry when I was a student at Seattle Pacific University, but they added them years ago, and now that school has appointed him as a professor of missiology, which I endorsed with enthusiasm.

Ray Bakke
Chancellor and Professor of Global Urban Studies
Bakke Graduate University
Seattle, Washington

Preface

A S AN UNDERGRADUATE STUDENT at the University of Washington in
1996, I attended Chinese Baptist Church on Beacon Hill in south
Seattle. As I gradually became involved in student ministry there, I had
no idea that I would later become fascinated with the neighborhood
and its people. Since that time, I have lived, worked, and worshipped in
southeast Seattle as a resident, citizen, and neighbor. The Rainier Valley,
one of the most ethnically and socioeconomically diverse communities
in the U.S., has become my home and my missiological laboratory, and
the journey has transformed my family, my vocation, and my sense of
God's work in the world. The following reflection is my attempt to honor
the people and places of the Valley, and to invite others into the beauty
that I have discovered in its stories.

In October of 2006, at a special Southeast District Council meeting, tensions were running high as city officials began to explain several
particular redevelopment initiatives as a part of the larger Southeast
Seattle Action Agenda, an "exciting time of growth and renewal for the
Rainier Valley" according to Seattle mayor Greg Nickels. Throughout
the meeting, the large and diverse crowd that had gathered murmured
suspiciously about displacement, gentrification, and a history of the city
making empty promises. Amidst the many local residents and business
owners who had filled every seat in the Rainier Valley Cultural Center, a
lone voice cried out, interrupting the presentation.

"The Valley is for poor people!" she exclaimed. The proclamation
was met with enthusiastic cheers and applause from the crowd, an immediate and vigorous affirmation of her abrupt but honest sentiment.
As I sat quietly in my seat listening to my neighbors, I realized at that
moment that change in the community was not only on the horizon as a
distant possibility; but rather, change had already arrived, and in many
ways, I was a part of this unstoppable tidal wave of development.

According to the lengthy presentation put together by the Southeast District Council, several key demographic indicators characterized the Rainier Valley. Namely, the people living there were 80 percent people of color, 40 percent foreign born, 45 percent spoke a second language, and 50 percent were renters. Afterwards, in what began as an open session of question and answer with the facilitators, an overabundance of heated complaints quickly snowballed into a borderline chaotic gathering of angry residents. Many of the questions focused on the challenge of how to ensure that the proposed changes coming to the neighborhood would benefit the people currently living in the neighborhood, enabling the existing residents to enjoy the "revitalized" community as opposed to being forcibly displaced due to the large and often unrestrained forces of gentrification. These difficult questions existed long before this particular meeting, and they continue to persist in the Rainier Valley today.

Over the years, I have come to genuinely appreciate the Valley's wonderfully diverse community, rich history, and strong sense of neighborhood identity. Though some of its challenges lie in its geographic and cultural isolation, history of discrimination and segregation, and uncertain future, many of its merits have been forged in the furnace of adversity. The Valley's future is intimately connected with the success of southeast Seattle, and ultimately Seattle's larger metropolitan area, which continues to shape the Northwest as a major port city of the Pacific Rim and a regional center for industry, education, and the arts.

The challenge of engaging the density, diversity, and disparity of the Valley is what initially prompted my research on cultural engagement, urban exegesis, and contextual theology. As I began to construct a loose methodology for observing and interpreting the complexities of the built environment of the urban context, I began to recognize that there was a particular universality to the city that was exhibited very uniquely through the street corners and back alleys of my neighborhood. This project is the culmination of that recognition, and my intent is to construct a distinctly interdisciplinary lens for practicing theological reading of the city.

Overall, this dissertation critically examines the cultural and theological significance of the urban context as an exercise in missiological contextualization. Through a dialectical exploration of the locality of Seattle's Rainier Valley and the universality of the street corner, three different lenses are used to examine the intersection of faith and culture in the city. First, through developing a missional theology of cultural engagement, the themes of incarnation, confrontation, and imagination inform a theological posture that is conversant with urbanism. Second, an interdisciplinary method of urban exegesis that synthesizes the symbolic systems of urban semiotics and the missional theology of cultural exegesis is applied to particular settings in Seattle's Rainier Valley as a form of observing and interpreting urban communities. Third, an urban contextual theology that is situated in an environment of physical density, social diversity, and economic disparity emphasizes the necessity of engaging the city with theologies of place, neighbor, and community.

In an effort to equip and empower the church and others to engage the city as thoughtful, missional people, this research seeks to cultivate a combination of critical observational skills in the urban context and a constructive understanding of the holistic Christian mission among the poor and disenfranchised in our urban communities. From the street corner in the ghetto to newly gentrified enclaves of hipsters, "street signs" are all around us; they point us in the right direction toward deeper understanding, alert us to the presence of injustice and suffering among our neighbors, and draw our attention to the redemptive beauty of the city that is revealed in the light of the gospel.

Acknowledgments

A DISSERTATION IS NEVER a solo project, and often the supporting cast plays just as significant a role as the one who is credited with authorship. This research is in many ways a mosaic of perspectives that has been undoubtedly shaped by numerous other voices, and as such I am grateful for the support and partnership of the many people who made this dissertation possible.

To Jude Tiersma Watson, Ryan Bolger, and Chuck Van Engen in the School of Intercultural Studies at Fuller Theological Seminary: thank you for your wisdom and oversight as my doctoral committee. I am also very appreciative of Ray Bakke, Priscilla Pope-Levison, Ron Ruthruff, and Michael Mata, each of whom offered helpful insights at various stages of my research. My colleagues in the School of Theology at Seattle Pacific University and my students also deserve credit for constantly challenging me to think about the integration of theology and praxis throughout this process. Lastly, I am deeply grateful for my family and neighbors in the Rainier Valley as they have shared their lives and stories with me along the way.

Figures

Introduction

A BDI, SAFIA, AND THEIR eight young children are a vibrant, generous family of Somali refugees living in Seattle. They were brought to the city by the refugee resettlement arm of World Relief, a Christian humanitarian relief and development organization. Sponsored by a partnership between the U.S. Office of Refugee Resettlement and the Office of the United Nations High Commissioner for Refugees, their first experience on an airplane was a series of flights that lasted more than twenty hours, and relocated them from an established refugee camp in Kakuma,[1] Kenya—a place they had lived for many years—to urban Seattle, a place as foreign as any they had ever encountered. Exhausted and bewildered as they arrived at the airport in their matching "USRP" (United States Refugee Program) sweatshirts, they could not have conceived of the challenges and adventures they would experience in the days ahead.

Several years later, having largely acclimated to the "American way of life" in the city, the family has learned a lot about the urban context. First, they have embraced the opportunity of education as the best possibility of improving their lives. And even though the public schools in their neighborhood are underserved and low-performing, the children in particular have demonstrated discipline and determination in their studies and language acquisition. They have also naturally adopted many habits and influences of the local urban culture, from the ubiquity of fast food and convenience stores to the music and media saturation of the city.

However, some discoveries along the way have been more difficult to navigate. The family has often struggled financially, facing the

---

1. Kakuma is a town in northwestern Kenya that is home to one of the largest refugee camps in the world. Kakuma Refugee Camp was founded in the early 1990s and hosts more than 75,000 international refugees from various countries throughout eastern Africa. "Kakuma" means "nowhere" in Swahili. For a contemporary perspective on Kakuma, see Simpson, *Horror to Hopelessness*.

harsh realities of economic scarcity in urban areas with a high cost of living. Additionally, they have encountered the ongoing challenges of cultural dislocation. While there are many African Americans in their surrounding neighborhood, relations between African Americans and African immigrants in the community are sometimes strained by ethnic tensions. On top of it all, they have wrestled with maintaining their Muslim faith in the pluralistic context of the city. As the children are learning English and adapting quickly to new surroundings, the cultural gap between their shifting worldview and the traditions of their parents is growing. On weekends, they attend a *madrassa*[2] at the local Somali mosque, but on weekdays they are immersed in the Seattle public school system. All of these cultural intricacies function as both obstacles and opportunities in the urban context.

These kinds of social, economic, political, and religious complexities within the urban context are some of the most prominent cultural realities shaping our global cities today. Cities represent the convergence of identities, industries, and ideologies in a dynamic urban ecosystem of pluralism and globalization. Far more than just the incidental built environment[3] that houses such phenomena, a city is a living, breathing organism with vital systems and infrastructure that function as a means of sustenance for its inhabitants. Ultimately, cities are a cultural reflection of our common humanity in all of its beauty and depravity.

In moving between the macro-geographic analysis of cities and the micro-ethnographic exploration of urban communities, we find that the city, like much of society, is arranged in particular patterns that reflect a larger urban system of cultural hierarchies, social stratification, and economic disparities. Even the most intricate, seemingly insignificant details of neighborhoods are subject to the structure and priorities of this system, and in a world that is marked by pervasive urbanization, we each interact with the particularities of this urban context every day.

---

2. A *madrassa* is a Muslim school for religious education. In Seattle, most *madrassas* are attached to a mosque and their programs offer supplemental Islamic instruction in language-specific programs.

3. The "built environment" is a concept widely used in various fields, from architecture and urban planning to environmental psychology and cognitive geography. Its most basic definition refers to the constructed physical context of human activity and settlement, or more simply, the whole of our human-made surroundings. Its most common usage is usually in reference to issues of design or planning. See McClure and Bartuska, *Built Environment*.

As we navigate the city, from wherever we may choose to live and work to how we engage our neighbors on the sidewalk, the ethical and therefore theological implications within the urban system often elude us.[4] But for those who are disenfranchised from the narratives of meritocracy and upward mobility, the deck often seems stacked against them. If, as Jesus proclaims in Luke's Gospel,[5] it is indeed the poor who are blessed, then it might be more difficult to immediately recognize this claim as truth from a street corner in the ghetto or the margins of an urban squatter settlement.

Understanding the basic components of the urban context is an essential step in the process of cultivating and sustaining the interconnected web of community that God speaks into being in the shalom of creation. Speaking of *shalom*, in the frequently quoted twenty-ninth chapter of Jeremiah, YHWH gives some challenging[6] urban advice to the community of uprooted exiles living in the city of Babylon. For YHWH to insist that settling down and seeking the shalom of Babylon (and by implication, its population of pagan oppressors) would actually secure *the Israelites' own* peace and prosperity flew in the face of conventional wisdom about God's sovereignty and his purpose of Israel's election.

At the very end of the book of Jonah, in a similarly unexpected expression of God's concern for the "great city" of Nineveh, YHWH overturns Jonah's assumptions about what he perceived to be a bastion of Assyrian brutality and evil. Much to his surprise and subsequent disappointment, Jonah's message of divine condemnation on the city's wickedness is actually received with contrition, and the people of Nineveh are shown to be a pious, penitent community from the top down.

In Isaiah 56, as a post-exilic community is returning to the city of Jerusalem in ruins, the prophet casts a vision of the temple as a "house

---

4. This generalization is made under the assertion that many upwardly-mobile people of privilege are simply not trained to see the urban context with its ethical implications in mind. Even those who are intellectually cognizant of something as basic as urban stratification are often socially conditioned into more consumer-driven, value-neutral perceptions of place in the city. This assertion will be qualified further throughout this research.

5. Luke 6:20–49, the "Sermon on the Plain," is an important interlocutor with the Sermon on the Mount in Matt 5–7.

6. Because of the way that language of "God's plan to give a hope and a future" has been co-opted by well-intentioned equivalents of the greeting card industry, the original impact and context of these words has been largely lost.

of prayer for all peoples,"⁷ an urban center of inclusive worship for a
diverse community. But the Second Temple Judaism of Jesus' day had
embraced a more ethnically exclusive position on who was invited into
the worshipping life of Israel, and the gospels describe in great detail the
judgment and condemnation that Jesus delivers in the cleansing of the
temple in Jerusalem.

These brief perspectives from the Prophets serve to illustrate the
plurality of ways that God's economy often dismantles human presuppositions about the city. Israel's vocation through the Abrahamic covenant
to be a channel of blessing to the nations was not to be fulfilled *in spite of*
the perceived paganism or impurity of these cities; quite to the contrary,
the people of God were being called to live into the reality of this vocation *in, through,* and ultimately *for* these cities. The church's mission to
today's cities is often marked by the same urban prejudices that obscured
Israel's ability to see God's great compassion toward those they perceived
as outsiders. Thankfully, YHWH continues to be "gracious and merciful,
slow to anger and abounding in steadfast love."⁸

Rather than seeing those in the urban context as stigmatized "others," victims of their own circumstances, or perpetuators of institutional
dependencies, a missional contextualization of the gospel in the city
reveals both the common humanity of urban dwellers and the complex
intricacy of the urban environment. In other words, a missional theology of urban cultural engagement has the potential to equip the church
with fresh eyes and ears, effective analytical approaches, and contextual
methodological tools for interpreting the city. In the research and reflection that follows, through the street signs that are pointing the way, this
desire to exegete the urban context with the sociocultural and theological rigor that it deserves is a constant consideration.

RESEARCH DESIGN

The purpose, goal, and central research issue of this study are outlined
in this brief summary description. First, the purpose of this study is to
examine the cultural and theological significance of the locality and
universality of the city through the lenses of cultural engagement, ur-

7. Isa 56:7.
8. Ps 145:8.

ban exegesis,[9] and contextual theology. Subsequently, the goal of this research is to develop a *contextual* and *missional* theology of urban cultural engagement, both for Seattle's Rainier Valley in particular and the urban context in general. Therefore, the central research issue is focused on the development of an urban contextual theology through the lens of an urban exegesis of Seattle's Rainier Valley.

Research Questions

The primary research questions are focused on the three lenses that are used to examine the intersection of faith and culture in the city, in both a local and universal context. First, in a broad sense, what is a *missional* theology of cultural engagement? Does missiology in a particular place shape our approach to contextualization, and if so, what are the contours and emphases of such an approach? Second, what is urban exegesis, and how can it be applied in a specific urban setting? How does an urban exegesis of the Rainier Valley inform the process of observing and interpreting urban communities? Third, how can the locality of urban exegesis shape the universality of urban contextual theology? How could an urban contextual theology engage the culture of the city, both locally and universally? These research questions determine the scope and shape of this study as it moves between the locality and universality of the theology and culture conversation.

Methodology

Methodologically, a variety of approaches are employed throughout this research. As in all missiological inquiry, theological reflection is done in conjunction with the social sciences; perspectives from cultural anthropology, urban sociology, and cultural semiotics are consistently referenced.[10] Part 1 builds a contextual foundation for the major themes of urbanism and contextualization, and then part 2 establishes a theological lens that is sustained throughout the remaining chapters. Theological reflection is examined primarily through biblical exegesis, systematic

9. The origin and definition of "urban exegesis" is a point of research and exploration that is examined in detail in chapter 6.

10. Though this initial section on methodology merely outlines some of the research methods in each chapter, the methods themselves will be examined in more depth within the text of those chapters themselves, particularly as parts 3 and 4 address methods in urban exegesis and contextual theology respectively.

theology, and an exploration of historical and contemporary voices that speak to the city, the church, and God's larger mission in the world.

The second and third lenses in parts 3 and 4 then share a similar methodological structure by combining cultural and theological analysis. Cultural analysis is conducted in various ways, from the thick description of cultural semiotics to the interdisciplinary approach of cultural studies.[11] Much of the local urban research is conducted through several qualitative methods, including direct observation of the built environment and participant observation in the community. Once the cultural research is in place, the remaining theological analysis is constructed primarily as contextual theology, which integrates cultural semiotics and theologizing in mission.

Though there is an intentionality in the sequence and structure of the overall methodology, as a whole, most of this research process—much like the ethnographic process of discovery—has also operated as a dialectical[12] conversation in which the exploration and interaction of ideas organically leads the research into an inevitable hermeneutic circle.[13] But the cyclical nature of this research is also progressive[14] as it reforms and refines the cultural and theological propositions that are subject to suspicion. For example, as the complexities of the urban con-

11. Thick description, cultural studies, and semiotics will be examined in detail in the chapter 9.

12. "Dialectical" in this context is not intended as a explicit reference to either classical Socractic dialogical methods or modern Hegelian dialectics. Rather, the term "dialectical conversation" is merely meant to connote the conversational aspects of discourse that inform both sides of the dialogue. For more on Socratic and Hegelian approaches to dialectics, see Kahn, *Plato and the Socratic Dialogue*; and Beiser, *Cambridge Companion to Hegel*.

13. Juan Luis Segundo's "hermeneutic circle" is a cyclical process that moves from social context and ideological suspicion to exegetical suspicion and a new hermeneutic. See Segundo, *Liberation of Theology*, 9. My use of the term here is not a specific reference to the particular forms of "suspicion" that broadly inform the tradition of Latin American liberation theology (though some of its political suspicions of power, hegemony, and oppression are relevant). Rather, it is an indication that the starting point for theology is not merely "tradition" or a text, and can often be difficult to discern. In Segundo's hermeneutic circle, there is a dynamic fluidity and interdependence between the social context and the theological propositions that arise out of the context. In this sense, the stages do not always have clear boundaries, but what does remain salient is that the stages influence one another significantly as the circle progresses.

14. "Progressive" is being used in the sense that the stages of the hermeneutic circle do not merely spiral in repetition; they are also constructive as they progress toward a goal of "mutual critique and affirmation." See Magesa, *Anatomy of Inculturation*, 5.

text reveal the necessity of constructing a model for urban exegesis, an urban exegesis of the Rainier Valley then demonstrates the importance of developing a missional theology of cultural engagement for the city at large.

OVERVIEW

Part 1 explores the initial tensions in *urbanism* and *contextualization* through an examination of Seattle's Rainier Valley and the street Corner as archetypal street signs for the locality and universality of the city. After this foundational perspective on these dimensions of the urban context, I will then situate my research within the framework of the larger dialogue between *faith* and *culture.*

Part 2 examines the Valley and the Corner through the first lens of cultural engagement, or more specifically, a *missional* theology of cultural engagement that is focused on *incarnation* as the missional task, *confrontation* as the prophetic task, and *imagination* as the creative task. This embodied, prophetic, and subversive approach to engaging culture is constructed in conversation with various perspectives from missiology, biblical theology, and cultural studies.

Part 3 examines the Valley and the Corner through the second lens of urban exegesis as an interdisciplinary synthesis of the observational methods of *urban semiotics* and the interpretive methods of *cultural exegesis.* This model is then applied to specific urban contexts in Seattle's Rainier Valley in order to interpret signs of density, diversity, and disparity in this particular urban community. Theologically, this application focuses on the themes of *incarnational place-making, prophetic neighborly justice,* and *imaginative communities of redistribution.*

Part 4 examines the Valley and the Corner through the third and final lens of contextual theology. This process explores methods in cultural analysis and moves more broadly into the universalities of the urban context in order to develop an *urban contextual theology.* The primary urban attributes of *density, diversity,* and *disparity* are examined with semiotic description and subsequently categorized according to physical, social, and economic domains of meaning. Based on this cultural analysis of the city, local theologies of *place, neighboring,* and *community* are constructed in the process of contextualizing faith in the urban context.

The conclusion presents a theological vision of the church engaging the city. Through revisiting the Valley and the Corner one final time as local and universal street signs, cultural engagement, urban exegesis, and contextual theology are held together as important methods for interpreting the city. Lastly, an urban, missional *ecclesiology* is explored as the particular community on which a missional theology of urban cultural engagement ultimately depends.

Part 1

Urbanism and Contextualization

Look what we have built . . . low-income projects that become worse centers of delinquency, vandalism, and general social hopelessness than the slums they were supposed to replace . . . cultural centers that are unable to support a good bookstore. Civic centers that are avoided by everyone but bums, who have fewer choices of loitering place than others. Commercial centers that are lackluster imitations of standardized suburban chain-store shopping. Promenades that go from no place to nowhere and have no promenaders. Expressways that eviscerate great cities. This is not the rebuilding of cities. This is the sacking of cities.

—Jane Jacobs, *The Death and Life of Great American Cities*, 1961

1

Urbanization in Context

FOR MOST OF THE global population, the consequences of living in a world that has undergone significant urbanization, particularly since the middle of the twentieth century,[1] have been both distinctly formative and relatively recent. As a phenomenon arising from the complex confluence of rapid population growth, international development, and mass rural migration to teeming city centers, urbanization has catalyzed enormous social and economic shifts from villages and agriculture to slum tenements and industry. But for many in the long established urban context of the West,[2] the significance of urbanization has not been as acutely felt; rather, it is simply the pragmatic reality of highly developed metropolitan economies, existing urban infrastructure, and a seemingly constant flow of capital in and out of cities that feeds their steady growth. In other words, a rapidly urbanizing world disproportionally affects the two-thirds world, while many in the developed West carry on with business as usual.

1. Numerous reports and organizations have documented the rapid urbanization of our world in recent years. The United Nations in particular has committed considerable resources to this research. See U.N. Population Fund, "State of World Population 2007."

2. The terms "West" and "Western"—though problematic in many ways—will be used to indicate the broad cultural-geographic grouping of North America, Western Europe, Australia, New Zealand, and various places in between theses traditionally "Western" nations. Unfortunately, despite the hegemonic and Western-centric connotation of the terms, I have not come across sufficiently specific functional equivalents, and "the West" is certainly preferred to terms like the "first" or "developed" world. In response to the "non-West" sometimes being called the "majority" or "two-thirds" world, some have suggested "minority" or "one-third" world, but at this point those terms may obscure more than they clarify, and so "the West" remains for now.

For this reason and others, in the Western context, it is important to move beyond the relatively static, physical reality[3] of urbanization to the more dynamic, holistic process of *urbanism*, or the interdisciplinary study of the characteristically urban dimensions of life in cities.[4] Understanding the city as a way of life certainly must take the reality of urbanization into account, but it also must draw on the stories and experiences of people living at the nexus of cities' geopolitical, socioeconomic, and ethnocultural systems, all of which have theological and therefore missiological implications.

Cities have shaped the Christian story from the very beginning of the biblical record, from Jericho and Babylon to Rome and the New Jerusalem, and many places in between. Long before the Apostle Paul's explicitly *missionary* journeys throughout the Mediterranean and Asia Minor, the cities of the ancient Near East had always played a significant role in the *contextualization* of the Christian faith, an essential element in the discipline of missiology.[5] Generally defined as the process by which the Christian faith finds its unique, local expression in a particular cultural setting, contextualization is part and parcel of the task of theology,[6] regardless of the specifics of settlement space. But cities do shape the process and character of contextualization in a uniquely urban way, one that is informed by and therefore congruent with the contours of the city.

The task of contextualizing Christianity in the city has always created both challenges and opportunities, but in a twenty-first-century context of rampant globalization and urbanization (and hence globalism and urbanism), the emerging challenges facing the church in our global cities abroad and at home are increasingly urgent. Particularly in the

3. Although urbanization continues to progress in the Western context, its growth is markedly slower than that of the two-thirds world; some assert that the continued growth of Western cities is only marginally increasing in this post-industrial era where urban expansion has "reached capacity" in many existing areas. As such, urbanization is primarily a function of the built environment, or a "physical reality" as I've mentioned here.

4. This shift in focus from urbanization to urbanism was noted by Harvie Conn, among others, in the early 1990s. See Van Engen and Tiersma, *God So Loves the City*, vi.

5. My assertion is simply that the embodied nature of the Christian faith has always been and will always be an exercise in contextualization; therefore, all theology is expressed missiologically.

6. The history of varied forms of contextualization and different models of contextual theology will be explored in part 4.

urbanism of the North American city, contextualization confronts our own presuppositions and biases about the *density, diversity,* and *disparity*[7] of the urban context. It is one thing to engage the seemingly distant poverty of our world's billion slum dwellers, but to also consider our own complicity in the structural injustices that perpetuate inequalities in our local neighborhoods sometimes hits—quite literally—a little too close to home. Why, after decades of civil rights legislation and seemingly so much progress toward social equality, are our schools, churches, neighborhoods, and cities so often just as socioeconomically segregated now as they have ever been?[8]

THE COLUMBIA CITY NEIGHBORHOOD

Contained in a relatively short, four-block stretch of Rainier Avenue South, right in the heart of Seattle's Rainier Valley, the Columbia City Landmark District is on the National Register of Historic Places. Today, quaint storefronts and turn-of-the-century architecture frame each urban block in a seemingly innocuous restoration of this once dilapidated business district. Yet behind the trendy boutiques and restaurants is a very particular history, one that connotes community pride and successful revitalization for some, but class tensions and deep resentment for others. Whenever a neighborhood changes, there are always people on both sides of the change. Developers, investors, business owners, families, and residents interact in a complex, dynamic process that can shift the socioeconomic trajectory of a community, and sometimes evidence of these changes is inscribed in the physical geography of the built environment.

---

7. These three characteristics of the urban context will be significant interlocutors throughout this research.

8. Naturally, this is a broad, complex claim, but substantial evidence in urban research across the U.S. points to this growing trend. See Sharkey, "Neighborhoods and Black-White Mobility"; and Cashin, *Failures of Integration.* Additionally, for recent national research on racial and economic inequity, see Wessler, "Race and Recession," for localized research on urban resegregation; see Shaw, "Resegregation of Seattle's Schools," for an exploration of residential resegregation; see Benjamin, *Searching for Whitopia;* and for research on segregation in churches see Emerson and Smith, *Divided by Faith,* and Rah, *Next Evangelicalism.* Though integration of these varying kinds of research is difficult, overwhelming evidence points to the large-scale and widespread resegregation of U.S. society, particularly in urban areas.

Angie's Cocktails, a fixture of the "original" Columbia City, is a symbolic tavern of the old neighborhood. Described by some as a classic "dive bar," Angie's has been a favorite watering hole of local clientele for decades, particularly among the African-American community as a business with primarily black customers. With as many surveillance cameras as there are barstools,[9] regulars come to shoot pool and enjoy cheap drinks, but for many newcomers in the neighborhood, a few too many incidents of seedy activity have soiled Angie's reputation in recent years.[10] Polarizing perspectives on the controversial bar have fragmented the community.

In 2000, directly across the street from Angie's, the opening of the Columbia City Ale House signaled the changing demographics of the community. Offering "fine ales and splendid food" according to their full-service menu, the new Ale House catered to a growing population of hipsters and professionals with very different tastes than those of the regulars at Angie's. Noticeably more upscale and attentive to aesthetics, the Ale House predictably attracts a customer base that is mostly white. And as one might naturally expect, the Angie's and Ale House crowds do not mix.

To the casual observer, these two bars, one on the west side of Rainier Avenue and the other on the east, are divided by what would appear to be little more than fifty feet of asphalt and sidewalks. But locals know all too well that the cultural, socioeconomic, and historical distance is much greater. In this particular context, Rainier Avenue signifies an invisible boundary that segregates the gentrifiers of the future from the working class of the past. Both groups are working through these tensions in the present, but they are doing so independent of one another and on either side of Rainier Avenue. And as simply one point of interest among many in the Rainier Valley, one of the more "churched" areas in the city of Seattle,[11] these kinds of boundaries and obstacles pose

9. Lewis, "Angie's Keeps Columbia City's 'Essence.'"

10. Accusations of crack dealing, prostitution, underage drinking, and gang activity have plagued Angie's for years. Recent changes in ownership have made attempts at cleaning up the bar's tarnished image, but the reputation remains. Currently, there is ongoing litigation, with community-based support, to revoke Angie's liquor license. See McNerthney, "City Targets South Seattle Bar."

11. The Rainier Valley has more churches per capita than many other residential regions in the city, many of which are relatively small, ethnic congregations. Common

specific challenges to the process of contextualization in a community marked by the pervasive and entrenched realities of urbanism.

READING THE STREET SIGNS

While taking these complexities of urbanism and contextualization into account, observing and interpreting the city is one of the primary tasks of both urban anthropology and urban missiology. At the intersection of these two disciplines, *urban exegesis* is an interpretive method at the ideological center of this research. Drawing on perspectives from semiotics, sociology, cultural anthropology, and missiology, my definition and application of urban exegesis aims to provide a structured approach to theological interpretation of the urban context.[12] One of the basic principles in urban exegesis, or "reading the city as a text," is breaking down the complex systems of the urban context into smaller units of pseudo-textual analysis, or "cultural texts."[13] These urban cultural texts (or urban "sign objects") are often physical objects in or aspects of the built environment of the city, and exploring the different dimensions of these cultural texts is one of the methods that enables urban exegesis as an analytical tool. Urban cultural texts are fundamentally *street signs* that carry messages and convey meaning in the city.

From the Valley to the Corner

Valleys and street corners are ubiquitous physical objects in the urban context, but as street signs they serve a variety of functions. Though a valley is a larger geographic feature, and a street corner is a much more specific location, both can function as cultural texts that are embedded with layers of meaning. Most importantly, both objects have a representative role to play in this research and each carries a plurality of messages. The Rainier Valley represents the locality of the city; the street corner represents the universality of the city. Understanding the aspects of both types of cultural texts is crucial for the process of reading and interpreting the signs in the urban context.

---

denominations are the Church of God in Christ, Missionary Baptist, Assemblies of God, and various Pentecostal and non-denominational/evangelical.

12. A full discussion of the specifics of urban exegesis will be explored in chapter 6.

13. Or simply "culture texts." Robert Schreiter uses this particular language in his semiotic approach to cultural analysis. See Schreiter, *Constructing Local Theologies*.

Much more than a physical boundary of an intersection, the street corner is a particular place that has long been the subject of both academic inquiry and popular culture. Noted urban ethnographer Elijah Anderson focused much of his early research on the culture of the corner. In his classic book, *A Place on the Corner*, Anderson explored street corners as "important gathering places for people of the 'urban villages' and ghetto areas of the city. Often they are special hangouts for the urban poor and working-class people, serving as more formal social clubs or domestic circles do for the middle and upper classes."[14] Rich with sociological information, the corner has also been an urban symbol in more popular reflections, like *The Corner: A Year in the Life of an Inner-City Neighborhood*, which spawned two successful HBO projects.[15] The literal corner is merely the physical form of what many recognize as a deeply symbolic place in the urban context. Hip-hop artist Common explains the significance of the corner this way:

> The corner, where struggle and greed fight
> We write songs about wrong 'cuz it's hard to see right
> Look to the sky, hoping it will bleed light . . .
> The corner was our magic, our music, our politics
> Fires raised as tribal dances and war cries
> Broke out on different corners
> Power to the people
> Black power
> Black is beautiful . . .
> The corner was our Rock of Gibraltar, our Stonehenge
> Our Taj Mahal, our monument
> Our testimonial to freedom, to peace, and to love
> Down on the corner[16]

Though the corner can be a harsh place, it is a tribute to the gritty realities of urban life. For Common, the very identity of the inner city was forged and defended on the concrete curbs of the street corner.

In geographic terms, a valley is an elongated geological depression, or more generally, a directional low point between surrounding land of a higher elevation. Valleys often receive the runoff of adjacent hills or

14. Anderson, *A Place on the Corner*, 1.

15. The mini-series by the same name (2000) and *The Wire* (2002–2008) both relied heavily on *The Corner* according to series creator David Simon.

16. Lyrics from "The Corner," featuring the Last Poets, from Common's 2005 album, *Be*.

mountains, serving as a natural drainage system for whatever is trickling down from the heights. In some cities, this metaphor carries over in a similar fashion. Urban valleys can function as literal and figurative low points in urban communities; they are frequently bounded by elevated land in proximity to more valuable commodities.[17] Territorial views, closer access to waterfront properties, and residential privacy are all benefits of living higher up. Meanwhile, those in the valley typically deal with whatever is left over. The reality that sewage, storm water, and waste runoff all seek the lowest geographic points for drainage is more than a function of gravity and fluid dynamics; it is also an everyday condition of life for those occupying the space at the bottom. In this regard, a valley and a gutter bear many similarities.

Signs in the Rainier Valley

Running about six miles through southeast Seattle, the Rainier Valley is a community in this tradition of urban valleys that suffers from both neglect and dumping from its surrounding areas. Historically, the Rainier Valley was developed later than other areas of Seattle for a number of reasons. First, its dense forests were outside of the relatively small footprint of the urban core as it existed in the late nineteenth century. Second, because some of the land was under water until the construction of the Lake Washington Ship Canal was completed in the early twentieth century, it simply was not suitable for development. Though early attempts at settlement resulted in the area's annexation into the city of Seattle, the Ship Canal to the north permanently altered the Valley's hopes of becoming a thriving port community. As the redirected waters receded, revealing low-lying swamplands and marshes, settlement continued, but the Valley was never the same.[18]

Early residents in the area were entrepreneurs and immigrants looking for economic opportunities in the new development; but after a relatively short boom fueled by the timber industry, the Valley entered into a slow but long downward spiral of neglect after the 1930s. Wetlands

---

17. Obviously not every geographic valley falls into this category. On a larger scale, some valleys thrive because the land is fertile in contrast to surrounding mountains with rockier terrain. Urban valleys are distinct because they are typically geographic low points within an already settled area, as opposed to a settled area bounded by underdeveloped land, in which case the valley may be thriving in comparison to its surroundings.

18. Speidel, *Sons of the Profits*, 216.

and other unused properties were used for dumping whatever was unwanted, whether marginalized populations, industrial waste, or just garbage. Development continued, but the local population always seemed
to be in transition. Because of the large number of Italian immigrants
in the Valley, the area was nicknamed the "Garlic Gulch," but the white
flight of the 1960s and 70s saw the community change dramatically with
a large influx of African Americans. The next wave came in the form
of families and refugees of Southeast Asian and East African descent,
many of whom are well established in the community today.[19] What
each group held in common was the urban reality of being surrounded
by neighborhoods that were higher in elevation and usually even higher
on the social ladder. Over time, the Valley became the default drainage
ditch of southeast Seattle.

The government-subsidized public housing projects built in the
Rainier Valley just after World War II solidified the Valley's reputation
as a low-income community, and many similar organizations and services followed. This momentum has been largely carried through to the
present as refugee resettlement agencies, transitional housing, and various social and health services serve a large population of the working
poor, many of whom are foreign born and people of color. Lower rates of
home ownership combined with lower overall property values perpetuate problems in the public school system, a situation that is complicated
further still by a systemic lack of healthy family support structures. As
with many urban communities that face similar challenges, these characteristics have significant consequences for children and youth. Poverty
undercuts educational achievement, gang violence fragments families,
and large pockets of the Valley's younger population are "at-risk" of repeating this damaging cycle.

However, this portrayal of the Valley as a dumping ground is not
the whole picture; thankfully, hard times have produced many positive
elements in the community as well. Resilient and deeply rooted, longtime residents of Rainier Valley take pride in the vast cultural, ethnic,
and socioeconomic diversity present in the neighborhoods. As a community with a strong identity and social conscience, many have worked
hard to preserve the rich history of the area and cultivate a community
of inclusion that values its multicultural heritage. Despite many ongoing
historic problems, a high level of social capital has made the Valley an

19. Woodward, *Rainier Valley Food Stories Cookbook*, 27.

organized community, though this has not necessarily translated into tangible political capital. Nevertheless, the Valley has also undergone a significant amount of redevelopment in recent years, and though there have been costs along with the widespread gentrification, high levels of diversity and community involvement remain.

This brief overview of the Valley is intended to serve as a basic, foundational context for the research that follows. Throughout this study, the Valley has been an ethnographic field site, a laboratory for urban exegesis, and a backdrop for theological reflection. And though the Valley is a specific locale with a very particular history, the universality of the Valley's characteristics also has wider applicability in a variety of different urban contexts.

SIGNS ON THE CORNER

If the street corner is a crucial place in shaping urban identity, then the corner store is a particular cultural text in the built environment that further accentuates the full dimensionality of the corner. As a reflection of the neighborhood, a corner store often embodies the social, economic, and cultural realities of the surrounding community. Typically categorized as a convenience store or "mini-mart," the urban corner store is both a market and a social hub, but its significance in the urban context is much greater than its transactional value as a vendor of goods and services.

In the process of interpreting the city, the corner store represents a fixture of the urban context which conveys meaning that is more than the sum of its parts. As a cultural text, it is a vehicle for denotation and connotation, loaded with intertwined and encoded messages.[20] Decoding this meaning, prior to the theological reflection that distinguishes urban exegesis from mere urban interpretation, is a process that utilizes sociological, anthropological, and semiotic perspectives. Before an observer can engage in thinking theologically about the city, a contextual understanding of these urban complexities must guide and inform the theological process.

Just a few blocks north of the Rainier Valley, Parnell's Mini Mart is a convenience store that sits on the northwest corner of Twenty-Third Avenue and Dearborn Street in the Central District, a historically black

---

20. Denotation and connotation are semiotic categories for how signs function in a coded text. Urban semiotics will be explored in detail in chapter six.

neighborhood.[21] This intersection has many characteristics that are fairly typical of the urban context in Seattle, aspects that distinguish Seattle's "urban" neighborhoods from the traditional "inner-city" blocks that have been likened to "concrete jungles."[22] On the surface, the street is well-maintained and the surrounding buildings are in decent condition. Facing north on 23rd Avenue, the open green space of Judkins Park[23] is visible on the east and the downtown Seattle skyline peaks over the tree line on the horizon. Though the worn, faded white paint is peeling off the siding, and black wrought iron bars on the windows of Parnell's are suggestive of urban blight, the overall physical structure does not appear to be anything out of the ordinary. But appearances do not tell the whole story; below the surface, the history and controversy surrounding Parnell's is as rich and personal as the story of the neighborhood itself.

Parnell was a local police officer who opened the corner store as a service to the neighborhood, and though he later sold the business the established name stuck through the transition. Over the years, as the Central District has struggled with cycles of crime along the 23rd Avenue corridor, Parnell's has been a point of interest for local community organizations, concerned neighbors, and law enforcement officials alike. From protesting about the pay phone in Parnell's parking lot to lobbying the city for restrictions on Parnell's liquor license, some neighbors view the corner store as a trouble spot in the community. Richard Wells, a twenty-year resident of Judkins Park, describes Parnell's from this perspective:

> Parnell's meets all the requirements of a neighborhood gathering spot: non-resident owners, non-resident operators, a large, asphalt parking lot for easy access, cluttered windows, bars on the

21. Until the widespread gentrification of the 1990s and early 2000s, the Central District was the only residential neighborhood in a five-state region with a majority black population. Though many have left in recent years, a fairly sizable (~35–40 percent) African American (and increasingly, African immigrant) population remains.

22. Seattle has no "inner city" in the traditional sense. The term "inner city" developed in the Chicago School of Urban Sociology because the slums and ghettos of the industrial cities on the East Coast and in the Midwest (New York, Detroit, Chicago, etc.) tended to be near the urban core. As an emerging or post-industrial city, Seattle's urban neighborhoods are distributed throughout the city, but also tend to cluster along the southeast (and increasingly, southwest) corridor.

23. Judkins Park is both a specific park in the Central District and also the name of a smaller neighborhood within the southern region of the Central Area, sometimes referred to as the Colman Neighborhood.

doors, and a conveniently located pay-phone for entrepreneurs who have yet to get their first cell phones. And Parnell's offers a wide range of products for the discriminating consumer: cigarettes, alcohol, super-sized t-shirts, candy, deep-fry, newspapers, and even milk. But it's not the interior (dark and a little dingy), nor the variety that attracts shoppers from all over Seattle, but the truly awesome deals on "non-prescription drugs," and "crack-ho-hookups" available in the parking lot. Now Parnell's is not one stop shopping: deals are made in the parking lot, but the goods are collected a half-a-block up 23rd. Slightly inconvenient (for a convenience store), but not as inconvenient as, say, a bullet to the head. I would recommend Parnell's Parking Lot to anyone with the courage to live the neighborhood high-life, and even more to the point, for its hassle free shopping—the police won't bother you—maybe they just don't care.[24]

Wells' portrayal of Parnell's, though polemical in its rhetoric, is largely shared by many residents and members of the Colman Neighborhood Association of Judkins Park, a group of active citizens in the immediate neighborhood.

However, on the other side of the fence, Parnell's also has its local advocates. When community support threatened removal of the infamous parking lot pay phone, the American Civil Liberties Union of Washington State got involved and fought for its necessity. Arguing that the pay phone supported local entrepreneurs without access to other means of communication, the ACLU sided with neighbors who felt that losing the pay phone would impact the community negatively.[25] Also, despite criticism and a questionable reputation among some, many argue that the steady flow of customers at Parnell's indicates that the business is meeting real economic needs. Given Parnell's long and colorful history in the neighborhood, still others have suggested its eligibility for landmark status, a recognition that would place the locally famous corner store on the National Register of Historic Places. Though this designation is unlikely to occur for a number of different reasons, the significance of Parnell's is clear: as a corner store, its cultural and historical meaning far exceeds its face value.

24. Wells, "Parnells Mini-Mart."

25. According to *Central District News* contributor "Falcon," a thirty-year resident of the Central District.

In a broad sense, while not every corner store in the urban context carries the depth of meaning contained in Parnell's unique history,
for the purposes of this research, the corner store is representative of
the reality that certain aspects of the built environment in the city can
communicate complex meaning in a way that requires an interpretive
framework beyond simple, surface-level analysis. The corner store is not
merely a generic physical space where financial transactions of convenience occur; rather, it is a *particular* place, bounded by particular stories and people, shaped by particular societal influences, and reflective
of particular cultural, economic, and theological implications. Thus the
corner store is a universal symbol of the multilayered meaning inherent
in the urban context, a complexity often shared by the grocery store,
night club, café, pub, park, community center, apartment building, and
homeless shelter.

Therefore, to move rhetorically from the Valley to the Corner, as
this research aims to do, is to move from the local particularity of the
Rainier Valley to the universality of the Corner in every urban context,
but in a way that allows for a dialectical fluidity between the locality and
universality of the city. Understanding urbanization in context requires
this sort of dialogical reflection if we are to grasp both the complexities
of contemporary urbanism and the challenges of theological contextualization therein.

2

Faith and Culture

SITUATED AT THE INTERSECTION of theology and culture, this research
aims to flesh out the particularities of contextualization in urban settings. Theologizing about faith and culture is certainly nothing new, nor
is the process of engaging in such reflection for the city. Thus, in order to
locate and distinguish the specific contours of urban contextualization
that inform this study, it is important to frame this process within the
broader faith and culture conversation that has been ongoing for quite
some time.

From the earliest record of the Christian faith, the question of how
to rightly interpret and practice religious belief in societal context has
been an ever-present concern.[1] Partly because an inherent limitation in
what it means to be human is to be bound[2] within culture, this question
is in many ways unavoidable. But in the wake of the post-Enlightenment
rationalism that characterized the modern era and the formal study of
"culture" as a disciplinary inquiry of academia, the question of faith and
culture began to take a particular shape.[3]

1. At this preliminary stage, it is hopefully understood as unnecessary to launch
into a full discussion of all the ways this assertion is true. From God's calling of "a
people" in Israel, to the first-century, Second Temple Judaism of Jesus of Nazareth, to
the Hellenistic culture of the Apostle Paul's context and beyond, both Scripture and
history bear witness to the essentially "contextual" nature of Christian theology.

2. Or more specifically, according to many cultural anthropologists and sociologists, epistemologically constrained by ethnocentric, naive realism and the "socially
constructed reality" of our enculturation. See Kraft, *Christianity in Culture*; and Berger
and Luckmann, *Social Construction of Reality*.

3. My rationale for skipping over the "premodern" discussion of faith and culture
is that I am trying to distinguish the reflection of the church fathers, monastics, and
reformers that was inherently about faith and culture from the explicit construction of
"culture" as understood in the modern era by the development of sociology, anthropol-

Countless works have been written to address the challenges of Christian living "in, but not of"[4] the world. In the modern era, many credit Richard Niebuhr's classic *Christ and Culture* with inaugurating a new genre of theological discourse about "the double wrestle of the church with its Lord and with the cultural society with which it lives in symbiosis."[5] As a theologian and Christian ethicist, Niebuhr in *Christ and Culture* presented a framework of five typologies that characterized a spectrum of theological interaction with culture, ranging from separatism and rejection to syncretism and transformation. In each typology—Christ against culture, Christ of culture, Christ above culture, Christ and culture in paradox, and Christ the transformer of culture—Niebuhr identifies both his affirmations and objections regarding these different motifs that inform the church's posture toward the world. And while many praise his work and still hold *Christ and Culture* in high regard, much has been written since Niebuhr that has broadened and deepened the faith and culture conversation.[6]

FORMATIVE PERSPECTIVES

Though more categories could be added to classify a broader diversity of perspectives in the field, for the sake of simplicity I will focus on two basic approaches to identifying the influential factors that have shaped the variety of perspectives on faith and culture. First, there are those who have written about faith and culture primarily from a particular theological or denominational tradition, and second, those who have approached faith and culture from a distinctive disciplinary perspective. Naturally, these categories connect and overlap in a number of works that are marked as much by an individual's faith tradition as they are by an author's area of academic or vocational expertise. Nevertheless, the construct serves the functional purpose of identifying and grouping the

---

ogy, and related disciplines. Surely Tertullian, Saint Augustine, Thomas Aquinas, and Martin Luther were theologizing about cultural realities in dialogue their contemporaries, but they were not, in the "modern" sense, working under the same assumptions and definitions in the "faith and culture" dialogue today.

4. John 17.

5. Niebuhr, *Christ and Culture*, xi.

6. The following section will flesh out the particularities of this claim through an overview of different types of methodological approaches in what I am loosely categorizing as the "faith and culture genre."

formative aspects of many of the modern, foundational works in faith and culture.

Tradition-Oriented Approaches

For the first category, many have approached the faith and culture dialogue from the viewpoint of their respective faith traditions. Evangelicals, for example, have long sought to distinguish themselves from their counterparts in the mainline church. As an attempt to establish a periodical that would create a unique cultural space for evangelicals in America, in 1956, evangelist Billy Graham and theologian Carl F. H. Henry founded *Christianity Today*, an evangelical magazine that provided an alternative to the mainline Protestantism characterized by publications like *The Christian Century*. Graham had hoped that *Christianity Today* would "plant the evangelical flag in the middle of the road, taking the conservative theological position but a definite liberal approach to social problems. It would combine the best in liberalism and the best in fundamentalism without compromising theologically."[7]

For Graham and Henry, the essential cultural issue that defined evangelicalism was finding a *via media* between the conservative, anti-intellectualism of fundamentalism and the more liberal, academic positions of the mainline church. Henry's desire to cultivate this middle ground, particularly through his scholarship and his work in establishing both the National Association of Evangelicals and Fuller Theological Seminary in the 1940s, left an indelible mark on the development of evangelicalism in America and its mode of engagement with the broader culture.

Another perspective on faith and culture that is definitively shaped by a particular Christian tradition is that of the Mennonite theologian John Howard Yoder. Though Yoder is most often recognized for his contribution to Christian ethics in works like *The Politics of Jesus*, as theologian Paul Tillich reminds us, the moral philosophy of Christian ethics and "theology of culture"[8] are always closely related.[9] Yoder's claim that

7. Marsden, *Reforming Fundamentalism*, 158.

8. Tillich and Kimball, *Theology of Culture*.

9. Twentieth-century Christian ethicists like Reinhold and Richard Niebuhr and Dietrich Bonhoeffer were never theologizing in a vacuum; quite to the contrary, their moral and philosophical inquiries always reflected the tensions and ethical implications of the social, political, cultural issues in their contemporary context.

"Jesus is, according to the biblical witness, a model of radical political action"[10] goes hand in hand with his Anabaptist heritage and its commitment to Christian pacifism and nonviolent resistance in a culture of "just wars."

It is precisely this emphasis on the ethics of peacemaking and social justice that infuses the work of Stanley Hauerwas, whose popular book *Resident Aliens* presents a vision of the church as a "Christian colony," or "an island of one culture in the middle of another."[11] Positioned as a perspective that would help to redefine the church's identity in an increasingly postmodern and post-Christendom culture, Hauerwas and Willimon consistently draw on Yoder's wisdom and Mennonite tradition in their call for the church to radically re-envision its place in and posture toward the world.[12]

Discipline-Oriented Approaches

Though all the perspectives on faith and culture do inherently incorporate elements of their respective theological traditions to some degree, the second category is marked not primarily by a denominational identifier or historical affiliation, but instead by the terminology and definitions of a particular academic discipline or vocational expertise. Where this distinction holds the most significance is in its discussion of "culture."

For Niebuhr, Henry, Yoder, and many others writing primarily in and for a Western context, *culture* is used almost synonymously with *society* or *civilization*. The ideas are virtually interchangeable because culture is meant to signify and encapsulate the breadth of particular societal phenomena in the West, from war and politics to economics and the arts. At times broad and abstract, culture in this sense is "the world" in which theology navigates between secularism, *Zeitgeist*, and tradition. But for anthropologists and missionaries working in cross-cultural contexts, "culture" often means something else entirely. Rather than speaking implicitly about faith and culture as theology "in, but not of" the world, cultural anthropologists and missiologists have estab-

10. Yoder, *Politics of Jesus*, 2.

11. Hauerwas and Willimon, *Resident Aliens*, 12.

12. For other tradition-oriented perspectives on faith and culture, see (in no particular order) Clapp, *Peculiar People*; Henry et al., *God and Culture*; Schaeffer, *How Should We Then Live?*; and Eliot, *Christianity and Culture*.

lished numerous explicit, systematic descriptions of culture that draw
on the social sciences and other academic disciplines that explore the
complex dynamics of interaction between different human cultures.
Thus, this second category of perspectives on faith and culture is heavily
influenced by the language and research methods of diverse disciplines
that engage in the wide range of cultural studies.[13]

The work of Charles H. Kraft, a Christian anthropologist with extensive cross-cultural experience, represents the significant contribution
that cultural anthropology has made to the faith and culture conversation, both in the west and globally. Kraft's *Christianity in Culture* develops an "anthropologically informed theology" that recognizes that "we
are culture-bound in our understandings and interpretations of God's
truth. Our understanding of the relationship of culture to hermeneutics
is therefore crucial."[14] Like many other Christian anthropologists and
missionaries, Kraft's experience of communicating theology cross-culturally made him keenly aware of the tacit cultural baggage that often
accompanies intercultural expressions of theological propositions, from
the forms and practices of liturgy to the nature of the gospel itself. While
Western perspectives frequently posit faith and culture as separate entities that must be reconciled, anthropologists like Kraft are often remind-
ing us that they must be held together.[15]

In a similar fashion, the life and scholarship of Bishop Lesslie
Newbigin was marked by his experiences as a career missionary in India.
In addition to his ministry as an ordained Presbyterian missionary of the
Church of Scotland, Newbigin pioneered new ecumenical partnerships
through the Church of South India and the World Council of Churches.
However, it was not until Newbigin "retired" from the mission field and
returned home to the United Kingdom that his work as a missiologist
began to catch the attention of theologians thinking critically about the
intersection of the gospel and culture.

13. Cultural studies is an increasingly broad and diverse academic field that draws
on perspectives from sociology, anthropology, political science, linguistics, philosophy,
literary theory, and so on. It often directs this interdisciplinary research toward contemporary issues of gender, ethnicity, social class, sexuality, and political ideology. See
Hoggart, *Contemporary Cultural Studies*.

14. Kraft, *Christianity in Culture*, 116.

15. For other anthropological perspectives on faith and culture, see Hiebert,
Anthropological Reflections; Kraft, *Anthropology for Christian Witness*; Lingenfelter,
Transforming Culture; and Mayers, *Christianity Confronts Culture*.

While he taught missiology as a lecturer at Selly Oak Colleges and pastored a small congregation in "a typical inner-city area"[16] of urban Birmingham, Newbigin became increasingly convinced that the most urgent emerging mission field of the twentieth century was the vast array of peoples and places shaped primarily by "modern Western culture," a culture that Newbigin deemed the most globally pervasive and resistant to the gospel. Somewhat ironically, it was Newbigin's lifelong experience overseas that fueled his scathing insights into the plurality of ways that Christianity had been largely domesticated and co-opted by Western ideologies.

By the early 1980s, Newbigin's work in seeking a genuine missionary encounter between the gospel and Western culture had already planted the seeds for The Gospel and Our Culture Network, a collaborative project begun in the 1990s that traces its origins to the kinds of questions raised in Newbigin's *The Other Side of 1984*, a short book that challenged churches to think missiologically about their interaction with modern culture. Today, The Gospel and Our Culture Network is continuing to carry on this task among scholars and practitioners for academic research and congregational ministry around issues of faith and culture in the West.

Hybrid Approaches

Bridging these two large categories of tradition-oriented and discipline-oriented approaches to the faith and culture dialogue is the work of Robert Schreiter, a Roman Catholic theologian with expertise in global theologies, inculturation, and the world mission of the church. As a professor who also served as dean of the Catholic Theological Union in Chicago, Schreiter is thoroughly committed to the spirit of the Second Vatican Council and the development of Catholic missiology.[17]

However, he is also firmly rooted in an interdisciplinary approach to understanding contextual theology. Schreiter's *Constructing Local Theologies* "is as interdisciplinary as single writer is able to muster . . .

---

16. Newbigin, *Foolishness to the Greeks*, 1.

17. Another important Roman Catholic missiologist who serves as a primary interlocutor in much of Schreiter's work is Louis J. Luzbetak. See Luzbetak, *Church and Cultures*. Many additional missiologists could be cited under this heading of "hybrid approaches," but for the sake of maintaining the particular scope of this preliminary chapter, I have chosen not to interact with any additional perspectives at this time.

the social sciences play the principal role of dialogue partner with the theology being shaped."[18] In a broad sense, Schreiter's work is representative of the foundational research that grew into Orbis Books' Faith and Culture Series, a corpus that explores contextual theologies around the world today as local and global perspectives continue to converge in an age of "glocalization."[19]

HEADING TOWARD THE CITY

Each of these varied perspectives on faith and culture makes a unique contribution the contours of the field, and while much has changed since Niebuhr's seminal *Christ and Culture*, much also remains the same. As the cultural shifts of the twenty-first century continue to present the church with challenges, the study of faith and culture persists. And though the ground has certainly shifted under the massive pressures of forces like widespread globalization and urbanization, Niebuhr's essential questions about the spectrum of contextualization remain.

In *Making the Best of It: Following Christ in the Real World*, theologian John G. Stackhouse returns to Niebuhr's classic typologies as an important starting point for understanding a theology of culture, or more simply, what it means "to be Christian in the world." Stackhouse reflects on Dietrich Bonhoeffer's classic theological question, "Who is Jesus Christ, for us, today?"[20] And in response, he turns the question around under the assertion that the anthropological question naturally follows. The primary ethical question is therefore: "Who are we, for Jesus Christ, today?"[21] This "simple" inquiry proves to be a deceptively complex question. Further, if this ethical inquiry is contextualized for the city, surely one of the most influential cultural settings of our day, the question ultimately becomes: "Who are we, for Jesus Christ, in the urban context, today?"

Contrary to popular Western notions of the city being an incidental reality of geography and infrastructure, one of the primary assertions of this research is that the urban context is a vital front of the emerging faith and culture conversation on the near horizon. Today's global cities

---

18. Schreiter, *Constructing Local Theologies*, xii.

19. The localization of global realities in the onset of globalization.

20. Bonhoeffer et al., *Testament to Freedom*, 375.

21. Stackhouse, *Making the Best of It*.

are at the center of our common future, shaping both the destinies of nations and the everyday fabric of our societies. If the church is to have a stake in this future, then the contextualization of the gospel in the city must engage the density, diversity, and disparity of the urban context with an effective, holistic witness to the transformative encounter that true contextualization brings.

However, prior to actual engagement with the complexities of the city, it is important to examine what sort of theology informs our cultural engagement more broadly. Given the variety of approaches to faith and culture briefly explored here, how does a theological perspective of God's larger mission in the world shape the ideology of "engaging culture"? Or more specifically, what exactly is a *missional theology of cultural engagement*? Answering this question is the task of part 2, and though its approach does not initially address the specifics of the urban context at this preliminary juncture, the subtext is conscientiously aware of the issues of urbanism and contextualization imminently on the horizon.

PART TWO

A Missional Theology
of Cultural Engagement

IN THE LARGER FRAMEWORK of this research context, constructing a missional theology of cultural engagement is a foundational element of understanding how the urban context provides a unique seedbed for a particular type of contextualization. From the soil of the city, a theology of culture grows with deep urban roots, and this culture has to be engaged in particular ways. My intent in part 2 is to develop a theology of cultural engagement that draws on the large body of aforementioned work, but does so in a way that is uniquely positioned for deployment in the urban context.

One of the primary descriptors of this theology of cultural engagement is its fundamentally *missional* character, an aspect that sends the entire construction on a particular trajectory. With these considerations in mind, how does a missional theology of cultural engagement sit in congruence or dissonance with the perspectives offered in tradition or discipline-oriented approaches to the faith and culture dialogue? My interdisciplinary approach draws on the strengths of a diversity of perspectives, ranging from missiologists and Christian ethicists to theologians and biblical scholars, and also engages the contemporary context as an important interlocutor. Overall, this approach seeks to construct a *distinctly missional*[1] theology that emphasizes the essentially radical nature of engaging with culture, or in other words, a *missional engagement* that goes beyond the merely "contextual" nature of engagement as it is traditionally used.

---

1. My definition of "missional" has two primary layers of meaning. On one level, I am initially interacting with missional in the way that The Gospel and Our Culture Network uses the term. See Guder and Barrett, *Missional Church*. But on a broader scale, I am also defining all three recurring themes of incarnation, confrontation, and imagination as integral components of a missional theology. This latter definition will be fleshed out in the subsequent chapters.

Ultimately, this approach places less emphasis on systematic theological analyses of particular cultural issues, and instead views the process holistically as a work of cultivation in which faith and culture are dynamic, creative conversation partners. The dialogical ideals developed in this context are presented as three interconnected components of the larger whole; each task is both sequential and dialectical. This *embodied*, *prophetic*, and *subversive* missional theology of cultural engagement focuses on the themes of *incarnation, confrontation*, and *imagination*.

When incarnation (the missional task), confrontation (the prophetic task), and imagination (the creative task) are combined in dynamic relationality, these themes work together to inform one another and cast a theological vision of a covenant community that is somehow both authentically present within and yet stands in prophetic contradistinction with the paradox of the "already but not yet" reign of God in the world. And as this missional theology of cultural engagement looks ahead to the city, its embodied witness aims to lay the groundwork for creative and subversive engagement with the urban context.

It should also be stated that though this development of a missional theology of cultural engagement is the first lens for examining the Valley and the Corner as signs of the locality and universality of the city, the specific attributes of the urban context may not be clear until the end. This is in part because part 2 places more emphasis on looking *at* the lens than *through* it as a prerequisite to understanding how to look through the later lenses of urban exegesis and contextual theology. In this sense, this missional theology of cultural engagement is a like a base lens which provides a theological foundation for the later lenses. As the process unfolds, the lenses overlap in particular ways that are intended to help the reader to see the complex dimensions of the city more clearly.

3

Incarnation: The Missional Task

BEGINNING WITH *INCARNATION AS the missional task* shapes the first steps of this missional theology of cultural engagement. Fundamental to this task is the affirmation that the incarnation of the triune God in the person of Jesus Christ serves as the theological foundation for God's mission in the world. Through an examination of the incarnation in John's Gospel as an orthodox and Trinitarian commitment of Christianity, I will propose a working definition of contemporary "missional theology" as distinct from "theology of mission." I will then present incarnational ministry as a "missional theology of culture"[1] and focus on the necessity of an *embodied* theology in our current cultural context that is both kenotic and downwardly mobile. The missional task is therefore the process of moving from the "enfleshment" of *sarx egeneto*[2] to the shape and character of mission in today's society.

THE WORD BECAME FLESH

As a central and definitive doctrine of Christianity, the incarnation has a rich and complex history of interpretation. Merely distinguishing between the concepts of *the* incarnation as a specific event and incarnation without the definitive article as a broad theological process is an important distinction to make in any academic discussion of this theological affirmation.[3] To be able to move from the incarnation as a study of the second person of the Godhead into the incarnational aspects of mis-

---

1. Or more simply, a missional theology in context.

2. The "word made flesh" from John 1:14.

3. Though I agree with Langmead's assertion here, because of my research scope, I will not engage in the exhaustive, systematic discussion of incarnational missiology that he has already outlined quite well. See Langmead, *Word Made Flesh*.

siology is not an automatic assumption, and only a careful investigation of this process can uncover the theological significance of holding
these concepts together. Asserting that the embodiment of God informs
the shape of God's mission in the world is a radical claim at the heart
of incarnational missiology, and understanding this claim echoes Karl
Barth's declaration that

> God with us [is] the core of the Christian message, the decisive
> general statement of the Christian community. . . . To put it in
> the simplest way, what unites God and us men is that He does
> not will to be God without us, that He creates us rather to share
> with us and therefore with our being and life and act His own
> incomparable being and life and act, that He does not allow His
> history to be His and ours ours, but causes them to take place as
> a common history. That is the special truth which the Christian
> message has to proclaim at its very heart.[4]

In other words, the incarnate "God with us" is "the central reality of the
Christian message in terms of which the rest of theology is to be worked
out."[5] Throughout the Christian Scriptures, few texts are as explicit about
this message as the first chapter of the Gospel of John.

The dramatic opening of John's Gospel draws heavily on the language and imagery of the Greek culture of the late first century. The
Hellenistic philosophical concept of the *Logos* as a pervasive ideal that
ordered the universe was widely accepted as a part of the cultural and
philosophical vernacular.[6] Knowing this about his audience, John begins
with the Logos but immediately starts to shift its meaning as he prepares
to redefine the Logos as an actual person of flesh and blood.

> [1] In the beginning was the Word, and the Word was with God,
> and the Word was God. [2] He was in the beginning with God. [3] All
> things came into being through him, and without him not one
> thing came into being. What has come into being [4] in him was

---

4. Barth, *Church Dogmatics*, 5–8.

5. Langmead, *Word Made Flesh*, 15.

6. Barrett also identifies the flexibility and range of meaning contained in the Logos,
considering its use in Platonism, Stoicism, and variants in between. Regardless, the
theological significance rests in the unique ways that John's Gospel works from popular understandings of Logos to transform its meaning in the incarnation. See Barrett,
Gospel according to St. John, 35.

life, and the life was the light of all people. ⁵ The light shines in the
darkness, and the darkness did not overcome it.[7]

By just the second verse, John has already made his radical move
from an impersonal creative force to a personal Creator. This sets the
stage for the most radical claim of all: that this all-powerful Creator,
the sole source of true light and life in the universe, has actually come
near in the physical presence of Jesus Christ. "And the Word became
flesh and lived among us, and we have seen his glory, the glory as of a
father's only son, full of grace and truth."[8] Given the pervasive dualism
that characterized the Greek philosophical worldview of the time, the
assertion that the Logos had a physical, material body would have been a
fairly scandalous claim in the first century, and the unique incarnational
proposition of this orthodox Christian commitment continues to challenge us today.

However, the orthodoxy of the doctrine of the incarnation was not
established without difficulty. Before Saint Athanasius of Alexandria fa-
mously defended the doctrine of the incarnation in the face of the Arian
heresy at the first ecumenical Council of Nicaea in 325, his short book
On the Incarnation of the Word of God had already laid the groundwork
for this fundamental commitment of early Christianity. Through emphasizing the centrality and totality of the incarnation in his discussion
of creation, Athanasius leans on John's Gospel, stating that "St. John,
speaking all inclusively, says, 'All things became by Him and without
Him came nothing into being.'"[9] He further elaborates on this affirmation by placing the incarnate God at the center of the Christian story
between creation and salvation.

> He has been manifested in a human body for this reason only,
> out of the love and goodness of His Father, for the salvation of
> us men. We will begin then, with the creation of the world and
> with God its Maker, for the first fact that you must grasp is this:
> the renewal of creation has been wrought by the Self-same Word
> Who made it in the beginning. There is thus no inconsistency
> between creation and salvation; for the One Father has employed

7. John 1:1–5.

8. John 1:14.

9. Athanasius, *On the Incarnation*, 27.

the same Agent for both works, effecting the salvation of the
world through the same Word Who made it in the beginning.[10]

This assertion that connects creation and salvation with the common
presence and authority of the incarnation identifies the purpose of the
word made flesh. God takes on a human body in Jesus out of love for
creation and in order to enact its salvation. Jesus is *sent* as an embodiment of YHWH's purpose: to carry out God's mission of reconciliation
in bodily form.

In a similar fashion, for Lesslie Newbigin, understanding the incarnation is always situated within a firmly rooted Trinitarian affirmation
of the Father, Son, and Holy Spirit. Having spent much of his life as a
missionary in India engaging the theological pluralism of the Hindu
pantheon, Newbigin understood that an appropriate conception of Jesus
Christ hinged on a robust commitment to the triune God. Neglecting
the creedal declaration of the Father, Son, and Holy Spirit as "coequal,
coeternal, and consubstantial" relegated Jesus to an esteemed but ultimately confined seat among the human prophets.

The radical challenge of asserting that Jesus was both fully human
and somehow beyond his humanity—actually God in the flesh—was
that it contradicted the presuppositions of not only the Hellenistic
worldview of the first century, but also the Judaism of which Jesus was
a part. "Fundamental among these presuppositions was that the really
real, the ultimate source of being, must be beyond and above the ordinary world which we see and hear, taste, and handle."[11] Newbigin calls
this worldview a "classical dichotomy" that separates the ineffable and
divine from the "real" time, space, and substance of history.[12] Popular
thought could not conceive of the Logos as being corrupted by the frailty
and temporality of human flesh. But the early church, led by its doctors
and fathers like Athanasius, fought for the deity of Christ in Jesus of
Nazareth, even unto martyrdom.

10. Ibid., 26.

11. Newbigin, *Open Secret*, 24.

12. Of course we see themes of this classical dichotomy in the work of Plato, its
subsequent neo-Platonic dualism, Gnosticism, and other contemporary philosophies
of the era. Notably, this "classical" dichotomy between God and the "real" world has not
necessarily gone out of fashion in the last two thousand years.

> The absolutely crucial point was this: in the man Jesus God had actually suffered for the sin of the world. For that assurance Christians were ready to go to the lions. If it was true, the whole classical worldview was false and had to be replaced by something radically different . . . this new way of understanding was embodied in the doctrine of the Trinity. . . . thus, on this new basis the dichotomy between the sensible and the intelligible worlds is healed, for God himself has actually been made flesh.[13]

In the incarnation, the triune God has overturned the expectations of the classically dichotomized world and redefined the boundaries of divinity by making his dwelling among us. Just as YHWH made his dwelling within Israel's tabernacle, so has Jesus come to "tabernacle" with his people.

While Newbigin holds to the importance of the Trinity in his understanding of the incarnation, there are also unique aspects of the Son as the sent one[14] of the Father that are central to God's mission in the world. From the beginning of his public ministry to the final week of his passion, Jesus was insistent on carrying out the mission of the Father in his proclamation of the kingdom of God. The significance of the incarnation is that in this gospel announcement was not only a proclamation of the kingdom, but also the *presence* of the kingdom. In the arrival of Jesus, the long awaited reign of God had become an *embodied* reality.

As Jesus commissioned his disciples to take up his ministry, the task of embodying the presence of the kingdom of God was given to the church. In John's Gospel account of this commissioning, Jesus says, "Peace be with you. As the Father has sent me, so I send you."[15] Newbigin notes that this greeting is indicative of the character of the mission.

> Peace, shalom, the all-embracing blessing of the God of Israel—this is what the presence of the kingdom is. The church is a movement launched into the life of the world to bear in its own life God's gift of peace for the life of the world. It is sent, therefore, not only to proclaim the kingdom but to bear in its own life the presence of the kingdom.[16]

13. Newbigin, *Open Secret*, 26.
14. John 20:19–23.
15. John 20:21.
16. Newbigin, The Open Secret, 49.

Echoing the opening lines of John's Gospel about the Word become flesh that "in him was life, and the life was the light of all people,"[17] the church is commissioned to proclaim the kingdom of the Father and bear witness to the life of Jesus through the power of the Holy Spirit. This mission, begun in the radical sending of the incarnation, is now entrusted to a community that is both called and sent: called into a covenant relationship with the triune, reconciling God, and sent into the world to redeem his creation.

Ultimately, the connections between the event of the incarnation and the process of embodying God's mission through the church are numerous. Langmead proposes three basic ways that incarnational mission takes shape in the world: (1) following Jesus as the pattern for mission, (2) participation in the presence of Christ, and (3) joining in the activity of God's incarnating mission through the church.[18] While each of these options corresponds to particular theological traditions that have embraced the incarnational contours of missiology, together they establish a theological foundation for God's mission in the world.

DEFINING MISSIONAL

Particularly among evangelicalism's "innovators" who catalyze the popular publishing and conference industries in the church, the word "missional" is becoming increasingly common, and "as church leaders continue to pile onto the missional bandwagon, the true meaning of the word may be getting buried under a pile of assumptions."[19] As a consequence of this development, what exactly is meant by "missional" has become increasingly difficult to decipher amidst competing voices and opinions seeking to promote their own unique definitions.

Author and church strategist Alan Hirsch, a self-proclaimed "missional activist," expressed his frustration with this situation in an article aimed at leadership development and appropriately titled *Defining Missional*. Through challenging communities of faith to understand the importance of guarding their theology, Hirsch argues that the widespread propagation of missional could have unintended consequences. "I am concerned about the confusion surrounding the meaning of the

17. John 1:4.

18. Langmead, *Word Made Flesh*, 58.

19. Hirsch, "Defining Missional," 1.

word *missional*. Maintaining the integrity of this word is critical, because recovering a missional understanding of God and the Church is essential not only for the advancement of our mission but, I believe, also for the survival of Christianity in the West."[20] Hirsch goes on to assert that "missional" should not be confused with a repackaged church frowth movement or other stylized attempts at outreach,[21] nor should it be perceived as an updated gloss on the liberal agenda for a social gospel, as others have positioned the term. Given the range of meaning in the field, finding a place to stand can be difficult. Nevertheless, as the church continues to work out its identity in the midst of this uncertainty, "it is especially important that the Christian church wrestle with its 'mission' in the sense of articulating the reason and purpose for which it exists."[22]

However, rather than surveying the broad variety of contemporary interpretations for points of reference, my approach to this preliminary definition of missional is to locate its origins in a particular historical frame so that the beginning of the concept can help to clarify the present circumstances. As a specific theological development with its genesis in the *missio Dei*[23] and its most prominent, recent emphasis through the work of The Gospel and Our Culture Network, *missional theology* has taken on a particular shape through the scholarship and research of several prominent perspectives.[24] According to the GOCN, at the heart of

20. Ibid.

21. This is probably one of the most common confusions about "missional" as it applies to congregational ministry and practices. "Outreach," no matter how creative or "outward-focused," is not inherently missional, nor can missional simply replace what some have traditionally called "evangelism." In short, calling something "missional"— as is increasingly common practice—does not necessarily make it so, however distantly it may be connected to someone's conception of mission.

22. Van Engen, "Mission Defined and Described," 2. Charles Van Engen has written extensively on theology of mission, and discusses various perspectives on the use of the terms mission and missional in both *God's Missionary People* and *Mission on the Way*. Notably, Van Engen departs from the GOCN on the issue of its emphasis on the local congregation, and a resemblance to the "Missionary Structures of the Congregation" of the WCC in the 1960s.

23. Latin for "the sending of God," *missio Dei* is sometimes translated more colloquially to mean "the mission of God." The complex early history of the term is explored in numerous works. See Vicedom, *Mission of God*; and Rosin, *"Missio Dei."*

24. Despite my heavy emphasis on the GOCN, it should be noted that the GOCN is not an "official" custodian of the term "missional." Various traditions (evangelical, mainline, ecumenical) and constituencies (academic institutions, popular Christian publishing, etc.) are continuing to work on defining the term. However, while a range

understanding what it means to be missional is a fundamental reorientation of our theology, ecclesiology, and missiology, or what the GOCN has called "a profoundly theocentric reconceptualization of Christian mission."[25] Only by recovering an understanding of the inherently missionary character of God will "missional" find its meaning for both the church and the world.

Origins of the Missio Dei

This missionary character is revealed most clearly in the *missio Dei* of the Christian Scriptures, which illuminate a rich Trinitarian narrative about the Father God who creates the world, the incarnate Son who reconciles the world, and the Holy Spirit who empowers the church for the sake of the world. As a missional narrative, the biblical story is rooted in the identity of the *missio Dei*, and the character of God's mission is interwoven with the story from beginning to end.[26] This affirmation of God as a fundamentally missionary God is at the ideological core of the *missio Dei*.

Noted South African missiologist David Bosch credits Karl Barth with being "one of the first theologians to articulate mission as an activity of God himself"[27] in the early 1930s. At the Brandenburg Missionary Conference in 1932, Barth presented a paper that portrayed mission as connected to the *actio Dei*, or the action of God in the world.[28] Soon after, German missiologist Karl Hartenstein began to express similar ideas in his writing on the theology of mission as rooted in the identity

---

of perspectives exists in the field, that of the GOCN is likely one of the most prolific and established. Most foundational among its many publications on missional theology is Guder and Barrett, *Missional Church: A Vision for the Sending of the Church in North America*, a book that some credit with popularizing the term "missional" by the early 2000s.

25. Guder and Barrett, *Missional Church*, 4.

26. Reading the whole of the biblical text through the lens of mission theology has been an increasingly common practice in the wake of the globalization of Christianity. See Wright, *Mission of God*; and Glasser et al., *Announcing the Kingdom*.

27. Bosch, *Transforming Mission*, 389. For an important earlier work, see Bosch, *Witness to the World*.

28. This particular emphasis of Barthian theology is still being explored today. See Chung, *Karl Barth*. However, not all missiologists agree on the role Barth may or may not have played in the early shaping of the *missio Dei*. With scant evidence from Barth himself on the mission of God in the world, we are left with the assertion of Bosch and the possibility of contradictory speculation.

and characteristics of God. However, the particular language of the *missio Dei* had not yet been thoroughly explicated in either the church, the academy, or the missionary councils.

One of the developments that helped to solidify a more explicitly theological understanding of mission was the third conference of the International Missionary Council in Tambaram, India, in 1938. In a global context "where peace was increasingly threatened by fascist-type regimes (Germany, Italy, Portugal, Spain, Japan), the discussions focused on the importance and centrality of the church, in particular the local church, in mission."[29] This emphasis on the ecclesiocentrism of this particular council is exemplified in this conference statement about the world mission of the church: "It is the Church and the Church alone which can carry the responsibility of transmitting the Gospel from one generation to another, of preserving its purity and of proclaiming it to all creatures. It is the Church and Church alone which can witness to the reality that man belongs to God in Christ with a higher right than that of any earthly institution which may claim his supreme allegiance."[30] In its effort to emphasize unity between the church and mission, the church was positioned as the primary instrument of God's mission in the world. This prominent place for ecclesiology in relationship with missiology would eventually lead to a kind of corrective[31] theological reflection on mission.

By the 1950s, particularly through the work of those in the IMC who objected to the Tambaram conference's emphasis on the church as the starting point for mission, the concept of the *missio Dei* was coming into clearer focus. At the 1952 World Missions Conference in Willingen, Hartenstein and others were declaring the missionary character of God as a primary attribute of his Trinitarian being.[32] Additional work like Georg Vicedom's *The Mission of God: An Introduction to a Theology of Mission* would also play a major role in popularizing the concept.[33] Within the next couple of decades, as the IMC was integrated into the

29. World Council of Churches, "History of World Mission and Evangelism."

30. *Philip, Edinburgh to Salvador*, 27.

31. Depending on your theological perspective, this "corrective" move could also be considered reactionary in the other direction by placing missiology above, or even apart from, ecclesiology.

32. Lienemann-Perrin, et al., *Reformed and Ecumenical*, 79.

33. Tennent, *Invitation to World Missions*, 55.

World Council of Churches, additional conciliar missiology contributed the growing momentum behind the *missio Dei*.[34] Prominent theological voices like Jurgen Moltmann would later follow suit and further affirm that "it is not the church that has a mission of salvation to fulfill in the world; it is the mission of the Son and the Spirit through the Father that includes the church."[35]

Along with Moltmann, Bosch elaborates on the *missio Dei* as theTrinitarian character of God whose very nature is to continually extend himself into creation. This active ontology defines the existence of God not as a condition of stasis but as a dynamic relationality of being. "Mission is understood as being derived from the very nature of God. It is thus put in the context of the doctrine of the Trinity, not of ecclesiology or soteriology. The classical doctrine of the *missio Dei* as God the Father sending the Son, and God the Father and Son sending the spirit is expanded to include yet another "movement": Father, Son, and Holy Spirit sending the church into the world."[36] This missional, Trinitarian trajectory informs the incarnational, pneumatological, and ecclesiological dimensions of being created in the image of the "sent one." Just as God is sent, so are God's image-bearing people sent to proclaim and embody the *euaggelion* that Jesus announced, empowered by the Spirit and called into a sent community.

Missiology and Ecclesiology

This reframed theological understanding of the triune God should therefore shape our understanding of the mission of the church. "Because

34. It is important to note here that even though I have only briefly glossed the 1950s–60s, for many, this was a tumultuous time in the development of mission theology. After WWII, the "fledgling World Council of Churches (founded in 1948) began to search for what they considered to be a more 'relevant' missiology. They wanted to mobilize the churches to become involved with what God was doing in the world. This new view of mission crystallized around the phrase missio Dei . . . and represented a radical secularization of mission. Missiologists like J. C. Hoekendijk demonstrated a deep pessimism about the church as a viable agent of God's mission" (Van Engen, "Mission Defined and Described"). This shift in conciliar missiology post-Willingen inadvertently de-emphasized the role of the church to such a degree that the result was an "undue separation of God's mission from the church" (Tennent, Invitation to World Missions, 56). Debate over this evangelical-ecumenical missiological divide continues today.

35. Moltmann, *Church in the Power*, 64.

36. Bosch, *Transforming Mission*, 390.

we are the "sent" people of God, the church is the instrument of God's mission in the world. As things stand, many people see it the other way around. They believe mission is an instrument of the church; a means by which the church is grown. Although we frequently say "the church has a mission," according to missional theology a more correct statement would be "the mission has a church."[37] Thus, churches seeking to be truly missional in this sense of the word must shift their understanding of mission from activity to identity, or from "doing mission" to "*being* a sent one." The former has to do with a programmatic understanding of mission, while the latter is about a fundamental reorientation of ecclesial posture toward the world. It is not that "mission programs" are inherently problematic, but there is a sense in which they can inhibit the cultivation of a *sent posture*. When theology of mission is domesticated within the church's self-understanding (its basic ecclesiology), then its missional efforts will always be limited to the kinds of bounded language and ideas commonly communicated in the "mission statement" of a church. But a truly "missional community sees the mission as both its originating impulse and its organizing principle."[38] Ultimately, though the church certainly plays a crucial role in God's mission in the world, the mission is initiated by and belongs to God.

This explicit commitment to the *missio Dei* as characteristic of the missional identity of God is one of the central distinctives that differentiates a Christendom perspective on theology of mission[39] from *missional theology*. The development of missional theology in the late twentieth century has shifted one particular emphasis in missiology by calling into question the Christendom project's emphasis on mission as belonging fundamentally to the church. As the foundation of Christendom began

37. Hirsch, "Defining Missional," 1. It should be noted in my citations of Hirsch that even though he is not an academic theologian or missiologist, as an author and practitioner, he has consistently been able to capture in accessible terms the issues facing missional theology for a mainstream context. In tracing his own theological influences in regard to missional theology, Hirsch has humorously stated that "in the beginning was Guder, and Guder was good." Here he is implicitly drawing on the GOCN, Newbigin, and Bosch.

38. Hirsch, "Defining Missional," 2.

39. The fourth-century Constantinian establishment of Christendom in the Roman Empire that would grow into a dominant cultural player in Western society shaped the church's understanding of mission for more than a thousand years. One major emphasis of Christendom missiology was the central role of ecclesiology in the domain of mission. See Bosch, *Believing in the Future*.

to erode in the increasing gap between the church and the nominally "Christian" West, it became apparent that mission could no longer be contained within an institutional, Constantinian assumption of needing to reach the "foreign and pagan" lands across the ocean. At the height of the Christendom era, "theology had no interest in the world outside the church, except insofar as the church might wrest 'territory' from the world and incorporate this into the church. As a matter of fact, when the modern Western foreign missionary enterprise was initiated, this is how mission was understood, to a significant extent: chunks of the pagan world outside Europe had to be conquered and incorporated into Christendom."[40]

However, despite the Christendom project's overemphasis on the centrality of the church in mission, and the remnants of a Christendom mentality that remain in the modern Western world, it would be a mistake to overreact in the other direction by too greatly diminishing the importance of the church as an instrument of God's mission in the world. In other words, "it is one thing to propose that mission should not be a subset of the doctrine of the church; it is entirely another to disconnect the *missio Dei* altogether from a robust ecclesiology."[41] The need for a robust, missional ecclesiology is an important recognition in the affirmation that God's mission does indeed have a church. Evangelical missiologist Charles Van Engen asserts that it is crucial to "emphasize the essential nature and vocation of the church as God's called and sent people . . . the word missional, with reference to the church, sees the church as the instrument of God's mission in God's world."[42]

Missional and Missiological

After centuries of a primary expression of mission being ecclesial programs that sent Western missionaries abroad to "unreached people groups," many church historians and missiologists now recognize that the fervent missionary impulse of the nineteenth and twentieth centuries has been hugely successful in Asia, Africa, and Latin America.[43]

40. Ibid., 29.

41. Tennent, *Invitation to World Missions*, 56.

42. Van Engen, "Mission Defined and Described," 12.

43. Without launching into a full discussion of mission history outside of the West, my use of the general term "successful" is in reference to the establishment of a substantial indigenous church outside of the West, which now far outnumbers Western

And as the balance of global Christianity has shifted heavily in favor of the non-Western world, missional theology has begun to reexamine the West as an important missionary context.[44] While missional theology is not limited by geography *per se,* much of the current research reflects a distinct type of missional theologizing that is heavily focused on the West as an emerging mission field, in addition to an interest in the national, ethnic, and geopolitical boundaries that have blurred in the onset of globalization.

This constantly shifting "center" of global Christianity keeps the momentum of the global church, and hence the character of global mission, on the move. A potential danger in the current emphasis on a Western, missional theology *over against* or *over-differentiated* from a global, *missiological* theology is a false dichotomy that removes the essential elements of theology of mission[45] that have shaped the discipline for centuries from the growing corpus of so-called missional theology. As the market-driven demand for "all things missional" continues to grow at a rate that threatens to dilute its meaning, there is a pressing need for the inclusion of grounded missiological theory in the propagation of missional theology. Without such theology of mission as a foundational qualifier of "missional," the trajectory of "all things missional" may be hijacked by little more than a slick marketing agenda and a "style" of mission without actual missiological substance.

Given the current climate of popularity around missional theology, an important question must always be asked in defining "missional": is this *missional* theology truly *missiological* enough to share a common root in God's mission? As this conversation continues to move forward, the terms "missional" and "missiological" need to mutually inform and define one another as twin attributes and close siblings of the same

---

Christians. See Jenkins, *Next Christendom*; Noll, *New Shape of World Christianity*; Marty, *Christian World*; and Adeney, *Kingdom without Borders.*

44. Whether or not the West can truly be considered a "missionary" context continues to be debated. While some assert that "first world re-evangelization" is more of a renewal movement than a missionary movement, others argue that the vast secularization of the West and the erosion of its Christian identity has left only a shell of nominal Christian affiliation in its place. In some ways, "missional" as distinct from "missionary" is intended to point to this nuance.

45. These "essential elements" of missiology could be broadly construed as the foundational aspects of biblical theology of mission, mission history, cross-cultural and intercultural contextualization, cultural anthropology, globalization studies, issues in interfaith dialogue, and so forth.

mother discipline of missiology. And if it is true, as systematic theologian Martin Kahler suggested in 1908, that "mission is the mother of theology,"[46] then retaining a missiological emphasis in missional theology is crucial to the integrity of theology itself.[47]

Ultimately, in returning to the role of the church, a missional *and* missiological theology recognizes that the mission of God—much like the "already but not yet" kingdom of God—is always out beyond the church, even as the church seeks to faithfully embody the mission. The Christian community of faith, as sent ones of the triune God, is a people called into the dynamic relationality and *ekstasis* of the Father, Son, and Holy Spirit. And it is only in this ecstatic participation in the divine community that the church is commissioned by God to be sent into the world as agents of the gospel.

INCARNATIONAL MINISTRY AS MISSIONAL THEOLOGY

Now, having briefly examined the incarnation and defined missional theology, the final movement in this initial task of constructing a missional theology of cultural engagement is to explore incarnational ministry as a missional theology of culture, or a missional theology in context.[48] If the incarnation is foundational to missional theology, and missional theology focuses on the *missio Dei*, then a contextualization of missional theology should demonstrate that incarnational ministry

46. Guder, *Continuing Conversion of the Church*, 21.

47. This inclusion of the "missional" and "missiological" clarification is more than a theological turf war. As more and more "missional" literature is published and promoted without a missiological foundation, the meaning of basic terms like "mission," "culture," "context," and "contextualization" become lost in an ideological gap between disciplines. The most relevant example of this gap is in defining "culture." In missional theology's predominantly Western context, many local cultural assumptions have not been questioned. In this way, defining cultural engagement becomes domesticated within one dominant cultural worldview. Missiology, on the other hand, has robust models of cultural analysis that have been developed in cross-cultural contexts, and these kinds of research methods have much to offer a young, growing corpus of missional theology.

48. In this section, I am using the words "culture" and "world" somewhat interchangeably in describing how incarnational ministry interacts with its context missionally. However, subsequent chapters will discuss a more specific, nuanced definition of "culture."

describes a particular approach to culture that is both *kenotic*[49] and downwardly mobile.

Much like the word "missional," descriptions of "incarnational ministry" abound. For some, "missional" and "incarnational" are used interchangeably, with the latter at times being a preferred term for those with a pejorative impression of the colonialist and imperialist connotations of the *mission* in "missional." But if incarnational ministry is intended to be distinct from the broad banner of missional theology and more than a convenient label for "doing ministry in the way of Jesus," then we must explore the specific character of what it means to minister to others in the spirit of the incarnation. In particular, the Apostle Paul's call on the church to embrace a Christlike *kenosis* in the second chapter of Philippians illuminates the dramatic humility of Jesus "being born in human likeness."[50] In turn, this kenotic ethic works in conjunction with Jesus' pronounced concern for a downward mobility with social and economic implications. These two themes are defining characteristics of incarnational ministry, and they provide tangible markers for contextualizing missional theology.

Christlike Kenosis

The depth and diversity of Pauline theology reveals the Apostle Paul's passionate commitment to the early church. As a theologian, pastor, church planter, missionary, and cultural emissary between Jews and Gentiles, Paul's life and body were literally marked by the trials and triumphs of preaching the gospel of Jesus Christ. In his epistle to the church in Philippi, Paul encouraged this community of faith to a joyful and steadfast unity, even as he wrote "in chains" from Rome. But this challenge to "live your life in a manner worthy of the gospel of Christ"[51]

49. *Kenosis* is the Greek concept of "self-emptying" described in Phil 2:7, and the kenotic theology in this text has a long and complex history in the church, from the Chalcedonian formulation of incarnational Christology to the controversial "kenosis theory" of late-nineteenth-century Lutherans. Though the research on *kenosis* is ongoing and substantial, my intent is not to systematically rehash the various positions on appropriating kenotic theology. Rather, I am seeking to connect the concept of *kenosis* with downward mobility in consideration of both its spiritual and practical implications. For more systematic approaches to kenotic theology, see Evans, *Exploring Kenotic Christology*; and Gorman, *Inhabiting the Cruciform God*.

50. Phil 2:7.

51. Phil 1:27. This verse is what leads into the "therefore" that opens the second chapter.

was not a call to joy without cost; rather, it was an invitation to joyful obedience under the radical humility of Christ. Their unity would only be found as "citizens of heaven," who must live as citizens of the Roman Empire while remembering that their higher allegiance was to the way of Jesus.

> Philippians 2: Imitating Christ's Humility
>
> [1] If then there is any encouragement in Christ, any consolation from love, any sharing in the Spirit, any compassion and sympathy, [2] make my joy complete: be of the same mind, having the same love, being in full accord and of one mind. [3] Do nothing from selfish ambition or conceit, but in humility regard others as better than yourselves. [4] Let each of you look not to your own interests, but to the interests of others. [5] Let the same mind be in you that was in Christ Jesus,
> [6] who, though he was in the form of God,
> did not regard equality with God
> as something to be exploited,
> [7] but emptied himself,
> taking the form of a slave,
> being born in human likeness.
> And being found in human form,
> [8] he humbled himself
> and became obedient to the point of death—
> even death on a cross.

The structured prose of this well known christological hymn in verses 6–11 points to its liturgical use in the early church,[52] and the incarnational focus of verses 6–8 emphasizes the theological context of *kenosis*. "Though he was in the form of God," with all of God's true *morphe*, or nature, Jesus intentionally denounces this equality with God. Instead, as the object of self-emptying, Jesus "made himself nothing" (*heauton ekenosen*) by taking on the nature of a *doulos*, or slave. The Son of God becomes enfleshed as the Son of Man in order to literally pour out his life for the sake of others. To worship this Christ is to submit to his lordship, "the lordship of one who became a servant, who poured himself out, even for his enemies (Rom. 5:10), of one who identified with the humble and downtrodden, who implacably opposed the forces of price,

---

52. The structure and meaning of the Carmen Christi has been parsed extensively. See Martin, *Carmen Christi*.

violence, injustice, and inequality. It is a lordship that does not domineer over its subjects but gives itself utterly for their sakes (Mk 10:42–45)."[53]

Notably, for the church in Philippi, this self-emptying was not intended to be an individual act of selflessness carried out in the hopes of attaining the exaltation of verses 9–11; rather, it is motivated in this context by a commitment to the community of faith. Paul's encouragement in verse 2 is to "be of the same mind, having the same love, being in full accord and of one mind." This unity is both the evidence of fellowship with Christ and the standard by which the church would testify to the truth of this union.

Incarnational ministry is therefore a self-denying service to others both *on behalf of the church* and *for its witness in the world.* Paul is admonishing the Philippians that unless the life of their community is marked by a Christlike *kenosis*, their unity in the face of suffering and persecution will fall apart. Further, their witness of the kingdom of God to the surrounding culture which makes high demands of their Roman citizenship would be compromised. The unity in the body of Christ that Paul desires is part and parcel of living "in a manner worthy of the gospel." In this sense, their very identity as Christ-followers hinges on their ability to allow "the same mind" or attitude to "be in [them] that was in Christ Jesus" by pouring out their lives for the sake of the world.

The contemporary relevance of this kenotic ethic in incarnational ministry remains critical for the church in the world today. First, the church is only the church when its inward life reflects the unity and mutual submission of being united with Christ through a common "sharing in the Spirit." When the church is divided, it has neglected the reconciling capacity of *kenosis* that cuts through "selfish ambition and conceit." Secondly, incarnational ministry as a missional theology in context calls the church to a sacrificial humility as opposed to embracing the imperial agenda[54] of citizenship in this world. The kenotic Christ "is opposed to all oppressive cultural, political, and ideological forces that claim universal or ultimate allegiance. To come under Jesus' lordship is to be liberated from all claims of these would-be lords."[55] In a context of competing

---

53. Finger, *Contemporary Anabaptist Theology*, 286.

54. Much like the Pax Romana, the contemporary demands of "the world" are often reflective of the Roman Empire's quest for dominance, affluence, and "development." This idea will be explored further in the sections on confrontation and imagination.

55. Ibid., 286.

loyalties, can the church remain faithful to a lordship that leads to the cross? The call to incarnational ministry demands a posture of service and thus a rejection of the ideology of entitlement that selfishly grasps at status in the eyes of the dominant culture. But what does *kenosis* look like in the real world where the Western church is struggling to recover its identity in the *missio Dei*?

Downward Mobility

Connected to this kenotic ethic of incarnational ministry is a commitment to a socially and economically downward mobility. Linking *kenosis* with the idea of downward mobility is not necessarily an unorthodox read of Philippians 2, though definitions of downward mobility can vary. According to theologian Michael Gorman, in reference to the narrative of Philippians 2:6–8, "Joseph Hellerman argues that it is a '*cursus pudorum*,' or downward-bound succession of ignominies, constructed in contrast to Rome's *cursus honorum*,[56] the elite's upward-bound race for honors, imitated in various ways throughout the provinces and colonies."[57] Hellerman himself goes on to say that Paul's portrayal of Jesus' "utter degradation" in the *Carmen Christi* happens through "three progressively degrading positions of social status in the Roman world;"[58] from God to humanity, humanity to slavery, and slavery to humiliation on the cross. Though Gorman does not explicitly move from the social and political aspects of downward mobility to the particularities of its economic implications as well, the connections can naturally be inferred.[59]

Though challenging our loyalty to accumulating social status and economic capital is often a quick route to the seemingly inevitable accusations of Marxist sympathies along with a condemnation of the social gospel, we must resist the temptation to solely spiritualize the implications of *kenosis*.[60] Henri Nouwen's legacy of writing on Christian spiri-

56. Latin for "course of honors."

57. Gorman, *Inhabiting the Cruciform God*, 16.

58. Hellerman, *Reconstructing Honor in Roman Philippi*, 130.

59. The cultural systems that link social and political capital with economic capital are complex, yet undeniable in the modern world. See Farmer, *Pathologies of Power*.

60. In Catholic, Protestant, and Eastern Orthodox traditions, various perspectives on *kenosis* portray its emphasis as an inward reality of emptying one's will in submission to God. Though valid spiritually, my intent has been to show that its corresponding

tuality demonstrates how holding the inward and outward dynamics of *kenosis* together is essential to the "Christian's responsibility to live an actively compassionate life for others."[61] Through connecting compassion, solidarity, and social action, "Nouwen's insistence on downward mobility" showed that his "ethic was kenotic, within the tradition of the self-emptying and self-denying model of Jesus."[62] But for those who would reduce the *kenosis* of Jesus to merely a model of spirituality, the problems are clear.

The tangible social trajectory of the incarnation is much more than a figurative humility that asks Christian believers to simply think less of themselves. Quite to the contrary, the downward movement from all-powerful God to a crucified human servant is an incarnational reality that demands imitation. To reduce the incarnation to anything less than a radical challenge to follow in the footsteps of the King of Kings who was born in a feeding trough for livestock is to denigrate the path to the cross and make empty metaphors of Christ's strong, repeated imperative to "take up your cross and follow me."[63] Cheap slogans that embrace the benign "nature of a servant" without coming to terms with the material sacrifice of the cost of discipleship[64] make light of the incarnation and replace Christlike humility with a self-congratulatory charity. That God has come in the flesh to redeem his creation through death on its behalf is not an invitation to mere charity.

The radical nature of the proclamation that in Jesus the *euaggelion* had arrived in bodily form was a controversial announcement that divided "father and mother, wife and children, brothers and sisters,"[65] and an invitation to be considered carefully because those who would seek to embrace this good news would find that it would cost them everything— "yes, and even life itself."[66] And if life in this world is often ruled by the social and economic commodities for which we toil, compete, and com-

---

outward expression is just as theologically justifiable and significant. For "a historical analysis of the kenotic motif," see Dawe, *Form of a Servant*.

61. LaNoue, *Spiritual Legacy of Henri Nouwen*, 135.

62. Ibid., 138.

63. Matt 10:38; 16:24; Mark 8:34; Luke 9:23; 14:27.

64. Parallels to Dietrich Bonhoeffer's concept of "costly grace" are appropriate here. See Bonhoeffer, *Cost of Discipleship*.

65. Luke 14:26.

66. Ibid.

mit idolatry, then it follows that the *kenosis* of Jesus Christ should call into question those priorities.

But is incarnational ministry about merely giving up status and capital to pursue self-inflicted suffering, a potentially false humility, or a mandatory, legalistic vow of poverty? As an expression of missional theology in context, incarnational ministry calls the church to a radical service of others in which the powerful forces of status and capital are dismantled and shown for what they are: broken "powers and principalities"[67] that have been removed from their proper context under the kenotic rule of Christ as "the image of the invisible God"[68] for which they were created. This selfless, kenotic service to which the church is called invites communities of faith into the delicate tension of challenging the powers without demonizing status and capital.

Ultimately, incarnational ministry must always operate in serious consideration of the dramatic reversals of upside-down economics and the descending social ladder of the kingdom of God. Under the reign of God pronounced in Jesus, the poor are blessed, the last are first, the outsiders are welcomed in, and the greatest are slaves to all. In a Western culture of upward mobility that highly prizes the consumer impulse to needlessly accumulate capital goods as symbols of social status, incarnational ministry is born out of a missional theology that is inherently backwards in the eyes of the world.

In Paul's Second Epistle to the Corinthians, he describes the importance of financial stewardship to the church in the wealthy city of Corinth. "For you know the generous act of our Lord Jesus Christ, that though he was rich, yet for your sakes he became poor, so that by his poverty you might become rich."[69] In typical Pauline fashion, echoing the "foolishness" of the cross in the opening chapter of his First Epistle to the Corinthians, just as "God's foolishness is wiser than human wisdom, and God's weakness is stronger than human strength,"[70] so is God's poverty richer than human wealth. The paradoxical reality of incarnational ministry is that only in the self-emptying, downwardly mobile posture of the church does the community of faith find true richness in the mission of God.

67. Col 1:16; 2:15.
68. Col 1:15.
69. 2 Cor 8:9.
70. 1 Cor 1:25.

4

Confrontation: The Prophetic Task

THE SECOND COMPONENT OF constructing this missional theology of
cultural engagement continues with *confrontation as the prophetic
task*. To move from the incarnational nature of the missional task to
the confrontational nature of the prophetic task is to recognize that the
enfleshment of God, while foundational theologically, is not a terminal
moment for the *missio Dei*. Rather, the incarnate God in the person of
Jesus of Nazareth has a mission: to proclaim that the kingdom of God
had arrived, that the inbreaking of God's reign had been made present
in his personhood. The very nature of this embodiment of the gospel
is an announcement of a confrontational event—God drawing near to
his creation to meet the challenges of humanity head-on. Just as God's
encounter with humanity is "up close and personal" in Jesus, so is Jesus'
life and ministry marked by the confrontational encounters that occur
as he declares the reign of God in an age of empire. Further, Jesus invites
his followers into this prophetic confrontation through the vocation of
the people of God in the world.

The structure of this cumulative prophetic task is threefold: first, by
defining "cultural engagement" in conversation with John Stackhouse's
use of Reinhold Niebuhr's Christian Realism and Stephen Bevans's
countercultural model of contextual theology, the task of *confronting*
culture is presented as an imperative of being the church in the world.
Secondly, through Walter Brueggemann's *Prophetic Imagination*, I will
emphasize the importance of *criticizing* and *energizing* in prophetic
cultural engagement. Thirdly, an exposition of the shape of prophetic
justice in the Old Testament in conjunction with the gospel narrative of
Mark 11:12–25 will then serve as a model of Jesus' approach to the task

of prophetic ministry, which is carried out in great continuity with the traditions of the Law and the Prophets.

ENGAGING CULTURE

"Engaging" the cultural context in which we find ourselves is often portrayed as a reasonable compromise between the two poles of antagonistic cultural rejection or syncretistic cultural embrace. While there is relevance to this middle ground approach, I will argue that "engagement" must have an inherently *embedded, countercultural ethic* if it is to be *missional*. To engage culture is not merely to walk the safe path of the *via media*. Instead, missional engagement always requires a confrontational encounter, one that enables the gospel to both incarnate and deconstruct the presuppositions of every cultural context.

Newfound interest in "culture"[1] is a theme that has seemingly become a popular trend among those who Robert Webber has labeled the emerging "younger evangelicals."[2] Desiring to distance themselves from the so-called "culture wars" of fundamentalism, and disenchanted by the theocratic visions of coalitions like the Moral Majority,[3] many of these "younger" North American evangelicals in particular have sought after softer language and a more redemptive view of secular culture. In other Christian circles, those of a more "missional" persuasion have emphasized the importance of understanding culture in order to resituate the church in a Western context that is increasingly being viewed as an emerging mission field. Still others have held on to the dream of theocracy, and with the resurgence of neoconservatism[4] in America, many

1. Though in this immediate context, "culture" is roughly equivalent to popular culture and the arts, elsewhere I am continuing to use a more general definition of "culture" as the whole of human context in which we communicate, make meaning, and share knowledge. I will touch on other anthropological, ethnographic, and sociological approaches to culture as a complex concept of our contemporary societal reality in later chapters.

2. Webber identifies several paradigms among younger evangelicals that indicate they are breaking away from the polarizations (e.g., fundamentalism vs. liberalism) of the past to embrace cultural thought and practice in new ways. See Webber, *Younger Evangelicals*.

3. The Moral Majority was a political lobbying group organized by Christian fundamentalist Jerry Falwell in 1979 that advocated for "conservative evangelical values" in the U.S. government throughout the 1980s. See Martin, *With God on Our Side*.

4. The term "neoconservative" remains controversial in American politics. Nevertheless, with the dominance of "Reaganite" thought in the presidencies of the Bush

politicians are consistently pandering to this religious base by positioning themselves as potential leaders of a "Christian nation."

Realism and Radicalism

Regardless of one's varied perspectives on these options, theologian John
Stackhouse argues that most Western Christians "encounter one or both
of only two models of serious Christian engagement with the world . . .
the one extant option is the option of cultural transformation, of totally
reshaping society according to Christian values. This is the option espoused by the American religious right—and left."[5] Corresponding with
Niebuhr's "Christ the Transformer of Culture"[6] typology, minor varia-
tions of this approach are also represented by Roman Catholicism on
the right and liberation theology on the left. The second option is the
"response of holy distinctness, of a definite Christian community living
in contradistinction to the rest of society and thus offering the beneficial
example and influence of an alternative way of life."[7] This alternative to
cultural transformation is most closely aligned with Niebuhr's "Christ
Against Culture" paradigm and can be found in the Amish, Mennonites,
and Anabaptists who choose to avoid becoming entangled with societal
attachments in comparison to more culturally accommodated Christian
traditions.

In response to this functional dichotomy which leaves the church
to choose either the total transformation of culture or complete with-
drawal from society, Stackhouse proposes a predictably balanced *via
media*, which slightly modifies Richard Niebuhr's "Christ and Culture
in Paradox" typology with a leaning towards "Christ the Transformer
of Culture." In conversation with C. S. Lewis, Reinhold Niebuhr, and
Dietrich Bonhoeffer, Stackhouse sketches the contours of a "new
Christian Realism,"[8] which invites people of faith into the delicate ten-

---

presidents, the connection between evangelicalism and the political process cannot be
denied. See Fukuyama, *America at the Crossroads*.

5. Stackhouse, *Making the Best of It*, 6.

6. Niebuhr, *Christ and Culture*.

7. Stackhouse, *Making the Best of It*, 6.

8. Stackhouse presents a renewed vision of Reinhold Niebuhr's Christian realism
as a realistic and pragmatic approach to the world which acknowledges the church-
culture tension as it recognizes the "already but not yet" paradox of the kingdom of
God. This nuanced take on Christian Realism sees the "all-or-nothing" perspectives of

sion between Christianity and the world, a tension that he describes as dangerously ambiguous in its pursuit of balancing the Christ and culture paradox. While presenting a solidly academic and thoughtful "third way" to engage culture, Stackhouse's assessment is not without its problems.

First, his oversimplification of the extremes tends to mischaracterize the variety of nuanced expressions present in both transformation and contradistinction approaches. Surprisingly, Stackhouse aligns the North American religious right and left by identifying them both as transformationalists in their desire to wield Christian power. However, even a cursory examination of the realities on the ground reveals that in comparison to the American religious right, very few in the religious left are operating under any illusion of "totally reshaping society according to Christian values,"[9] nor is their approach as top-down in its aspirational power structures.[10] In fact, the religious right and left in American politics often have entirely different modes of engagement with the broader culture, with starkly contrasting means and ends driving their movements. From the organizational ethics of power structures to the methods of enacting social change, in many ways the religious right and left are, as it would seem semantically, diametrically opposed.[11] Merely because they both aim at various forms of cultural transformation does not merit their being grouped together as dominionists.[12]

---

radicalism as unrealistic and therefore embraces a compromised, but hopeful view of the reign of God on earth. Throughout *Making the Best of It*, Stackhouse consistently posits this Christian Realism as a more reasoned, balanced, mainstream, and effective approach than the "radical contradistinction model" he sees in Yoder and Hauerwas.

9. Stackhouse, *Making the Best of It*, 6.

10. Granted, this is somewhat speculative, but I think one would be hard pressed to identify leaders within America's "Christian Left" (Jim Wallis, Ron Sider, etc.), who, in comparison to the religious right, are comparably oriented towards "wielding Christian power" in secular society. If anything, the religious left is seeking to translate Christian values into more widely palatable policies.

11. See Neuhaus and Cromartie, *Piety and Politics*.

12. Like neoconservativism, the ideology of Christian dominionism is similarly controversial in its desire to reshape American society according to conservative Christian values primarily through political action. Given the way Stackhouse describes the use of power in the "Christ the Transformer of Culture" typology, it sounds more like dominionism than perhaps what Niebuhr originally intended. For examples of Christian dominionism, see Hedges, *American Fascists*.

In the same way, significant variance within the contradistinction camp exists as well. The Amish and Mennonites, for example, surely share a historical connection in the larger Anabaptist tradition, but it would be irresponsible, given the diversity of their respective sectarian differences, to group them all under the "Christ against culture" banner when clearly many Anabaptists are increasingly enmeshed with a plurality of cultural institutions in the modern world. Mennonite theologian Thomas Finger, in his substantial construction of *A Contemporary Anabaptist Theology*, argues that in addition to the variety of positions on church-world interaction in historic Anabaptism, "over the last half century Anabaptists have been increasingly involved in society."[13] From new monastic communities to missional Mennonites, Anabaptists today are hardly withdrawn from the culture.

Stackhouse is surely aware of these many nuances, and much like his recovery of Richard Niebuhr's *Christ and Culture*, perhaps his binary grouping is merely an attempt at a broad *typology*, and not a systematic *taxonomy*. But beyond these categorical critiques, the most significant flaw in Stackhouse's new Christian Realism is rooted in a deeper problem, one that fails to grasp both the gravity of the current cultural context of the Western church, and the capacity of contradistinction approaches to transform this same context. If the church must, as the Gospel and Our Culture Network suggests, radically revisit its assumptions about its place *in* and interaction *with* the world, then perhaps "this is a time for a dramatically new vision. The current predicament of churches in North America requires more than a mere tinkering with long-assumed notions about the identity and mission of the church. Instead, as many knowledgeable observers have noted, there is a need for reinventing and rediscovering the church in this new kind of world."[14] This new world of a twenty-first century post-Christendom context in North America is in many ways vastly different from the early to mid-twentieth century West that Reinhold Niebuhr addressed in his approach to Christian Realism.

Thus, as Stackhouse channels a "new" but essentially very Niebuhrian view of cultural engagement that opts for "realistic" compromise as opposed to "idealistic" radicalism in Christian ethics, two questions arise. First, are these realistic and idealistic qualifiers mutually exclusive in the realm of Christian interaction with society? Or could they pos-

13. Finger, *Contemporary Anabaptist Theology*, 290.
14. Guder and Barrett, *Missional Church*, 77.

sibly be two sides of the same ethical coin of the church's vocation to be "in but not of the world"? Secondly, recognizing that neither a "realistic idealism" nor "idealistic realism" can be quantitatively assessed as "balanced," the essential question becomes focused on which emphasis takes priority, and whether or not fair consideration is given to the other side of the coin.

Though there is certainly valuable wisdom in Reinhold Niebuhr's pragmatic[15] approach to ethics that seeks "neither the sentimental affirmation of an alternative reality that, in the end, means nothing for present choices, nor the fanatic realization of a vision that must, in the end, be corrected by a wiser reason,"[16] there are also limitations in Niebuhr's emphasis on the individual over the community of faith, and his "insistence that responsible Christianity requires a compromise of the demands of Jesus' ethics."[17] While Stackhouse recognizes these limitations, he nevertheless remains critical of Niebuhr's opponents whom he characterizes as totalizing radicals who encourage others to have such "single-minded confidence"[18] in their opposition to the corrupt power structures of secular society.[19]

Unfortunately, in Stackhouse's response to more radical critics of Niebuhr's Christian realism, he has in some ways swung the pendulum too far to the other side, and in so doing neglected the significance and relevance of the more "uncompromising" ethical methods embodied in contradistinction approaches to culture. This disregard for the more

---

15. Robin Lovin notes that "by 1957, Niebuhr himself acknowledged that his work could be called a 'Christian pragmatism'" (Lovin, *Reinhold Niebuhr and Christian Realism*, 48) which he described as "the application of Christian freedom and a sense of responsibility to the complex issues of economics and politics, with the firm resolve that inherited dogmas and generalizations will not be accepted, no matter how revered or venerable, if they do not contribute to the establishment of justice in a given situation" (Niebuhr, *Faith and Politics*, 55). In this statement, Niebuhr rejects the authority of doctrinal certainty when it does not serve the purpose of a Christian sense of "ethical pragmatism."

16. Lovin, *Reinhold Niebuhr and Christian Realism*, 118.

17. Ibid., 94.

18. Stackhouse, *Making the Best of It*, 6.

19. It should also be noted that Stackhouse makes several concessions to Yoder and Hauerwas, but frequently qualifies those concessions by indicating that "it is best that *most* Christians take another, more . . . ambiguous stance" (ibid., 279) in regard to the practicality of radicalism.

subtly pragmatic[20] value of Christian radicalism as espoused by Yoder and Hauerwas is especially unfortunate given our contemporary circumstances which point to the simultaneous cultural dislocation and accommodation of the North American church,[21] a situation in need of alternative communities which can witness to the uniquely countercultural life and work of the gospel in society.

There are two unintentional costs of elevating Christian Realism over Christian radicalism. First, the emphasis on realistic pragmatism inherently downplays the urgency and severity of the issues facing the Western church in its current cultural context. Second, there is a dismissal of the very real potential within alternative Christian communities to directly impact the larger society. Though Stackhouse's call to a reasoned and balanced approach to engagement with culture is a praiseworthy attempt at "making the best of it," the cogency of its compelling vision can get lost in a moderate compromise. On one hand, the church is certainly in need of biblically rooted and theologically sound approaches to faith and culture that can function realistically and pragmatically in the complexities of the everyday world. However, on the other hand, the community of faith is *also* in desperate need of more idealistic, radical perspectives on cultural engagement that can counter society's massive gravitational momentum that pulls the church into a compromise that is more "not yet" than "already" as it seeks to embody the kingdom of God. At what point does Christian Realism's pragmatic compromise actually serve as justification for no longer seeking to transform the paradox of Christ and culture? In this regard, radical communities of contradistinction serve to awaken the church's conscience to the urgency of its contemporary crises.

As we examine the current cultural context of the Western church, certain alarming trends may require more than just realism. While the church of the global South explodes in exponential growth, Western Christians are increasingly marginalized through the widespread de-

20. One of reasons radicalism is often dismissed as untenable is because of its alleged "impracticality." However, I would argue that there are indeed pragmatic (not necessarily in the same way Niebuhr uses the term) aspects of the idealism in radical Christian movements, buts its practical value may not be seen on the surface, and is hence more subtle in nature.

21. The church's "dislocation and accommodation" will be discussed further in conjunction with the creative task of imagination, which serves as the third component of this overall missional theology of cultural engagement.

cline of both numbers and influence in society.[22] Given this dramatic shift, much of which has occurred within the last century, is ideological moderation the only appropriate response? When it is no longer entirely clear what distinguishes the worldview and social praxis of "Christians" from non-Christians in many Western contexts,[23] is that widespread cultural accommodation just a reality of how things are that must be accepted? Can a compromised realism significantly counteract this societal phenomenon? When economic disparity between North America and the two-thirds world (where, coincidentally, two-thirds of the global Christian church resides) is shockingly disproportionate to what we know to be just in the eyes of God, is "making the best of it" really the *best* that we can do in the face of such stark injustice?

Though it would be unwise for the church to solely advocate for radical extremism in its societal engagement at the cost of the compromised Christian Realism offered in Stackhouse's cultural analysis, it would be equally unwise to overlook the severity of our contemporary situation and the significance of our need for a more radical re-visioning of the church's vocation in the dire circumstances of *this* world as we now know it. To dismiss the necessity of cultivating radical Christian communities of contradistinction as unrealistic is to abandon the countercultural imagination that has always characterized the people of God and catalyzed social change within the church for the sake of the world.

Engagement as Countercultural

Because of this necessity of holding realism and radicalism together, it is my assertion that a *missional* theology of cultural engagement must go beyond the balanced Christian Realism that Stackhouse proposes. If cultural engagement calls the church only to thoughtful compromise in the already but not yet reality of the reign of God, then the means by

22. Guder and Barrett, *Missional Church.*

23. Significant sociological research on religious identification and corresponding participation in religious activities/behavioral patterns (prayer, church attendance, political beliefs, etc) has demonstrated that an enormous gap exists between nominal religious affiliation and consistent praxis of religious beliefs. Additional studies examining the distinctions between those who self-identify as either "non-religious" or "Christian" show no statistically significant differences in many social indicators like divorce rates, moral values, economic outlook, political inclinations, and so on, especially when socioeconomic classification remains constant. See the Pew Forum's "U.S. Religious Landscape Survey."

which the church pursues the kingdom of heaven on earth will reflect this moderation. And although there are certainly occasions when the moderation of Christian realism is the wisest choice, the suggestion that true engagement with our current cultural context can also call the church to something more should not be considered an impractical radicalism. In a perspective that emphasizes the confrontational nature of cultural engagement, Catholic missiologist Steven Bevans describes one particular approach to contextual theology that he calls "the countercultural model."

In Bevans' countercultural model which draws heavily on Newbigin and the Gospel and Our Culture Network, engagement is seen as bringing about a prophetic encounter with culture. Bevans emphasizes the inherently countercultural nature of the gospel itself in his conviction that "there is always something in a communication of the gospel that calls a particular human experience, a particular culture, a particular social location and historical situation to judgment."[24] This affirmation of the gospel as a message that calls into question the assumptions and presuppositions of every society is what defines the encounter with culture. Without this encounter, there is no real "engagement" at all. However, the challenge in the countercultural model is resisting the potential to become *anti*-cultural and judgmental toward the world. The goal of engaging culture must be to present a "challenging relevance" to the culture; one that works as a critique from within and in the language of the culture. If it is indeed true that when it comes to communicating the gospel culturally, "good contextualization offends,"[25] then it should offend because of the radical content of the gospel message, and not the way in which the message is communicated.

Clarifying this distinction between being against culture and countercultural is an important priority in defining cultural engagement. Though the communications scholar Marshall McLuhan cautions attempts to separate the medium and message,[26] Christians must remember that countercultural engagement is still essentially a form of thoughtful contextualization. Therefore, the medium must be received as relevant and contextual, even if the message is one of confrontation and radical challenge. To communicate the gospel without local, con-

---

24. Bevans, *Models of Contextual Theology*, 117.

25. Whiteman, "Contextualization," 3.

26. McLuhan and Terrence, *Understanding Media*.

textual considerations inevitably leads to cultural imperialism, but to neglect the challenging relevance of engagement is to dilute and distort the true nature of the gospel itself. For this reason, the essentially countercultural nature of engagement must be *embedded*, or below the surface level of communication. That is to say, the confrontational element is subversive, not readily apparent at first glance. Christian cultural engagement must always wrestle with this fundamental tension, not as a bait-and-switch tactic, but as a paradoxical already but not yet reality of the countercultural kingdom of God. Recovering this confrontational aspect of engagement requires an examination of how faith and culture are often positioned in relationship with one another.

On the spectrum of faith's interaction with culture, there is usually a progression that moves from the relevance of embracing culture on one side to the irrelevance of rejecting culture on the other. The former leads to syncretism and assimilation, while the latter leads to sectarianism and isolation.[27] The problem with this arrangement is that it does not always take into account the reality that few people live on the extremes on this spectrum. Just as it is unlikely to find Christians who proudly and uncritically embrace *all* elements of culture, so is it difficult to find Christians who are adamantly committed to rejecting all of culture (as if that were even possible). Thus, once again, "cultural engagement" has often been positioned as a healthy compromise between the two.

However, while it seems like placing engagement in the ideological center is a natural compromise, this positioning neglects the complication that people do not approach the spectrum with a neutral perspective, nor are people evenly distributed across the spectrum's variety of positions. In fact, the reality of Western Christianity, much like the basic tendencies of human social behavior, is that *relevance* is highly valued while *irrelevance* is rarely sought. Few are actively involved in the process of seeking to be culturally *irrelevant* in their lives, and even those who would claim such an ideal typically do so as a part of a subculture that values the relevance of its commonly shared "countercultural" values.[28] On the other hand, most would be hard pressed to find churches

27. This basic dichotomy has defined the traditional contextualization options for centuries, again as illustrated by Richard Niebuhr's respective "Christ of Culture" and "Christ against Culture" paradigms.

28. See Stapel and Suls, *Assimilation and Contrast*.

or Christians that are *not* concerned with, on some level, being relevant to their context, whatever it may be.

With this inherent human bias toward relevance and hence affinity with others in mind, it becomes clearer that "cultural engagement," if merely placed in the center of the spectrum, does not pose much of a challenge to those already on the side of relevance. With very few proponents of irrelevance on the spectrum, if cultural engagement is equally distanced from both relevance and irrelevance, then it is not truly in the center. In other words, if cultural engagement is thought of as the fulcrum on which the balance of faith and culture between assimilation and isolation turns, the lever is already weighted heavily toward the side of relevance. Thus, to truly find a "balanced" approach to culture, more weight must be placed on the side of irrelevance in order to correct the inherent inclination toward relevance. This emphasis on the countercultural nature of balanced engagement pushes the center towards radical confrontation, and there is no better model of this ethic than the prophetic tradition of the Old Testament.

PROPHETIC CONFRONTATION

The prophetic confrontation of culture is therefore an embrace of "holy irrelevance" that seeks to restore a balanced perspective to the faith and culture conversation. It is not enough to merely "engage" a culture in which popular forms of syncretism are already the norm;[29] rather, the mode of prophetic critique must serve as a foundational component of true cultural engagement. The unique vibrancy and authority of the prophetic tradition in the Christian Scriptures is the bold "irrelevance" and poetic beauty of its language and message. In countless circumstances of joy and grief, proclamation and lament, judgment and promise, the biblical prophets were captured by an alternative vision of the world in which the kingdom of God was looming, imminent, and powerfully real in the present.

---

29. Syncretism between Christianity and culture takes various forms in North American society; individualism, consumerism, nationalism, patriotism, imperialism, democracy, and other ideologies have been readily adopted into the church, often unintentionally. See Van Gelder, *Confident Witness*.

Criticizing and Energizing

Among contemporary perspectives on prophetic ministry, few are as compelling and creative as the prolific Old Testament scholar Walter Brueggemann. Though Brueggemann's work is contested in some circles,[30] his advocacy for rhetorical criticism as "an indispensable complement to sociological analysis"[31] consistently explores the meaning of the text with a passionate concern for its contemporary message to society. With a particular emphasis on the "major breakpoint of Western culture" that requires a deconstruction of "the interpretive engine of the dominant modes of Western Christendom," Brueggemann argues for the necessity of understanding a "new sociopolitical-interpretive situation" which he labels simply as "postmodern."[32] While this new postmodern interpretive method is conversant with several foundational modern works of Old Testament theology,[33] Brueggemann focuses heavily on the pluralistic, rhetorical, narrative, and imaginative aspects of reading and interpreting the text.

Though Brueggemann's *Theology of the Old Testament* represents his most exhaustive and systematic explanation of this postmodern approach, much of this same method was already evident in his very first book, *The Prophetic Imagination*, which examined the contemporary implications of the words of the prophets with piercing clarity. This relatively brief exposition of the prophetic vocation of the church in society is as fresh and relevant today as it was when it was first published in 1978. The interpretive themes in *The Prophetic Imagination* would go on to characterize much of Brueggemann's research in Old Testament studies as well as his active teaching and preaching ministry in the church.

In contrast to the popular notion that the ministry of the prophets in the Old Testament had to do primarily with forms of cultural forecast-

---

30. Arguably Brueggemann's *magnum opus*, *Theology of the Old Testament* is a bold attempt at a truly comprehensive and "postmodern" Old Testament theology from an established scholarly perspective. Though many received his development of a "counter-testimony" in Israel's narrative as a positive consideration of the plurality of voices in the canonical witness of the OT, others found this view to be too much of a departure from more centrist perspectives on the overall arc of the OT metanarrative.

31. Brueggemann, *Theology of the Old Testament*, 53.

32. Ibid., 60–61.

33. Brueggemann notes Gerhard Von Rad and Walter Eichrodt as particularly formative interlocutors among relatively recent contributions in the field. See Von Rad, *Message of the Prophets*; and Eichrodt and Baker, *Theology of the Old Testament*.

ing and future-telling, Brueggemann's fundamental thesis is that "the task of prophetic ministry is to nurture, nourish, and evoke a consciousness and perception alternative to the consciousness and perception of the world around us. Thus I suggest that prophetic ministry has to do not primarily with addressing specific public crises but with addressing, in season and out of season, the dominant crisis that is enduring and resilient, of having our alternative vocation co-opted and domesticated."[34] Within this call to a prophetic ministry that cultivates the alternative vocation of the church are two interdependent perspectives to be held in tension: "The alternative consciousness to be nurtured, on the one hand, serves to *criticize* in dismantling the dominant consciousness . . . to engage in a rejection and delegitimatizing of the present ordering of things. On the other hand, that alternative consciousness to be nurtured serves to *energize* persons and communities by its promise of another time and situation toward which the community of faith may move."[35] Brueggemann then moves on to an examination of Moses as an archetype of the prophetic leader who cultivates an alternative community in Israel by *criticizing* the imperial oppression of Pharaoh and *energizing* the enslaved Hebrews to have faith in the deliverance of YHWH.

It is precisely in the initiation of the Exodus narrative that Moses becomes the exemplar of prophetic ministry. As one appointed by God to reject, delegitimize, and dismantle the authority of Pharaoh, Moses moves in radical faith to confront the "gods" of the Egyptian empire. Captured by the alternative vision of an all-powerful YHWH who heard the cries of his people and was committed to their liberation, Moses harnesses the energy of the God who had covenanted Israel to himself. These prophetic characteristics of the ministry of Moses are later echoed in the ministry of Jesus as the Gospel of Matthew paints Jesus as a new Moses[36] figure in the first century of Second Temple Judaism.

Finding the balance between criticizing and energizing in prophetic ministry requires a dialogical approach to *deconstruction* and

---

34. Brueggemann, *Prophetic Imagination*, 13.

35. Ibid.

36. Jesus as the new Moses in Matthew is a paradigm explored in the parallel patterns of Israel receiving the Law. In the exodus, Moses wanders in the desert for forty years, goes up to Sinai, and then gives the Decalogue to Israel. In Matthew, Jesus wanders for in the desert for forty days, goes up to the Mount of Olives, and then delivers the Sermon on the Mount as a "fulfillment" of Torah. See Luz, *Theology of the Gospel of Matthew*.

reconstruction. If the prophetic confrontation of culture is only characterized by criticizing and dismantling, then the over-emphasis on deconstruction can be received as little more than incessant, angry protest.
Prophetic ministry is not equivalent to the agenda of social activism,
and Brueggemann repeatedly chastises the liberal movements within
Christianity that have limited the role of prophetic engagement with
culture as such. Criticizing in prophetic ministry must always be partnered with a reconstructive energizing of communities of faith that is
rooted in a *particular* alternative vision: that of God's kingdom of *shalom*
that rules with peace, justice, wholeness, and mutuality. Thus, to confront the culture in the spirit of the prophets is not only to challenge the
kind of "imperial consciousness" embodied in the exploitation of Israel
under Pharaoh; it is also to cast a restorative vision of what could be in
the already but not yet reign of God.

For Brueggemann, this exposition of prophetic ministry is not an
abstraction of Old Testament scholarship; rather, it is firmly rooted in
his concern for the vocation of the church and grows out of a conviction
that "the contemporary American church is so largely enculturated to the
American ethos of consumerism that it has little power to believe or act .
. . it may not be a new situation, but it is one that seems especially urgent
and pressing at this present time."[37] The contemporary relevance of prophetic confrontation lies in the prevalence of what Brueggemann calls
the "royal consciousness," a phenomenon exemplified in the kingdom of
Solomon. The opulence and religious pluralism of King Solomon's rule
marked a radical departure from the alternative community of Moses,
and even from that of his father, King David. "The economics of affluence and the politics of oppression are the most characteristic marks of
the Solomonic achievement."[38]

Consequently, the church is called to a prophetic condemnation
of the spirit of the Solomonic empire wherever it is found in our current cultural context. Wherever wealth is maintained and controlled in a
centralized establishment over against the cries of those on the margins,
and wherever faithfulness to YHWH is exchanged for relationships of
convenience for the sake of political gain, the church must cultivate an
alternative consciousness rooted in the memory of the Exodus and the
reality of the present kingdom. For Brueggemann, Solomon's empire,

37. Brueggemann, *Prophetic Imagination*, 11.
38. Ibid., 34.

like every imperial establishment of the past and the present in the world, is representative of the inherently systematic dehumanization that is consistently embodied in imperial aspirations. The dominant consciousness of the world is the spirit of empire, and YHWH, as the God of the oppressed in the Exodus, always stands against the self-interests of the empire.[39] Whether or not one agrees with Brueggemann's particular cultural analysis in this context,[40] it is the commitment to criticizing and energizing in prophetic ministry that lies at the center of cultural confrontation and, in many ways, at the heart of the gospel that Jesus himself preaches in continuity with the Old Testament prophetic tradition.

Prophetic Justice

In and through their ministries of criticizing and energizing, the prophets of Israel embody a rich tradition of proclamation and mediation throughout the Old Testament narrative. In proclaiming God's words, the prophets reveal the heart of YHWH, which is constantly extended to Israel in the patient love of discipline and the righteous anger of judgment. And it is through this ministry of proclamation that the prophets mediate the character of God's covenant, which defines the shape of YHWH's relationship with Israel. As mediators of this covenant relationship, the prophets are often in the position of proclaiming words of admonition when the communal life of Israel slips into the connected realities of idolatry and injustice,[41] both of which impact their collective identity and their interaction with neighboring nations.

---

39. A more in-depth discussion of what is meant by "empire" will be explored in chapter 5.

40. Brueggemann freely admits that his interpretive bias errs on the side of a "hermeneutic of suspicion" as opposed to a hermeneutic of trust. And though some consider his emphasis on the rhetorical authority of the text to be slightly "unorthodox," his prolific scholarship in Old Testament studies has demonstrated his ability to work within and also critique more "traditional" models of interpretation.

41. Idolatry and injustice are frequently connected in the judgment of the prophets; arguably they are two sides of the same coin. Idolatry violates the vertical dimensions of the covenant between God and Israel; injustice violates the horizontal dimensions of the covenant between Israel and her neighbors. Though in this sense you cannot have one without the other, because of my research context on prophetic engagement with culture, my focus in this section will be primarily on the social implications of God's desire for justice.

Again and again throughout Israel's history, the prophets engage their society's complicity in the problem of injustice, an issue that often arises in the wake of idolatry that distorts Israel's understanding of (and therefore their obedience to) their divine election. YHWH is depicted as a champion of justice in his advocacy for the powerless and marginalized.

> God's insistence on justice is dictated by his concern for those to whom justice is denied . . . it is for this reason that the biblical command to do justice is so often connected with the injunction to protect the rights of the weak and helpless. . . . It is the continually recurring accusation of the prophets that the people do not espouse the cause of the poor and the oppressed, that their denial of justice to the fatherless and needy is what brings on the anger of God . . . it is the denial of justice that causes God to exact justice. His anger has its source in the compassion for those who, by the denial of justice due to them, are made to carry the yoke of human wickedness . . . to seek justice is to relieve the oppressed.[42]

God's desire for justice is an undeniable thread that is woven through the whole of the prophets (and essentially the entire biblical narrative), but the justice of YHWH is not an ambiguous concern for the common good or a generic social ethic of inclusion, as it is sometimes portrayed. Rather, YHWH's justice is rooted in a *particular* good, and in a framework of communal ethics that are informed by a covenantal relationship with the living God of Israel.

The tenth chapter of the book of Deuteronomy provides a window into the shape of this covenant as it locates God's expectations of Israel within their cultural and theological context. The first half of the chapter describes the second pair of tablets on which the ten commandments were written by God, and the narrative implication is that Israel is graciously being given a second chance to avoid repeating the incident of blatant idolatry surrounding the golden calf. Given all that has occurred in the long and dramatic journey to Sinai, Moses is emphatic in his instruction on how Israel is to remain faithful to this second iteration of the Decalogue. Thus, the second half of the chapter focuses on God's requirements for keeping the commandments.

---

42. Berkovits and Hazony, *Essential Essays on Judaism*, 132–33.

Deuteronomy 10: The Essence of the Law

[12] So now, O Israel, what does the Lord your God require of you? Only to fear the Lord your God, to walk in all his ways, to love him, to serve the Lord your God with all your heart and with all your soul, [13] and to keep the commandments of the Lord your God and his decrees that I am commanding you today, for your own well-being. [14] Although heaven and the heaven of heavens belong to the Lord your God, the earth with all that is in it, [15] yet the Lord set his heart in love on your ancestors alone and chose you, their descendants after them, out of all the peoples, as it is today. [16] Circumcise, then, the foreskin of your heart, and do not be stubborn any longer. [17] For the Lord your God is God of gods and Lord of lords, the great God, mighty and awesome, who is not partial and takes no bribe, [18] who executes justice for the orphan and the widow, and who loves the strangers, providing them with food and clothing. [19] You shall also love the stranger, for you were strangers in the land of Egypt. [20] You shall fear the Lord your God; him alone you shall worship; to him you shall hold fast, and by his name you shall swear.

Part and parcel of the call to "fear the Lord your God" and "walk in all his ways" is to understand that the election of Israel described in verse 15 requires a "circumcision of the heart" in full submission to YHWH's will. Further, God's will is characterized by the divine impartiality of verse 17; the Lord cannot be bribed and does not "play favorites." However, there is an important turn in verse 18 that significantly shifts the conventional meaning of *mishpat* (judgment) as it is most commonly used in a legal sense prior to Deuteronomy 10. Though God "is not partial" to anyone, he *is* concerned for the *orphan*, the *widow*, and the *stranger*.

Mishpat is therefore not only about the judgment that God exercises; it is also about an overarching sense of *justice* that seeks the protection of the most marginalized groups in society. Simply put, as a righteous judge, the Lord sides with the oppressed because "God had particular concern that those in the community whose social and economic status was not secure should receive just and proper treatment."[43] This "holy triad"[44] of the orphan, widow, and stranger is a grouping that

---

43. Craigie, *Book of Deuteronomy*, 206.

44. Brueggemann, among others, uses this particular language in his description of the repeated occurrences of the orphan, widow, and foreigner in the OT. See Brueggemann, *Church in Joyous Obedience*.

echoes throughout the Old Testament in a recurring pattern whenever God's justice is at stake. In this context of the law, faithfulness to the true meaning of the fear and worship of the Lord is contingent on the just treatment of these particular people in society.

The ninth chapter of Jeremiah is another passage that reveals the specific shape of prophetic justice in the Old Testament. Though there is considerable historical and narrative distance between texts like Deuteronomy 10 and Jeremiah 9, the context and language describing the character of Israel's covenant with YHWH bears many similarities. In particular, it is Israel's inability to remain faithful to Torah in the way that Moses demanded in Deuteronomy 10 that similarly plagues the community of exiles in Jeremiah. The repeated injunctions to keep the commandments, maintain justice, and break the patterns of communal stubbornness in loving obedience to YHWH had not been honored, and Israel faced the consequences of God's discipline as a result.

Thus, as the prophet Jeremiah is witness to this "self-paved road to exile"[45] in Babylon, he laments Israel's unfaithfulness. The aptly named "weeping prophet" cries out in an "extended oracle of disaster"[46] as he surveys the suffering of his people. Jeremiah "paints a grim picture of the collapse of social solidarity and presents the desolation of the land and the dispersal of its people as inevitable consequences. The covenant triangle with Yahweh, Israel, and the land as its fixed points could continue no longer."[47] In the face of such loss and tragedy, the prophet asks the rhetorical "why" in his quest for deeper understanding.

> Jeremiah 9
>
> [12] Who is wise enough to understand this? To whom has the mouth of the Lord spoken, so that they may declare it? Why is the land ruined and laid waste like a wilderness, so that no one passes through? [13] And the Lord says: Because they have forsaken my law that I set before them, and have not obeyed my voice, or walked in accordance with it, [14] but have stubbornly followed their own hearts and have gone after the Baals, as their ancestors taught them. [15] Therefore, thus says the Lord of hosts, the God of Israel: I am feeding this people with wormwood, and giving them poisonous water to drink. [16] I will scatter them among nations

45. Allen, *Jeremiah*, 115.
46. Ibid., 113.
47. Ibid., 117.

that neither they nor their ancestors have known; and I will send
the sword after them, until I have consumed them.

The Lord's explanation in verses 13–14 is an unambiguous condemnation of Israel's failure to keep the same commandments issued in
Deuteronomy 10. In repeatedly forsaking the law, Israel clearly demonstrated that their hearts had not been circumcised, and that their "stiff-
necked" disposition still had not been broken. The form of their idolatry
may have shifted from the golden calf to the Baals, but the root problem
of infidelity was the same.

As the text continues to enumerate the disastrous consequences of
Israel's offenses against YHWH, the chapter draws to a close with this
sage advice from the mouth of the Lord: "Thus says the Lord: Do not
let the wise boast in their wisdom, do not let the mighty boast in their
might, do not let the wealthy boast in their wealth; but let those who
boast boast in this, that they understand and know me, that I am the
Lord; I act with steadfast love, justice, and righteousness in the earth,
for in these things I delight, says the Lord."[48] This "unholy triad" of
wisdom, might (or strength), and wealth echoes the misplaced trust
of the Solomonic empire, and stands in stark contrast with those who
understand and know the Lord. YHWH, the great "I Am," acts with
steadfast love (*hesed*), justice (*mishpat*), and righteousness (*tzedakah*)
throughout creation; moreover, God takes *pleasure* in exercising these
ethics in the world. This second holy triad of *hesed, mishpat,* and *tzedakah* corresponds to the first holy triad of widow, orphan, and stranger as
it prescribes the shape and character of just treatment for those on the
margins of society.

Though modern Western society tends to hold mercy and justice
apart as opposites, the prophetic tradition exemplified in Jeremiah surrounds justice with lovingkindness and charity in a way that infuses the
justice of God with a providential mercy toward the oppressed. Thus the
prophetic confrontation of culture, through criticizing and energizing, as
well as proclamation and mediation, is committed to solidarity with the
vulnerable and excluded because of a divine justice rooted in the delight
of YHWH. Rather than trusting in the wisdom, strength, and wealth of
the world, which the Apostle Paul declares to be foolishness, weakness,
and poverty in the eyes of God, the people of God are covenanted to the

---

48. Jer 9:23–24.

God of justice. This is the legacy of the prophetic tradition, and it is a rich tradition that Jesus embodies in his own prophetic vocation.

JESUS AS PROPHET

The *munus triplex*, or "threefold office" of Jesus Christ as Prophet, Priest, and King, was developed by John Calvin and largely adopted into both the Reformed and Roman Catholic traditions.[49] As a doctrine that describes the major paradigmatic roles of the ministry of Jesus, each category represents a unique characteristic of Jesus' vocation, and the offices of *priest* and *king* in particular have been the subject of robust theological discourse.[50] The priestly vocation of Jesus presents his role as the sacrificial mediator on the cross, an essential doctrine in atonement theology,[51] and Jesus' ministry as king appoints him as the triumphant head of the Church, an important role in both the present kingdom and the eschaton. However, in regard to the *prophetic vocation* of Jesus, "modern emphasis on the prophetic office of Christ . . . places the chief emphasis on Jesus as a teacher."[52] Though this prophetic instruction is broad in scope, it is essential to remember that in Calvin's designation of Christ as Prophet, he "does not intend this in the sense of a mere educator of those who needed only to be taught because they were ignorant. Christ's prophecy consisted in the proclamation of the Gospel . . . his anointing to prophetic office was not only that he should be the Prophet, but also that his people should be prophets."[53] To reduce the office of prophet to simply a didactic ministry is to miss the richness of the Old Testament prophetic tradition in which Jesus is deeply embedded.

The prophetic proclamations in Jesus' ministry evoke a deep, profound calling to embody a transformative vision of the world rooted in

49. Berkhof, *Systematic Theology*, 357.

50. See Migliore, *Faith Seeking Understanding*, 186–90. While some themes in the *munus triplex* can be traced all the way back to Eusebius of Caesarea, examining the use of Calvin's doctrine in the Westminster Shorter Catechism in comparison to Luther's Small Catechism reveals similar emphases on Jesus' offices of priest and king, while less theological discussion is given to the role of prophet. This trend has carried over into popular Christian conversations as well, where the threefold office has been commonly used as a motif for different roles in church leadership. See Driscoll, *On Church Leadership*.

51. See Sherman, *King, Prophet, and Priest*.

52. Berkhof, *Systematic Theology*, 359.

53. Parker, *Calvin*, 69.

the long-awaited kingdom of God. My assertion in this final section of the prophetic task in developing a missional theology of cultural engagement is that Jesus acts in a robust continuity with the prophets when he confronts the temple system in Mark 11:12–25. This narrative captures the essence of Jesus' prophetic vocation and the spirit behind his radical engagement with the social, religious, and economic context of his day.

The eleventh chapter of Mark's Gospel opens with the "Triumphal Entry," the dramatic beginning of Jesus' passion week which coincided with the heightened celebration of Passover in Jerusalem. With the culmination of Jesus' life and ministry just days away, his controversial actions in the temple would set into motion the events that would lead to his death. The infamous temple-cleansing scene is framed by the fig tree narrative, which bookends Jesus' confrontation with the heart of Israel's religious identity. I will argue that when taken as a whole, this passage exemplifies the prophetic ministry of Jesus which, in a reflection of Brueggemann's *Prophetic Imagination*, is characterized by both *criticizing* and dismantling the Jewish religious establishment and *energizing* and empowering the community of his disciples. Additionally, in so doing, Jesus embodies the justice of the prophets, a crucial element of prophetic confrontation.

Mark 11: Jesus Curses the Fig Tree

[12] On the following day, when they came from Bethany, he was hungry. [13] Seeing in the distance a fig tree in leaf, he went to see whether perhaps he would find anything on it. When he came to it, he found nothing but leaves, for it was not the season for figs. [14] He said to it, 'May no one ever eat fruit from you again.' And his disciples heard it.

Jesus Cleanses the Temple

[15] Then they came to Jerusalem. And he entered the temple and began to drive out those who were selling and those who were buying in the temple, and he overturned the tables of the money-changers and the seats of those who sold doves; [16] and he would not allow anyone to carry anything through the temple. [17] He was teaching and saying, 'Is it not written, "My house shall be called a house of prayer for all the nations"? But you have made it a den of robbers.' [18] And when the chief priests and the scribes heard it, they kept looking for a way to kill him; for they were afraid of him, because the whole crowd was spellbound by his teaching.

[19] And when evening came, Jesus and his disciples went out of the city.

The Lesson from the Withered Fig Tree

[20] In the morning as they passed by, they saw the fig tree withered away to its roots. [21] Then Peter remembered and said to him, "Rabbi, look! The fig tree that you cursed has withered." [22] Jesus answered them, "Have faith in God. [23] Truly I tell you, if you say to this mountain, 'Be taken up and thrown into the sea,' and if you do not doubt in your heart, but believe that what you say will come to pass, it will be done for you. [24] So I tell you, whatever you ask for in prayer, believe that you have received it, and it will be yours." [25-26] "Whenever you stand praying, forgive, if you have anything against anyone; so that your Father in heaven may also forgive you your trespasses."

The opening pericope about the fig tree sets the stage for the whole narrative as Jesus heads toward Jerusalem. As a cultural symbol, "the fig tree is an emblem of peace and prosperity; hope for the future is expressed in terms of sitting in security under one's vine and one's fig tree (e.g., Mic 4:4; Zech 3:10) and gathering fruit from them (Hag 2:19)."[54] And though various theories have been presented about why Jesus curses the tree if "it was not the season for figs,"[55] "the point is that Jesus has come and is ready to gather in God's people, but they are bearing no fruit at all. Here we see judgment on Israel in general."[56] As the disciples prepare to move toward the temple, Jesus uses the fruitless fig tree as a metaphor for the fruitlessness of Israel embodied in the religious system of the temple. Though the tree, like the temple, is intended to bear good fruit, it does not, and is therefore cursed. This pointed condemnation is echoed in Jesus' teaching in John 15 about the vine and the branches, where he teaches his disciples that fruitless branches are "gathered, thrown into the fire, and burned."[57]

54. Hooker, *Gospel according to Saint Mark*, 262.

55. Various commentaries have speculated about the timing of the fig tree's lack of fruit. Some say that Jesus knew it was not the season for figs, but that the leafing of the tree was out of season and indicated the possibility of fruit. Others point to an edible pre-fruit that fig trees bear before the fig, and say they were commonly eaten, hence Jesus' suspicion of fruit. See Boring, *Mark*. Regardless, the primary point is that the tree was fruitless.

56. Witherington, *Gospel of Mark*, 313.

57. John 15:6.

Upon arriving in Jerusalem in verse 15, Jesus immediately begins to enact the condemnation he declared on the fruitless fig tree. In a provocative display of righteous anger and zeal, Jesus confronts the corruption and empty religiosity of the temple by expelling those who sustain the marketable trade of selling sacrificial offerings. Notably, though doves were common offerings made by the poor, and John's Gospel alludes to the potential economic exploitation occurring here,[58] the synoptics do not make an explicit condemnation of the financial transactions themselves. These exchanges were necessary for the daily operation of the temple, and would have been especially busy during Passover. Rather, some theorize that it is location of these transactions in the temple courts, the only place where Gentiles were allowed to worship, that incites Jesus to action. In this context, the temple cleansing is "an expression of divine indignation at this callous act which prevented true worship from going on in the Court of Gentiles."[59]

After driving out[60] those who had committed these offenses, Jesus explains his actions further by quoting "My house shall be called a house of prayer for all the nations" from Isaiah 56:7, which describes how foreigners and eunuchs who keep the Sabbath and bind themselves to YHWH are included in Israel's worshipping community on the Temple Mount.

Isaiah 56: The Covenant Extended to All Who Obey

[1] Thus says the Lord:
Maintain justice, and do what is right
for soon my salvation will come,
and my deliverance be revealed.
[2] Happy is the mortal who does this,
the one who holds it fast,
who keeps the sabbath, not profaning it,
and refrains from doing any evil.
[3] Do not let the foreigner joined to the Lord say,
'The Lord will surely separate me from his people';
and do not let the eunuch say,
'I am just a dry tree.'
[4] For thus says the Lord:

---

58. In John 2:16, Jesus exclaims, "Stop making my Father's house a market-place!"

59. Witherington, *The Gospel of Mark : A Socio-Rhetorical Commentary*, 315.

60. Notably, *ekballo* (to eject or "cast out") is the same verb used repeatedly throughout Mark's Gospel to describe Jesus' numerous exorcisms of the demon-possessed.

To the eunuchs who keep my sabbaths,
who choose the things that please me
and hold fast my covenant,
⁵ I will give, in my house and within my walls,
a monument and a name
better than sons and daughters;
I will give them an everlasting name
that shall not be cut off.
⁶And the foreigners who join themselves to the Lord,
to minister to him, to love the name of the Lord,
and to be his servants,
all who keep the sabbath, and do not profane it,
and hold fast my covenant—
⁷ these I will bring to my holy mountain,
and make them joyful in my house of prayer;
their burnt-offerings and their sacrifices
will be accepted on my altar;
for my house shall be called a house of prayer
for all peoples.

As the opening text of Third Isaiah, chapter 56 begins as the postexilic community is returning from Babylon to find the city of Jerusalem in ruins. Isaiah's vision for an inclusive worshipping community where justice (*mishpat*) is maintained in the welcoming of foreigners and eunuchs who kept Torah was intended to set the trajectory of reconstruction. However, in their exclusion of Gentiles, the Jewish religious elite of the temple system had neglected their faithfulness to Isaiah's vision of a diverse worshipping community in Zion. More important than ethnicity or bloodline was a loving and just commitment to Sabbath, service, and faithfulness to the covenant with YHWH. "The point is made decisively that the 'servants' can include foreigners and outcasts who line themselves with the law of God over against the rebels and sinners within and without Israel who continue to resist his will."⁶¹ Jesus condemns the injustice and exclusivity of the second temple that had pushed out the very people God intended to gather together.

As he further explains his righteous indignation, Jesus goes on to quote "den of robbers" from Jeremiah 7, indicating his judgment on the temple system's hypocrisy and oppression of the foreigner, the orphan, and the widow.

61. Childs, *Isaiah*, 458.

Jeremiah 7: Jeremiah Proclaims God's Judgment on the Nation

[1] The word that came to Jeremiah from the Lord: [2] Stand in the gate of the Lord's house, and proclaim there this word, and say, "Hear the word of the Lord, all you people of Judah, you that enter these gates to worship the Lord. [3] Thus says the Lord of hosts, the God of Israel: Amend your ways and your doings, and let me dwell with you in this place. [4] Do not trust in these deceptive words: 'This is the temple of the Lord, the temple of the Lord, the temple of the Lord.' [5] For if you truly amend your ways and your doings, if you truly act justly one with another, [6] if you do not oppress the alien, the orphan, and the widow, or shed innocent blood in this place, and if you do not go after other gods to your own hurt, [7] then I will dwell with you in this place, in the land that I gave of old to your ancestors for ever and ever. [8] Here you are, trusting in deceptive words to no avail. [9] Will you steal, murder, commit adultery, swear falsely, make offerings to Baal, and go after other gods that you have not known, [10] and then come and stand before me in this house, which is called by my name, and say, 'We are safe!'—only to go on doing all these abominations? [11] Has this house, which is called by my name, become a den of robbers in your sight? You know, I too am watching, says the Lord."

Jesus could not have been clearer in his prophetic confrontation of the temple and all it represented. The "Temple Sermon" of Jeremiah 7 is "perhaps the clearest and most formidable statement we have of the basic themes of the Jeremiah tradition . . . in profound conflict with the dominant temple ideology on which the state relied."[62] The ethnocentric myopia, the hollow and meaningless rituals, the oppression of the alien, orphan and widow, and the idolatry of pagan religions over covenant with YHWH had all played a part in the fruitlessness of the temple. And Jesus would not stand for it. The litany of abominations was simply unacceptable. The Second Temple Judaism establishment, centered in the cultural and physical structure of the temple system, would all come crashing down under the powerful vision of Jesus' prophetic call to righteousness and justice.

The people gathered in the temple that day who witnessed Jesus in action responded to the truth in this vision, and "the whole crowd was spellbound by his teaching."[63] The language of amazement expressed in

62. Brueggemann, *Commentary on Jeremiah*, 77.
63. Mark 11:18b.

ekplesso conveys the abrupt physicality of being grasped by Jesus' presence; the people were literally struck with astonishment at the authority of Jesus' teaching. This prophetic *criticizing* of the broken system that upheld the chief priests and teachers of the law was birthed in the radical visions of Isaiah and Jeremiah, and Jesus harnesses their passion as he fulfills his own prophetic vocation. Naturally, the response of the religious establishment is fear. They see in Jesus (and rightfully so) an authentic threat to their positions of power over the people, and he therefore must be eliminated at all costs.

As Mark's narrative transitions away from the temple courts and into the evening, the withered fig tree provides Jesus with another teachable moment for his disciples. It is here that Jesus begins *energizing* his disciples for the trials and challenges ahead. Peter's recognition in verse 21 that the fig tree had indeed withered prompts Jesus to assure his followers that the same power that infuses his ministry is also available to them, if only they will have faith. "This mountain" that Jesus references in verse 23 could very well be *the* mountain—the Temple Mount itself. The significance of this prophetic declaration is that in "contrast to the Jewish expectation that at the Last Day 'the mountain of the house of the Lord' would be exalted and 'established as the highest of mountains' (Mic 4.1), Jesus now pronounces judgment on it and declares that it will be submerged in the sea . . . the place of destruction."[64] Faith to move mountains in this fashion would have seemed unimaginable at the time, but Jesus knew that the temple's days were numbered.

Finally, knowing that his prophetic confrontation of the temple would ultimately lead to his death and the persecution of his followers, Jesus encourages the disciples to model a community of faith and forgiveness in the days ahead. This timely wisdom of Jesus would serve to prepare his close friends for the suffering and hardship they would inevitably encounter in the coming trials of his crucifixion. Though they would initially falter, faith to move mountains and a commitment to forgive one another would eventually mark the community of the early church that went out in the power of the Holy Spirit convinced that the resurrected Jesus had commissioned them as his ambassadors. This communal *metanoia* is a result of the inspiring, transformative power of prophetic ministry in the world.

---

64. Hooker, *Gospel according to Saint Mark*, 270.

5

Imagination: The Creative Task

HAVING NOW CONSIDERED *INCARNATION* as the missional task and *confrontation* as the prophetic task, the final task of developing a missional theology of cultural engagement seeks to cultivate a *subversive imagination* as a crucial element of ensuring that an embodied, prophetic theology can take root and flourish in the shadow of the empire. While this final section draws on the incarnational and confrontational aspects of engaging culture, it also proposes creativity as a fundamental necessity of the church's character in a post-Christendom context. Through an exploration of New Monasticism as an expression of subversive Christianity, we will consider the shape and practices of alternative Christian communities emerging on the margins of society. Lastly, by returning to Brueggemann's prophetic creativity in *Hopeful Imagination* and *The Church in Joyous Obedience*, we will move toward cultivating an imaginative vision of cultural engagement.

HOPEFUL SUBVERSION

Though the language of Christian "subversion" can carry a sinister connotation of undermining authority, the validity of the metaphor is contingent on one's interpretation of contemporary Christianity's cultural circumstances in the West. If, as Stackhouse argued earlier, the Constantinian institutionalization of Western Christianity in Christendom is a situation best engaged through a compromised Christian realism, then the suggestion of Christian subversion may come across as too radical. However, if Western Christendom has in fact become more like the empire than a particular called and sent community, then perhaps a more subversive model of Christian engagement with culture is needed.

There is no shortage of perspectives on the imperial corruption of Western Christianity, and radical Christian movements have frequently drawn on a number of voices,[1] from Christian Anarchists to Liberation Theologians. French philosopher Jacques Ellul, who was heavily influenced by the uncompromising Christocentrism of Karl Barth and the scathing criticism of political Christendom in Soren Kierkegaard, describes "the heart of the problem"[2] this way:

> There is . . . a difficulty, for what the New Testament really means by being a Christian is the very opposite of what is natural to us. It is thus a scandal. We have either to revolt against it or at all costs to find cunning ways of avoiding the problem, such as by the trickery of calling Christianity what is in fact its exact antithesis, and then giving thanks to God for the great favor of being Christians. As Kierkegaard says, nothing displeases or revolts us more than New Testament Christianity when it is properly proclaimed . . .
>
> Here is the difficulty: it is not at all that of showing that official Christianity is not the Christianity of the New Testament, but that of showing that New Testament Christianity and what it implies to be a Christian are profoundly disagreeable to us. Never—no more today than in the year 30—can Christian revelation please us: in the depths of our hearts Christianity has always been a mortal enemy. History bears witness that in generation after generation there has been a highly respected social class (that of priests) whose task is to make of Christianity the very opposite of what it really is.[3]

Here Ellul captures a sentiment that encapsulates much of what drives Christian radicalism: a conviction that the authentic witness of the New Testament, particularly in the social and political ethics of Jesus, is a totalizing standard and "mortal enemy" of natural humanity.[4]

1. Surely many names culd be added to this list (John Howard Yoder, Martin Luther King, Jr., Dorothy Day, James Cone, Gustavo Gutierrez, Juan Luis Segundo, Oscar Romero, Lesslie Newbigin, and Desmond Tutu, just to name a few); my mention of Barth and Kierkegaard is a reflection of Jacques Ellul's explicit influences.

2. This is the title of the eighth chapter of Jacques Ellul's *The Subversion of Christianity*.

3. Ellul, *Subversion of Christianity*, 154.

4. Undoubtedly, this is a typical but no less bold claim of Ellul and his contemporary Christian anarchists. In *The Subversion of Christianity*, Ellul walks through a series of "contradictions" between the biblical witness and the contemporary expressions of Christendom, from power and politics to moralism and the sacred.

Because of this reality, "official Christianity" becomes in fact the opposite of what the New Testament intends. "The church has simply adopted wholesale the ideas and manners of modern society as it did those of past societies,"[5] and in so doing, "Christianity imbibes cultures like a sponge"[6] rather than calling those cultures into question. This is how, according to Ellul, the Christian faith became the empire of Christendom.

Though numerous references to the ideology of empire have been mentioned throughout this research, from the upward mobility of social status and economic capital to the affluence and oppression of the Solomonic kingdom, a clearer definition of "empire" is still needed to identify the substance of subversion. Brian J. Walsh offers this perspective: "Empires are totalizing by definition. In the words of the psalmist, imperial 'mouths lay claim to heaven, and their tongues take possession of the earth' (Ps 73:9 NIV). Empires are built on systemic centralizations of power and secured by structures of socioeconomic and military control. They are religiously legitimated by powerful myths that are rooted in foundational assumptions, and they are sustained by a proliferation of imperial images that captivate the imagination of the population."[7]

This contemporary description of imperial phenomena outlines the primary characteristics of empires:

1. Systematized, centralized power

2. Structured socioeconomic and military control

3. Religious legitimization by cultural myths

4. Widespread visual propaganda

Though mythologies[8] and imperial images[9] may look different in a Western-dominated, postcolonial era where imperialism has gone out

---

5. Ellul, *Subversion of Christianity*, 8.

6. Ibid., 18.

7. Walsh and Keesmaat, *Colossians Remixed*, 31.

8. Western "myths" like "progress," the "American Dream," or "democracy and development" are not inherently false, but the forms of their propagation can reach a kind of mythological status in a culture that idolizes such ideologies. See Boyd, *Myth of a Christian Nation*.

9. Probably the best example of imperial images in the West is the culture of television, mass media, and the marketing industrial complex. These images undoubtedly dominate the physical, social, and psychological space of Western culture. See Postman, *Amusing Ourselves to Death*.

of fashion politically, the widespread existence of contemporary empires by these standards should be obvious.[10] These imperial characteristics may be present in the explicit, traditional geopolitical conceptions of empire, as in the historical Roman Empire, or in the implicit ideological connotations of empire present in powerful entities that have no clear boundaries. The crucial point of understanding is in an awareness of the *spirit* of empire, which may be as obvious as an emperor or as subtle as a credit card.

Mark Van Steenwyk, founder of the Anabaptist intentional community Missio Dei, argues that one of the primary tasks of the Christian community in every age is to confront and subvert the spirit of empire, which requires a good deal of imagination. This perspective defines imagination not as the whimsical fantasy of "playing pretend," but instead as the creative ability to see things as they could be, or to imagine that which does not appear to be possible in the present reality. In this sense, faith requires a particular kind of imagination, one that has the capacity to believe in the unbelievable, even in the face of uncertainty. The author of Hebrews puts it this way: "Now faith is the assurance of things hoped for, the conviction of things not seen."[11] This kind of faith is the outcome of a spiritual imagination that trusts in the faithfulness of an "invisible God,"[12] and it is precisely this *faithful imagination* that has mobilized the people of God in the shadow of the empire for thousands of years.

When Jesus began his public ministry by proclaiming "the kingdom of God is at hand," this was a prophetic declaration over against the Roman Empire that named Caesar as "lord." While the empire ruled with hierarchy and violence, Jesus preached about a kingdom of inclusiveness and peacemaking. Equipped with the radical ethics of the Sermon on the Mount, Jesus prepared his followers for a different way of life in the empire, one that would subvert the power structures of dominance and control with servanthood and sacrifice. Ultimately, the cross was (and is) the pinnacle of subversion. Used as an instrument of fear and death,

10. The implicit allegation that the U.S. is an empire is understandably met with resistance among those who view the accusation as "un-American" or "unpatriotic." For those with that concern, I would suggest, along with historian Howard Zinn, that political dissent is a form of patriotism in line with the greatest ideals of our democratic liberties. See Zinn, *People's History of the United States*.

11. Heb 11:1.

12. Col 1:15.

the Roman Empire crucified criminals who would dare to confront the imperial agenda. But Jesus turns this symbol upside-down in the resurrection and conquers death through *kenosis* on the cross. That which the empire meant for defeat, Jesus uses to declare a cosmic victory. For the believing community of the early church, it would take more than a little faithful imagination at first to be convinced of the radical possibility in this unexpected turn of events.

In this same spirit, the church today is called to engage the empire(s) of our present age with the same kingdom message that requires the same faithful imagination. When the spirit of empire declares people to be fragmented autonomous individuals, the kingdom of God calls people into a family of wholeness and mutual interdependence. When the empire equates consumerism and entertainment with "the good life," the kingdom of God invites people to Sabbath rest and a ministry of hospitality.[13] When the imperial agenda conceals difficult truths under a façade of benevolence, the people of the kingdom must expose the falsehood of artificial magnanimity.[14] The church must embody this prophetic witness by cultivating an imagination that enables truth-telling in a society that values appearances and inauthenticity. If the people of God cannot discern life-giving alternatives from the death-dealing culture of narcissism, celebrity idolatry, corporate greed, and human exploitation, then we have lost our imagination.

This imaginative subversion of the imperial consciousness will only take root and flourish if it is exceedingly hopeful. "Being sure of what we hope for" is the element of faith that prompts an inner longing for something more than what the present has to offer. Hope is born in the *energizing* task of prophetic ministry, and is sustained in the vision of the Faithful One who honors his covenant with his people. Hope breeds creativity in adversity, just as the biblical prophets saw enduring hope and grace behind the judgment of God in the present. In *Hopeful Imagination: Prophetic Voices in Exile*, Brueggemann explains how the prophets "proclaim a new beginning with fresh actions from God that are wrought in this moment of exile, in this crisis of dismantling . . .

13. Van Steenwyk, *Christian Radicalism.*

14. For example, the spirit of empire often hides human suffering behind excuses of self-responsibility, rugged individualism, or inevitability. At best, it is suggested that charity can alleviate suffering. But in the kingdom of God, we are each responsible for and accountable to the suffering of our neighbors, and only authentic solidarity with our neighbors can begin to change the situation of their oppression.

these poets not only *discerned* the new actions of God that others did not discern, but they *wrought* the new actions of God by the power of their imagination, their tongues, their words. New poetic imagination evoked new realities in the community."[15] It is the hopefulness in their poetic imagination that enacts the work of God in their midst. In his exposition of Jeremiah 30, Ezekiel 36, and Isaiah 54, Brueggemann asserts that it is only in the double movement toward *relinquishing* the present world of suffering and *receiving* the new world under YHWH's sovereignty that "grief permits newness, holiness gives hope, and memory allows possibility."[16]

A *hopeful* subversion ensures that the faithful imagination of the church is constructive and creative, even in a context of pain and suffering. Agenda-driven imperial subversion can easily take on a harsh, deconstructive tone of binary oppositions, but a hopeful subversion that grows out of the faithful imagination of the prophets breathes life and newness into the age of empire. Brueggemann repeatedly emphasizes the importance of the *poetic vocation* of the prophets; that as poets, the creative energy behind their words is the catalyst in their ministry of subverting the empire.

NEW MONASTICISM

Alternative communities of faith that have embraced a hopeful subversion of empire are springing up in places around the world.[17] Though not all would identify themselves as associated with the movement that has come to be known as "New Monasticism," many share a common outlook on the deep-seated problems with imperial Christianity, especially in America. Most advocates of New Monasticism have readily admitted that there is nothing particularly "new" about their practice of monastic

---

15. Brueggemann, *Hopeful Imagination*, 2.

16. Ibid., 131.

17. Another important movement that shares some common themes with New Monasticism has been called the "New Friars." Though some are tentative about the presumptions that may go along with such a designation, the movement has been characterized by values that are "incarnational, devotional, communal, missional, and marginal." Where the New Friars would be most distinct from the New Monasticism is in their global and missiological emphasis while New Monasticism could be perceived as more local and missional. See Bessenecker, *New Friars*.

ideals, but their emphasis on the urgency of the present moment is always seeking fresh, new responses to our contemporary crises.

In doing so, they resonate with Dietrich Bonhoeffer's sentiment in 1935 that "the restoration of the church will surely come from a sort of new monasticism which has in common with the old only the uncompromising attitude of a life lived according to the Sermon on the Mount in the following of Christ. I believe it is now time to call people to this."[18] As Bonhoeffer wrote to his brother Karl during the rise of Nazi Germany, he understood that the secularization of the church which had precluded its prophetic witness to the German state could only be remedied by a return to the radical ideals exemplified in the Sermon on the Mount. This recognition is what inspired Bonhoeffer's underground seminary in Finkenwalde (and subsequently, *Life Together*), and much of the same perspective has motivated similar movements in New Monasticism.

Though the specific social and political circumstances which surrounded Bonhoeffer have passed, New Monasticism sees similar cultural crises in the context of a post-Christendom society.

> Two things have become quite clear to those who care about the church and its mission. On the one hand, the churches of North America have been dislocated from their prior social role of chaplain to the culture and society and have lost their once privileged positions of influence. Religious life in general and the churches in particular have increasingly been relegated to the private spheres of life. Too readily, the churches have accepted this as their proper place. At the same time, the churches have become so accommodated to the American way of life that they are now domesticated, and it is no longer obvious what justifies their existence as particular communities.[19]

Of particular concern to New Monasticism is what Guder describes as a cultural accommodation to American society to such a degree that the church has become domesticated within the dominant way of life. In much of this version of "Christian America," the church has little to offer by way of contradistinction to the culture. Rather, there is a sanitized mimicry of mainstream culture that has more to do with private values in a religious enclave than any sort of public, holistic

18. Bonhoeffer, *Testament to Freedom*, 424.
19. Guder and Barrett, *Missional Church*, 78.

truth. Consequently, for those committed to a more radical vision of the transformative, countercultural nature of the gospel, some cognitive dissonance develops. And just as the fourth century Constantinian adoption of the formerly marginalized Christian religion into the heart of the Roman Empire drove a monastic exodus into the desert, so has American imperial Christianity of the twenty-first century provoked a new monastic movement into "the abandoned places of empire."[20]

Growing out of a "movement of radical rebirth" at St. Johns Baptist Church in Durham, North Carolina, these twelve marks came to characterize this New Monasticism:

1. Relocation to the abandoned places of Empire.

2. Sharing economic resources with fellow community members and the needy among us.

3. Hospitality to the stranger.

4. Lament for racial divisions within the church and our communities combined with the active pursuit of a just reconciliation.

5. Humble submission to Christ's body, the church.

6. Intentional formation in the way of Christ and the rule of the community along the lines of the old novitiate.

7. Nurturing common life among members of intentional community.

8. Support for celibate singles alongside monogamous married couples and their children.

9. Geographical proximity to community members who share a common rule of life.

10. Care for the plot of God's earth given to us along with support of our local economies.

11. Peacemaking in the midst of violence and conflict resolution within communities along the lines of Matthew 18.

12. Commitment to a disciplined contemplative life.[21]

---

20. Rutba-House, *School(s) for Conversion*, xii.
21. Ibid.

Echoing their forebears in the Franciscan Orders, the Catholic Worker Movement, and the Bruderhof Communities, these new monastics committed themselves to re-imagining how the church could look in a society permeated with the spirit of empire. Each mark seeks to subvert the societal norms that have further fragmented a culture already mired in brokenness. Creative stewardship, generous hospitality, creation care, and intentional peacemaking are efforts directed at reconciling the many rifts in a globalizing consumer culture. In order to embody these twelve ideals, the missional, incarnational, and prophetic witness of a more radical Christianity would require a "re-baptizing of their imaginations," which would enable them to be captured by an alternative vision of the reign of God in the world.[22] This vision breaks with the status quo of segregation and hyper-individualism and instead embraces a community of wholeness and healing.

As an expression of Christian radicalism, New Monasticism is simply trying to get to the root of the problem. Radicals are labeled as such because of their desire to excavate the issue at the *radix*, which is Latin for "root." Peter Maurin, who cofounded the Catholic Worker Movement with Dorothy Day, said that this desire is rooted in "a vision so old it looks new." "In the history of the church, it's nothing new to look around and find our institutions severely compromised. Ours is a tragic story. But it is also a story of hope. In every era God has raised up new monastics to pledge their allegiance to God alone and remind the church of its true vocation . . . such radical hope is the heart of the monastic impulse, always calling the church back to its roots underground. If such a vision seems novel, it may be a sign of how far we've strayed from our story."[23] This hope for a powerfully subversive Christianity can only be realized when the vision of a faithful imagination is lived out in a called and sent community of people. In a post-Christendom context of enculturated, accommodated Christianity, a commitment to this kind of creative cultural engagement has the potential to work like yeast through the dough of a domesticated church that has lost its sense of imagination.

It should also be noted, however, that New Monasticism is not without its problems. First, imaginative potential and effectual change on the ground are two very different realities. Barriers to entry in these

22. Van Steenwyk, "Christian Radicalism."

23. Wilson-Hartgrove, *New Monasticism*, 54.

intentional communities remain high, and naturally the appeal of New Monasticism's "uncompromising" rule is quite limited. When an inability to geographically relocate or radically restructure one's communal life precludes participation in New Monasticism, the gulf between these younger monastics and their more "mainstream" Christian counterparts seems to grow. Along with this separation comes a criticism that cultivating radicalism actually breeds a form of spiritual elitism. Much like Stackhouse's critique of Yoder's advocacy for alternative Christian communities of contradistinction, this "canon within the canon"[24] treatment of the Sermon on the Mount can promote an unintentional "holier than thou" posture among its more radical adherents.

Secondly, despite all of its efforts directed at the ministry of reconciliation in socioeconomically stratified neighborhoods, New Monasticism has not often been able to live into this vision of a reconciled community with tangible markers of genuine diversity.

> Another problem the communities face is the challenge of transcending divisions along the lines of race and class. While those who do join are drawn to the scriptural norm of communities that transcend racial and financial barriers, they tend to be white, college-educated folks, despite great effort to reach out. For example, one of the Sojourners' original goals was to serve some of the tens of thousands of refugees displaced to San Francisco as a result of civil war in El Salvador. Three Salvadoran families joined the church and benefited from its legal clinic and job preparation aid. As soon as they acquired the resources, the families promptly bought minivans, left the church and moved to the suburbs. Perhaps those who have had less of a chance at pursuing the American dream are not yet ready to be disenchanted with it.[25]

The implicit assumption that marginalized people in established communities will look with favor upon Christians who, even with the best of intentions, relocate to these "abandoned places of empire" is a fundamentally flawed presupposition. The very fact that many proponents of New Monasticism are significantly shaped by the ethnic, educational, and economic privileges that they already have (and which they gladly eschew "for the sake of the gospel") demonstrates the con-

---

24. Stackhouse, *Making the Best of It.*

25. Byassee, "New Monastics," 45.

tradictory complexity in attempting to shed privilege for the purpose of serving others. There is nothing inherently glorious or spiritual about the cyclical oppression of poverty, and Jesus' teaching that the poor (in spirit and in wealth) are blessed must inform any attempt at downward mobility with compassion, wisdom, and intercultural competency.[26]

In spite of these criticisms, much of which adherents of New Monasticism are already aware, there is still a refreshing imagination in this movement that is both peculiar and compelling. Though its presence on the larger stage of emerging Christian communities may be understated, New Monasticism is—slowly but surely—transforming the church from the margins in small but significant ways with creativity, hope, and prophetic imagination.

IMPERIAL SCARCITY AND GOD'S ABUNDANCE

Imagination is a crucial necessity in a paradoxical world where the already and not yet overlap in an elusive fashion. And yet, "the history of imagination . . . indicates that since Aristotle, imagination has been regarded as an inadequate mode of knowledge, in contrast to reasonable, logical, or empirical discourse."[27] In a similar epistemological prejudice, "the classical theological tradition, with its bent toward the philosophical, has been reserved about imagination that moves beyond the logical or the empirical."[28] Given this heavy bias toward Enlightenment rationality, what role can imagination play beyond the cultural enclave of the arts?

In an effort to reframe the validity of imaginative theological thinking, Garrett Green suggests that "religion, in an age virtually defined by the paradigm of natural science, has generally been understood as the great alternative to science, as the chief example of the *other* way of thinking and acting. This dualism characterizes the leading interpretations of religion by friends and foes alike. Both . . . have shared an

26. I prefer the language of "competency" over "sensitivity" if for no other reason than its higher cost to the party in power in intercultural communication. Being "sensitive" to multicultural situations is not as demanding as developing relational competencies that function cross-culturally in an equitable manner.

27. Brueggemann, *Theology of the Old Testament*, 67. In supporting this claim, Brueggemann cites Kearney, *Wake of Imagination*; Green, *Imagining God*; and Bryant, *Faith and the Play of Imagination* as influential works.

28. Brueggemann, *Theology of the Old Testament*, 68.

underlying assumption that religion is a form of imagination."[29] As a proponent of this kind of thinking, Brueggemann joins Green in characterizing the work of theological imagination "as the capacity to generate, evoke, and articulate alternative images of reality, images that counter what hegemonic power and knowledge have declared to be impossible."[30] Thus, imaginative energy redefines "reality" with new possibilities, and "this countervision (sub-version) of reality thereby deabsolutizes and destabilizes what 'the world' regards as given, and invites the hearers of the text to recharacterize what is given or taken as real."[31]

Though this reality-altering capacity of imagination is significant in a theological sense, the creativity that is partnered with imagination is rarely deemed important in a society that cherishes the market value of tangible commodities. Imagination has seemingly little significance in the frenetic pace of our workaday world; it cannot be bought, sold, traded, or commercialized. But if we are able, as Brueggemann continually beckons, to back away from Western culture's obsession with supply and demand—even for just a moment—then we may see that imagination, though cheap in the eyes of the world, has priceless value in God's economy.

Returning to Moses as the prophet par excellence of the Old Testament, Brueggemann explores the remarkable imaginative capacity of Moses in the Exodus narrative in his 2008 lecture at Regent College, "From Exodus to Sinai: The Journey to the Common Good."[32] This journey leads Israel from slavery and oppression to covenant and freedom, and is fueled, at every turn, by the ability of the people of God to imagine a different way of life than what they have known all their lives.

Again positioning Pharaoh as the archetype of imperial consciousness, Brueggemann goes on to explain that the driving force behind Pharaoh's oppressive exploitation of the Hebrew slaves is *anxiety about scarcity*. This anxiety is indicative of the major impediment to the common good of all people. In Genesis 41, Pharaoh's nightmare about a coming famine in Egypt drives him to create a food monopoly which in turn enslaves the local population. A fear of scarcity creates an abusive

---

29. Green, *Imagining God*, 10.

30. Brueggemann, *Theology of the Old Testament*, 68.

31. Ibid.

32. Brueggemann, *Church in Joyous Obedience*.

system of anxiety, and the scarcity mentality becomes so ingrained in the people of Israel that they cannot imagine another way of life.[33]

In sharp contrast with this imperial anxiety caused by scarcity is the radical abundance of God's generosity. But even after having witnessed God's miraculous deliverance of Israel at the hand of Moses, the people cannot foster the faithful imagination necessary to believe that God will continue to provide for them. Instead, by Exodus 16, they already want to go back to Egypt, where revisionist history about an abundance of food has erased their memories of oppression. In response to this collective amnesia, a patient and gracious YHWH miraculously provides manna and quail for his people. This show of "YHWH's inestimable generosity stands in contrast to Pharaoh's nightmare of anxiety about scarcity."[34]

As the narrative progresses, we see that the journey from Egypt to Sinai is not only a geographic relocation of a group of freed slaves. In fact, it is more significantly a journey out of the enslaving anxiety system of scarcity under Pharaoh and into the freeing generosity covenant of God's abundance. The commandments given at Sinai are as much about neighborliness as they are about ethical norms under YHWH's rule. In God's economy, being a good neighbor means sharing in God's abundance and trusting in his provision. For a nation of slaves that had been trained in a scarcity system for generations, this new paradigm of YHWH's radical economics required an imaginative leap of faith. Without this faithful imagination, Israel would have remained bound to the ideology of empire and enslaved to the anxiety system of scarcity.

Scarcity of resources is perhaps the most prominent economic force in our world,[35] and the spirit of Pharaoh is alive and well in our contemporary anxiety. Empires can never have enough resources, even when our neighbors have so little. In our current cultural context, there is a

33. I am certain it is no accident that Brueggemann uses the term "scarcity" to parallel the concept in modern macroeconomics that drives the consumption engine of free market capitalism. Just as scarcity caused anxiety in Egypt, so it continues to cause anxiety in our age of consumerism and globalization. See Barrera, *God and the Evil of Scarcity.*

34. Brueggemann, *Church in Joyous Obedience.*

35. Whether the resources are natural (energy), material (commodities), or economic (capital), scarcity in all its forms, both perceived and genuine, is a pressing issue at the heart of many contemporary global crises. See Bardhan, *Scarcity, Conflicts, and Cooperation.*

desperate need for an imaginative revisioning of our economic systems that have cultivated fear and anxiety instead of freedom and generosity. While insurmountable debt enslaves the poorest of the world's poor, the empires of the West revel in overabundance.[36] This is not the imaginative vision of God's generosity in the world. Creative solutions like micro-finance, social venture projects, and grassroots economic development are being pioneered and championed by those outside of the church,[37] and the people of God must become better partners and leaders in these fields if the church is to offer a compelling vision of how the world could be when a more caring and generous neighborliness is a significant priority on God's agenda.

Brueggemann closes with the recognition that "people who live in anxiety and fear have no time or energy for the common good," and "it takes an immense act of generosity to break the grip of anxiety."[38] The quintessential act of God's generosity to his people is embodied in the person of Jesus Christ, who took on flesh and got down in the mud with his creation. The church remembers this gift whenever the Eucharist is celebrated. For it is in the broken body of the Suffering Servant that we can once again imagine a God who would empty himself on behalf of the world in order to demonstrate the abundant life readily given in his Son. And as we have sought to cultivate an imaginative vision of cultural engagement, it is good to remember that "those who receive the bread of abundance have energy beyond themselves for the sake of the world."[39] In the same way, may the church be ready and willing to be taken, blessed, broken, and given.

THE VALLEY AND THE CORNER REVISITED

Up until this point, the street signs in the Valley and on the Corner may have seemed curiously absent from this more explicitly theological conversation. However, as the transition is made from looking *at* the lens of cultural engagement to *through* the lens of a missional theology of cultural engagement, a few things become clearer.

---

36. Jochnick and Preston, *Sovereign Debt at the Crossroads*.

37. Yunus and Jolis, *Banker to the Poor*.

38. Brueggemann, *Church in Joyous Obedience*.

39. Ibid.

Overall, developing a missional theology of cultural engagement contributes a unique perspective to the existing faith and culture dialogue by challenging the church to consider a more embodied, prophetic, and subversive ethical encounter with the world, particularly in the urban context. Beginning with the incarnation, the *kenosis* of the church must inform the shape of missional engagement with a posture of radical humility and service in the city. Continuing with confrontation, the countercultural nature of the gospel must infuse prophetic engagement with an alternative vision of the kingdom over against the empire. And concluding with imagination, a subversive vision of hope must guide creative engagement with urban communities of faith that are committed to an imaginative generosity in a world that is stratified into ghettos, slums, suburbs, and gated communities.

Incarnation is the missional task; the Word becomes flesh and makes his dwelling among us in the city. This declaration of the embodied presence of God in the person of Jesus Christ is a fundamental affirmation of the church and a foundational component of the triune God's mission in the Valley and on the Corner. When theology of mission is liberated from its Christendom ecclesiology and recentered in the identity of the *missio Dei*, the missional character of the church is revealed in a Western, post-Christendom context. As an expression of missional theology in context, incarnational ministry cultivates a sent, downwardly mobile posture in the church by challenging urban communities of faith to pour out their lives on behalf of the city in the spirit of Christ's ultimate *kenosis* on the cross. In the process of developing a missional theology of cultural engagement, the incarnation initiates the missional task by calling the people of God to a truly embodied theology in both the locality of the Valley and the universality of the Corner.

Confrontation is the prophetic task in the urban context. Though "engaging culture" has often been presented as a mild compromise between the extremes of syncretism and irrelevance, the circumstances of the Western church's urban context require a more radical understanding of the countercultural implications of true engagement. When engaging culture is seen as prophetic confrontation in continuity with the biblical prophets' vision of steadfast love, justice, and righteousness, Brueggemann suggests that the church must learn to *criticize* and *energize* in the city. As one who passionately embodies this prophetic vocation, Jesus models this ministry as he confronts the cultural challenges of the Temple system in urban Jerusalem.

Imagination is the creative task in the city. With imagination functioning as the creative force that enables an incarnational, confrontational engagement with the city, the church must embody the essentially subversive nature of the Christian encounter with "empire" wherever it is found in the urban context. Through emerging radical movements in Christianity like the New Monasticism, the missional imagination of the church is inspiring those who are collectively conspiring to create alternative Christian communities in contexts like the Valley and the Corner. As a people of faithful and hopeful imagination, the creative capacity of the church can dismantle imperial anxiety in the city and construct urban communities of radical hospitality and generosity.

PART 3

An Urban Exegesis of the Rainier Valley

Thus says the LORD: I will return to Zion, and will dwell in the midst of Jerusalem; Jerusalem shall be called the faithful city, and the mountain of the LORD of hosts shall be called the holy mountain. Thus says the LORD of hosts: Old men and old women shall again sit in the streets of Jerusalem, each with staff in hand because of their great age. And the streets of the city shall be full of boys and girls playing in its streets.

—Zechariah 8:3–5

IN THE PROPHET ZECHARIAH's vision of a restored Jerusalem, the faithful city is rebuilt and once again becomes a holy dwelling place for YHWH. Children and the elderly—both vulnerable populations—play peacefully in the streets. Though the Babylonian exiles had experienced much urban despair, "the context for reflection about good times remains an urban reality . . . clearly, Zechariah is centrally concerned with Jerusalem and its immediate environs as the setting in which renewal will take place."[1] The renewal of the city was not only an eschatological hope; it was also a mission for the present. Urban exegesis, or *reading the city as a text*, is a means to participate in this ongoing mission in the contemporary city.

Having established a primary lens for *missional* cultural engagement in part 2, part 3 presents a new lens for the city by examining the local setting of Seattle's Rainier Valley in order to develop a model of urban exegesis. As a method of cultural analysis, this model utilizes semiotic description of culture[2] by exploring urban semiotics in a community, and as a method of theological analysis, emphasis is placed on cultural exegesis. Overall, this model also draws on part 2's missional

1. Petersen, *Haggai and Zechariah 1–8*, 300.

2. Semiotic description of culture is explained further in chapter 9.

theology of cultural engagement by contextualizing the themes of incarnation, confrontation, and imagination.

In chapter 6, I will unpack the process of urban exegesis by first interacting with a variety of missiological perspectives on understanding the local urban context. Then, through an emphasis on the anthropological categories of *observation* and *interpretation*, I will examine *urban socio-semiotics* as a method of observing the built environment of the urban community and *cultural exegesis* as a method of interpreting the missiological implications of the urban community.

In chapter 7, I will focus on the urban context of the Rainier Valley by applying the methods of the observation component of urban exegesis. Through a semiotic analysis of the Valley's density, diversity, and disparity, I will examine how the Valley's "street signs" shape the urban space and character of the community.

Lastly, in chapter 8, I will develop a local urban theology of the Rainier Valley by utilizing the methods of the interpretation component of urban exegesis. By focusing on the incarnational, confrontational, and imaginative issues of place, neighbor, and community, I will explore how a local theology can be firmly rooted in both the culture of the immediate context and the broader biblical narrative. Overall, this second lens of urban exegesis aims to highlight the indispensible locality of the city, and the significance of the particular neighborhood for the urban context at large.

6

Unpacking Urban Exegesis

IN THE ABSENCE OF an established, systematic definition of "urban exegesis," the somewhat ambiguous terminology has taken on a variety of meanings[1] as many different academic disciplines have implicitly or explicitly used several related metaphors. Urban sociology has discussed the possibility of an urban approach to social semiotics, and formal semioticians have in turn made contributions to the intersection of semiology and urbanism.[2] From cultural studies and geography, literary theorists and urban planners alike have described cities as "texts," or have discussed "reading" urban environments. Missiologists and theologians have developed models of cultural exegesis,[3] and many urban practitioners have examined the urban context as a complex mission field that requires critical interpretation. But despite the occasional overlap and interplay between these perspectives, very few in academic

---

1. In my early research on the origins of "urban exegesis," I connected with Ray Bakke at Bakke Graduate University, who directed me to the urban geographer Ronald Boyce. Boyce, Bakke, and BGU do use the term, but there is little consensus on its precise meaning. Subsequent citations will elaborate on its range of usage.

2. Most notable among these contributions are Gottdiener and Lagopoulos, *The City and the Sign*; and Barthes, "Semiology and the Urban." While both Gottdiener and Lagopoulos have published more recent works, *The City and the Sign* remains their most foundational work in urban semiotics. I will discuss these works further within the context of the observation component of urban exegesis.

3. "Cultural hermeneutics" is a more common area of study most closely associated with cultural exegesis. Though cultural hermeneutics often branches out into other areas like philosophical hermeneutics, my brief and limited exploration of cultural hermeneutics is looking more specifically at models of cultural interpretation that analyze cultural structures as a distinctly *textual* phenomenon. See Vanhoozer et al., *Everyday Theology*.

theology—if any—have attempted to lay out a more formal definition of urban exegesis.[4]

Consequently, I have chosen to define urban exegesis as a method of observing and interpreting urban communities that synthesizes the symbolic systems of *urban semiotics* and the missional theology of *cultural exegesis* in order to draw out the multifaceted meaning of complex environments in the city.[5]

OBSERVING AND INTERPRETING URBAN COMMUNITIES

The necessity of developing a model for urban exegesis arises out of the importance of understanding the many cultural and theological intricacies present in urban *communities*. The primary difference between the broad urban context of the city and the specificity of the urban community is the latter's emphasis on a particular locale within a larger urban area. An individual city is comprised of many different types of urban communities, and each of those communities may contain multiple neighborhoods.[6] At every level of analysis, there are unique dynamics at work defining the locality of each setting. And while semiotic description of the urban context is applicable for both the city at large as well as other types of urban environments, my definition of urban exegesis focuses more specifically on the community as a significant unit of urban analysis.[7]

4. To my knowledge, no formal academic publication has addressed the specific task of constructing a systematic, interdisciplinary definition of urban exegesis. The closest related perspective comes from Michael Mata's "Mailboxes, Stucco, and Graffiti" and "Entering the Community" in *Transforming the City*. Another important perspective comes from Glenn Smith's Lausanne occasional paper titled "Towards the Transformation of Our Cities/Regions."

5. There are further dimensions of this definition that will be unpacked under the broader categories of *semiotic observation* and *missiological interpretation*. Additionally, simpler versions of this definition are summarized at the end of the first section of this chapter.

6. The different types of urban areas, in order of size from largest to smallest, are typically: metropolitan area (market area), urban agglomeration (continuously built-up area), city (specific municipality), community (multiple neighborhoods), neighborhood (local unit of analysis). Though the definitions of *community* and *neighborhood* overlap at times, I am defining a community as a combination of neighborhoods (or space in between neighborhoods) because the physical boundaries are not always clearly defined.

7. With that said, I do not want to limit its applicability to urban communities alone. Because its observation component borrows heavily from urban semiotics, in

The need to exegete the urban community, like much of the city's unique settings, is rooted in its contextual complexities. Urban affairs journalist Grady Clay, in his book *Close-Up: How to Read the American City*, says "no true secrets are lurking in the landscape, but only undisclosed evidence, waiting for us. No true chaos in the urban scene, but only patterns and clues waiting to be organized."[8] Clay asserts that while a back alley may appear to be little more than an arbitrary and chaotic mess, the truly *observant* individual discovers evidence and clues in the patterned codes of urban space. In this sense, one of the basic keys to semiotic analysis in the urban context is a critical eye for the details and seemingly insignificant nuances that make neighborhoods and land-scapes uniquely urban. Communities in the city are full of these details; some are rather obvious, and others are quite subtle.

Urban exegesis seeks to identify these details in relation to cultural texts in the urban setting and then interpret them according to what urban ethnographer Elijah Anderson calls a "code of the street."[9] In Anderson's research, this code develops because inner city "despair is pervasive enough to have spawned an oppositional culture, that of 'the street,' whose norms are often consciously opposed to those of main-stream society . . . the street culture has evolved a 'code of the street,' which amounts to a set of informal rules governing interpersonal public behavior, particularly violence."[10] In addition to the codes that regulate personal interaction, street culture also creates other codes which shape a variety of elements in the urban context, from the built environment of the city to its economic and political structures. The challenge of decoding patterns like social stratification and urban territorial boundaries is that street culture takes on many different forms in the city. From one neighborhood to the next (or even one block to the next), the code of the street can change, requiring urban dwellers to be capable of "code-

---

theory, urban exegesis can be utilized at many levels of urban analysis, from a neighborhood setting to a metropolitan area. My immediate focus on the community is simply a reflection of the research scope.

8. Clay, *Close-Up*, 11.

9. Anderson's *Code of the Street* is an urban ethnography of inner-city Philadelphia which explores the ethical issues of morality and violence in urban culture. His approach may not be explicitly semiotic, but the analogy in his analytical methods is merited.

10. Anderson, *Code of the Street*, 32–33.

switching,"[11] or navigating the changing rules of different urban contexts. Many of the difficulties that people encounter in the city are rooted in an ignorance of these codes, an inability to read the appropriate signs, or both. This leads to the kinds of misunderstanding and misinterpretation that create conflict in urban communities.

Christian Approaches to the City

In order to engage these complexities, various urban missiologists, theologians, and practitioners have developed different approaches to understanding urban communities in the city. While methods vary in their respective emphases, most approaches tend to focus on the role of urban *ministry*[12] as it applies broadly to city-level analysis of the urban context. Four general categories in the literature of this urban ministry approach are *holistic-pastoral, academic-pastoral, geographic,* and *community-strategic.*[13]

The *holistic-pastoral* approach to understanding urban ministry is exemplified by Christian "urbanologist" Ray Bakke, and his longstanding work to develop "a theology as big as the city."[14] In Bakke's first book,

---

11. Ibid., 36. A simple example of code-switching in the urban context is the many different types of greetings appropriate in different settings and between people of varying levels of urban social status. These codes develop socially and have unique implications in each local setting.

12. In much of the urban Christian literature, perspectives on urban *ministry* have far outweighed those on urban *theology*, which is a reflection of the applied, practical, and missiological orientation of the field. Naturally there is considerable overlap between theology and ministry (as well as some exceptional works of urban theology), but the distinction—for better or worse—remains. On the other hand, it is likely that many urban theologians would protest the academic hierarchies within "formal" theology that often relegate missiology to an "applied" field. An example of an intentional distinction between urban ministry and urban theology is Harvey's *Theology in the City: A Theological Response to "Faith in the City."*

13. These labels are by no means mutually exclusive, all-encompassing categorical themes; rather, they are broad groupings intended to highlight certain emphases within the literature. Many of the titles and authors listed here could easily be perceived as in between or across categories.

14. Bakke's book of the same title is perhaps his most well-known as it outlines his general approach to urban ministry. Though predominantly narrative and heavily biographical, Bakke also outlines a canonical approach to reading the scriptures through an urban lens. See Bakke, *Theology as Big as the City*. Another important work in a similar area is Robert Linthicum's *City of God, City of Satan*. Like Bakke, Linthicum has also published extensively in urban ministry with a strong emphasis on urban churches.

The Urban Christian, he describes his calling to urban ministry. "I had a vision of what urban pastors and churches could do. The relationships of evangelistic, social, academic ministries with pastoral caring and political activity all came together."[15] As a pastor with extensive ministry experience in urban communities, Bakke emphasizes the importance of growing the church's ability to minister holistically within the varied contexts of the city. As urban congregations engage this mission, they must recognize that "a biblical holistic theology... includes not only the physical aspects of persons but also the geography in which we have identity and security."[16] Bakke also focuses heavily on historical context, believing that history significantly shapes the personality of cities by leaving a trail of formative moments in urban development.[17] Though Bakke's work is indeed practical and pastoral at a congregational level, it is also dynamic and missiological in a global context. Because of his high level involvement with the broad scope of organizations like International Urban Associates[18] and Bakke Graduate University,[19] much of his work is reflective of this priority on global macro-analysis of cities.[20]

Academic-pastoral approaches to urban ministry have typically been housed within the corpus of textbooks that address the diversity of issues at work in Christian mission to the city. Often written by ministers with experience in both the church and the academy, professors like Harvie Conn, Manuel Ortiz, and Roger Greenway are representative of this category. This approach still focuses on the importance of leadership development in pastoral training and church planting strategies in urban neighborhoods, but it also goes a step further in its academic analysis of cities as unique cultural contexts for missiological inquiry. With a

15. Bakke and Hart, *Urban Christian*, 20.

16. Bakke, *Theology as Big as the City*, 61.

17. Bakke and Sharpe, *Street Signs*.

18. Bakke founded IUA in 1989 as a network for "urban-minded" Christians in over one hundred cities around the world. Because of the size and global diversity of IUA, Bakke's work tends to think in terms of cities as opposed to neighborhoods, which is appropriate given the broad scope of IUA and BGU. My point is simply that cities break down into much smaller units of analysis, and more work should also be done to emphasize the importance of doing local micro-analysis of urban communities.

19. Bakke Graduate University's mission is to "strengthen leaders who steward resources with and for vulnerable people and places, by means of contextual, Christian-based education innovatively delivered throughout the urban world" (BGU 2010).

20. Macro, meso, and micro are geographic categories similar to global, regional, and local.

more comprehensive emphasis on the anthropological and sociological dimensions of urban settlements, the academic-pastoral approach also looks systematically at the theological issues in globalization, urbanization, and contextualization.[21] *Urban Ministry: The Kingdom, the City, and the People of God*, the last book Conn published before his death in 1999, is in many ways the quintessential urban ministry textbook for its significant depth, breadth, and scope.[22]

Another common approach to understanding urban communities focuses on breaking down large metropolitan areas into *geographic* categories. Glenn Smith, an urban missiologist and senior associate of urban mission for the Lausanne Movement, explains how geography shapes the urban context. "By grasping a geography of urban functions, we are looking at issues (the social dynamics, problems, needs, aspirations and worldviews) that are culturally and historically specific. Like the city itself, these issues reflect the prevailing values, ideology and structure of the prevailing social formation. A useful analytical, social and theological purpose is served by the empirical recognition that urban issues are manifest in geographical space."[23] As Smith presents a geographical paradigm for understanding urban phenomena, urban geographer Ronald Boyce further argues that this type of urban interpretation must apply to three levels of analysis: macro, meso, and micro, which represent regional, urban area, and neighborhood contexts. By focusing on the geographic and economic principles of proximity, interaction, and exchange, Boyce explores the ways that land, transit, and trade impact the characteristics of cities.[24] At the local level, both Smith and Boyce do uphold ethnographic analysis of urban culture as the best tool for understanding social interaction and behavior, but neither goes into much detail about how ethnography should be done specifically.[25] Rather, the

21. See Greenway and Monsma, *Cities*.

22. Harvie Conn also served as the editor of *Urban Mission*, an academic journal that grew out of his work with other urban ministers and missiologists at Westminster Theological Seminary in Philadelphia.

23. Smith, "Exegesis of a City."

24. Boyce, *Note on How to Exegete Cities*.

25. One exception may be that in his 2004 Lausanne occasional paper, Smith outlines a fairly comprehensive list of "Twenty Steps" on "How to do an exegesis of a city-region" (Smith, "Towards the Transformation of Our Cities/Regions"). However, while some attention is given to the local considerations of neighborhoods, the overall ethnographic emphasis still focuses predominantly on the city as a whole.

focus remains primarily on cities and the roles they play in metropolitan areas or urban agglomerations.

In contrast to the broad relevance and global scope of city-level analysis in pastoral, academic, and geographic approaches, the *community-strategic* approach is the most local in its emphasis on the specific inner workings of communities and neighborhoods. This approach is best modeled by Dr. John Perkins and the Christian Community Development Association,[26] which also includes many other ministry practitioners like Robert Lupton and Rudy Carrasco. Perkins, most well known for his "3 R's" model of relocation, reconciliation, and redistribution,[27] brings a local perspective to urban ministry that is honest, accessible, and focused on the hard work of community development in contexts of urban poverty and decay. Consistently authentic in his call for the church to go "beyond charity,"[28] Perkins is a prophetic strategist and coalition builder with the wisdom of decades of experience, the resolve of a civil rights leader, and the passion of a gospel preacher.

Another strategic thinker for urban communities is Michael Mata, Urban Development Director of World Vision's U.S. Programs. Mata presents a detailed method for understanding the urban context at the neighborhood level. While other perspectives acknowledge the benefits of using ethnographic research methods[29] at the neighborhood level, few are as thoroughly developed as Mata's outline for observing and interpreting an urban community. *Mailboxes, Stucco, and Graffiti* looks comprehensively at issues of space, structures, signage, symbols, social interaction, sensory experience, and other categories of meaning. These varied urban characteristics allow for a breadth and depth of research that engages both urban ethnography and urban sociology in a specific community. Mata's unique background as an urban planner, urban pastor, and Transformational Development Specialist for World Vision shapes his emphasis on direct observation, participant observa-

---

26. The CCDA was founded in 1989 as Dr. Perkins gathered like-minded Christians in Chicago for CCDA's first annual meeting. Today the CCDA is one of the largest organizations of its kind in the world.

27. Perkins, *With Justice for All*.

28. Perkins, *Beyond Charity*.

29. Ethnography traditionally utilizes a variety of qualitative research methods, which include (but are not limited to) participant observation, direct observation, ethnographic interviews, focus groups, genealogical methods, and case studies.

tion, and "socio-cultural analysis of the urban landscape."[30] Though his model is slightly thin on content for distinctly theological reflection, his basic themes of *observation* and *interpretation* are foundational to my definition of urban exegesis.

Practicing Observation and Interpretation

Given this plurality of Christian approaches to understanding urban communities, what unique perspective does urban exegesis have to offer, and how does it operate in the urban context? In addition to its distinct combination of urban semiotics and cultural exegesis that emphasizes both the city *and* its constitutive local communities, observation and interpretation in urban exegesis focus heavily on a *theological* understanding the *built environment* of neighborhoods.

For example, something as simple as an isolated concrete street curb can reveal significant information about a neighborhood.[31] It is quite common in urban communities that even in close proximity, some residential blocks may have street curbs while other adjacent blocks do not. Blocks with curbs have clear boundaries to the street that indicate where cars can park, and curbs, along with sidewalks, create walkable areas that serve as a buffer zone between the private property of homes and the public area of the street. However, residential blocks without curbs have streets with vague boundaries, often surrounded by gravel or an ambiguous area of dirt and debris. Cars can park in whatever arrangement the land will allow, or even on a front lawn if necessary. Walkable space is inhibited or nonexistent, and often homes will use stronger dividers like chain link fencing or iron gates to emphasize the public-private boundary since a curb is not present to delineate that distinction. The practice of critical observation seeks to notice these kinds of urban details in the context of a community.

In the process of interpreting this residential street curb phenomenon, a number of considerations must be explored. Curbs and sidewalks are often standard features of residential areas, but if certain blocks are

30. This kind of urban analysis, along with "assessing the social ecology of religious institutions in urban communities," is a part of Mata's specific research interests in his faculty biography for Bakke Graduate University.

31. This example applies to many North American urban contexts, but may not have the same kind of applicability outside of that particular model of urban planning and infrastructure.

annexed at a later date by a city municipality, a lack of street curbs may indicate that the area was either rezoned or an unincorporated county area at one time. Additionally, without curbs, streets tend to appear wider and thus larger commercial vehicles that may otherwise be unable to pass through residential streets are allowed access. How do these factors impact the residents on such a street? What does an old car parked on a front lawn inside a chain link fence communicate about the people that live on a particular block? And most importantly, is there any *theological* significance to streets without curbs where children play and cars often speed by because of the quick access to a major arterial? Is there an ethical consideration in having equal access to the same quality of street in the same neighborhood? The task of interpretation is to get at the root of these types of questions by processing the cultural and theological meaning of these everyday urban realities.

Thus, observation and interpretation are the two critical components of urban exegesis. By breaking down these two complex tasks into more systematic processes, observation applies the symbolic principles of urban semiotics, and interpretation draws on the missiological characteristics of cultural exegesis.

Urban Semiotics as Observation

"The city is a discourse and this discourse is truly a language: the city speaks to its inhabitants, we speak our city—the city where we are—simply by living in it, by wandering through it, by looking at it."[32] French philosopher, literary theorist, and semiotician Roland Barthes was one of the first to formulate an academic relationship between "the city and the sign" in his 1967 essay "Semiology and the Urban." Seeking the possibility of an urban expression of semiotics, Barthes was motivated by his love for the symbolic nature of the built environment in cities, and the social construction of meaning that occurs in the midst of everyday urban elements.

What Barthes posits as the critical issue in any potential urban semiology is the necessity to "bring an expression like 'the language of the city' out of the purely metaphorical stage. It is very easy metaphorically to speak of the language of the city as we speak of the language of the cinema or the language of flowers. The real scientific leap will be realized

---

32. Barthes, "Semiology and the Urban," 168.

when we speak of a language of the city without metaphor."[33] Identifying and articulating this urban language requires an understanding of the signs, texts, and codes of the city, but Barthes was convinced that the social sciences at the time lacked sufficient methodology to construct any coherent symbolic system for the city. Because of this need for new analytical tools, Barthes called for "a new scientific energy in order to transform these data, to pass from metaphor to the description of signification, and it is in this that semiology could perhaps, by a development yet unforeseeable, come to our aid."[34] However, before a systematic approach could be developed, Barthes felt that "it is not so important to multiply the surveys or the functional studies of the city, but to multiply the readings of the city, of which unfortunately only the writers have so far given us some examples."[35] Only from a more diverse plurality of urban readings could an empirical approach to urban semiotics be constructed. Therefore, in his subsequent reluctance to explore the procedures and mechanics of a potentially scientific model of urban semiotics, Barthes left the proposition open-ended.

In the modern city[36] after Barthes, physical, social, and economic systems of meaning continue to be intertwined in an urban context which creates cultural codes that can be difficult to decipher, and the social sciences have taken Barthes' challenge to task. As a response in part to a perceived lack of understanding of urban social symbolism in fields like cognitive geography and environmental psychology,[37] various attempts have been made to bolster a semiotic approach to cultural analysis. However, many have characterized the emerging field of urban semiotics as having "a wide variety of approaches with limited critical

33. Ibid.

34. Ibid.

35. Ibid., 171.

36. The "modern" city is not only "contemporary," but it is increasingly *postmodern* as well in terms of architecture, philosophy, and the arts. Barthes wrote about the urban context of Paris in "Semiology and the Urban," but the transformation of Paris's metropolitan area since the late 1960s has been significant, and in some cases, dramatic. For example, the 2005 conflict around predominantly Muslim ethnic ghettos in the Parisian suburbs altered the world's perception of Paris as a peaceful, idyllic European city. See Amara and Zappi, *Breaking the Silence.*

37. Both cognitive/behavioral geography and environmental psychology investigate similar areas of academic inquiry; namely, how an individual processes and interprets physical space. The former is rooted in human geography and the latter in interdisciplinary sciences.

review; a proliferation of terminology and a lack of its systematization...
a relative lack of general theories; and, finally, a weak sister relationship
with its more robust relative, architectural semiotics."[38] Despite this
ambiguity, generally speaking, urban sociology in particular has led the
way in formulating more systematic approaches to urban semiotics.[39]

Picking up where Barthes left off, urban sociologist Mark Gottdiener, in *The City and the Sign: An Introduction to Urban Semiotics*,
defines urban semiotics as "the inquiry into the social signification[40] of
urban forms, or, more generally, forms of settlement space . . . urban
semiotics represents a unique and perhaps improved way of studying
the social role of signification in settlement space."[41] He then elaborates
on this definition by identifying the physical framework of the urban
sign system. "For urban semiotics in particular, material objects are the
vehicles of signification, so that the symbolic act always involves some
physical object as well as social discourse on it. In the case of urban
semiotics these objects are the elements of urban space, for example,
streets, squares, buildings, and facades. Semiotic analysis can also be
extended to include codes of property ownership, written texts of planning, the plans of designers, urban discourse by the users of the city,
and real-estate advertising."[42] While Gottdiener employs a semiotic
paradigm in his analysis of the urban context, he also distinguishes his
approach from "purely semiotic"[43] methods by emphasizing his focus on
the social context and ideology behind the sign systems themselves. He
calls this "socio-semiotics," which "studies both systems of denotation[44]

38. Pipkin et al., *Remaking the City*, 101.

39. Though not formally engaging in semiotic analysis, architecture and literary
theorists have also contributed to the dialogue about the symbolic nature of the city.
Because interdisciplinary semiotic inquiry is by nature quite flexible, one could argue
that urban planners, literature studies, and other disciplines are also engaging in critical
analysis of the symbolic systems of the city. See Wirth-Nesher, *City Codes*; and Grange,
The City.

40. Signification is the process by which signs convey meaning.

41. Gottdiener and Lagopoulos, *City and the Sign*, 2.

42. Ibid., 3.

43. Gottdiener argues that "pure" semiotic models focus on "signification proper,"
independent of social context.

44. Denotation is the direct, literal, or explicit meaning of a sign/signifier.

and metalinguistic systems[45] in relation to the culturally specific systems of connotation operating behind them."[46]

Thus, socio-semiotics explores both the explicit meaning of the sign object and the implicit meaning of the sign object's cultural context. In the urban context, "every architectural or urban object is transformed, at the level of denotation, into a signified[47] of its own function. But beyond its conceptualized functional use, the object has another function as well, which is symbolic. Thus, it signifies on a second level also, that of connotation."[48] In other words, denotation identifies the explicit, specific purpose of an urban sign, while connotation implies the symbolic meaning of the sign in context. For example, a payday loans storefront denotes the location of a financial lending institution that deals in high-interest, short-term loans, but it also connotes a certain type of clientele and socioeconomic class that utilizes short-term loans and check cashing services.

Another way of thinking about the nature of urban sign objects is through *form* (the signifier) and *substance* (the signified concept). Form is the physical material itself, and substance is the conceptual understanding of what the form signifies. Therefore, in order to "read" (or observe and interpret) the city,

> A socio-semiotic analysis of an urban sign system or pseudo-text would then proceed as follows. On the one hand, observational data would be collected on both the form and the substance of the expression. In the first case (form), attention would be given to the specific spatial elements which are the vehicles of signification, while in the second (substance), a description of material urban space invested by signification would be obtained. On the other hand, cultural research is required to document the forms and substance of the content. Such a task requires, firstly, attention to historically and culturally established signification, realized through research into the general cultural traits of the society within which the settlement space is embedded. Research is required to document the codified ideology structuring the

45. Metalinguistic systems examine the relationship between language and culture.

46. Ibid., 5.

47. Linguist Ferdinand de Saussure described signs as "dyadic" (a two-part model). Every sign has a *signifier* (the form of the sign) and a *signified* (the concept the sign represents).

48. Ibid., 12.

signifieds of space... if we want to explain urban semiotic systems
rather than merely describe them, it is necessary to specify the
manner by which such systems are constituted socially.[49]

This method of urban socio-semiotic analysis is essentially a four-
part process:

1. Collect observational data on the form of the sign. What is the
   basic spatial essence of the object?

2. Describe observational data on the substance of the sign. What
   meaning or concept does the material object communicate?

3. Conduct cultural research on both the form and substance of
   the sign. What does the object symbolize in cultural and historical context?

4. Conduct research to determine how the sign functions in a
   coded structure. How does the object relate to the larger system
   of signs?

When applied to a specific urban context, the nature of this process of socio-semiotic analysis depends greatly on the type of sign being
observed.[50] While many sign objects are physical structures within the
built environment, not every sign has a physical, material essence. This
is particularly relevant for ethnographic signs. A personal gesture (wave,
wink, or walk) or sensory experience (sight, smell, or sound) denotes
and connotes differently than an apartment complex or a liquor store
on the corner. As the sign object varies, so does its explicit and implicit
meaning in context.

Gottdiener's approach to urban semiotics also has several similarities to Robert Schreiter's discussion of cultural semiotics in *Constructing
Local Theologies*. Like Schreiter's method of semiotic description of culture, urban semiotics aims to locate cultural texts (or "pseudo-texts")
in the city as basic units of analysis (urban sign objects), identify their
meaning in social and historical context, and then group them according to the codes within larger semiotic domains of physical, social, and
economic systems. Ultimately, as the observation component of urban
exegesis, urban socio-semiotic analysis collects and processes data on

---

49. Ibid., 17–19.

50. Like much of semiotic analysis, this dialectical process does not always work
systematically step-by-step; for some signs, steps blend together or operate out of order.

the built environment of the city in order to better understand the signs and symbols of urban space in the community.[51]

Cultural Exegesis as Interpretation

Moving from observation to interpretation in urban exegesis shifts the focus from urban semiotics to cultural exegesis. *Cultural exegesis* is a term used in both contextual theology and cultural hermeneutics to apply theological interpretation to cultural analysis. Given the complexity of cultural analysis itself, adding theological interpretation to the process can at times seem overwhelming. Nevertheless, theological interpretation of culture is an essential component of both urban exegesis and what theologian Kevin Vanhoozer simply calls "everyday theology."[52] Contextual theology and cultural hermeneutics take slightly different approaches to cultural exegesis, so each will be examined separately in succession.

While anthropologists and sociologists conduct cultural analysis according to the principles of social science, missiologists and contextual theologians conduct cultural exegesis as a synthesis of sociocultural analysis and theologizing about local cultures. Filipino theologian Jose De Mesa describes the process this way:

> Cultural exegesis is an interpretative activity. It is a form of cultural analysis for the purpose of theological examination and evaluation of the culture. As cultural analysis, it explicitly intends to make sense of the implicit cultural meanings arising from a tradition of experiences which are embodied in specific cultural elements or aspects. The culture is, as it were, a text which has been written by previous generations of people in a given society and which needs to be read and reinterpreted by the present one

---

51. While this process of urban socio-semiotic analysis contains elements of both observation (data collection) and interpretation (cultural research), for the purposes of defining urban exegesis, I am grouping both of these primary methods of urban semiotics within the *observation* component of urban exegesis. In other words, when I apply the principles of urban semiotics (which naturally includes some "interpretation") to a specific urban context in the process of doing urban exegesis, I am still operating primarily within the task of *observation*. An easier way to say this is perhaps that interpretation in urban semiotics is still just "observation" in urban exegesis. Consequently, the primary emphasis of the *interpretation* component of urban exegesis is directed towards *theological* interpretation, whereas urban semiotics has little to no interest in theological concerns, hence the distinction.

52. Vanhoozer et al., *Everyday Theology*.

for the present time. As exegesis aims to draw out meanings in biblical texts, so cultural exegesis intends to make explicit the implicit meanings a culture holds . . . it is not merely descriptive but prescriptive from an evangelical perspective: for inculturating the gospel.[53]

De Mesa identifies two main tasks in cultural exegesis: (1) *descriptive examination* of the culture, and (2) *prescriptive evaluation* of the culture. To "read" and interpret the culture as a text is to first examine its *content*—traditions, experiences, values—and then to evaluate this examination theologically according to its *context*—social, historical, religious, and so on. In a striking similarity to biblical exegesis, "good exegetical questions fall into two basic categories: questions of *content* (what is said) and of *context* (why it is said)."[54] Asking what a culture is "saying" and why it is being said in a particular way is the foundation of being able to "exegete"[55] its cultural and theological meaning.

Additionally, cultural exegesis recognizes that culture as a text is "authored" by both people and God, and must be evaluated as such. "Exegesis is primarily concerned with intentionality: What did the author intend his original readers to understand?"[56] Previous generations "write" or create cultural practices and process cultural knowledge within a specific context; cultural exegesis therefore must explore the original intent behind this process so that it can be contextualized in the present. Similarly, as God authors culture,[57] cultural exegesis aims to discover God's original intent for meaning and purpose in human cultures.

Thus, what distinguishes cultural exegesis from cultural analysis is its exegetical emphasis on the content, context, and intentionality of culture. Ultimately, cultural exegesis seeks to interpret (examine content and evaluate context) culture in consideration of the nature of the gospel, which is both missional and redemptive. As a missional narrative, the biblical story is rooted in the gospel of the *missio Dei*, which reveals

53. De Mesa, *Why Theology Is Never Far*, 115.

54. Fee, *New Testament Exegesis*, 31.

55. *Exegesis* comes from the Greek word *exagō*, meaning "to lead out." Thus the literal intent of exegesis is to lead the meaning out of the text (or pseudo-text).

56. Fee, *New Testament Exegesis*, 27.

57. The role that God plays in "authoring" culture is obviously very different from the role that humans play in inherently making meaning of their surroundings. Nevertheless, God authors *providentially* in his sovereignty as well as *incarnationally* through people created in his image.

God's intent from the beginning to extend God's self into creation for its ultimate shalom and restoration. Cultural exegesis calls for an interpretive method that can cultivate an active participation in that redemptive purpose.

Cultural hermeneutics[58] offers another perspective on cultural exegesis that seeks to interpret the text(s) of culture. Vanhoozer argues that "Christians must learn to read the signs of the times . . . most of us learn to read and write . . . what we do not learn, however, is *cultural literacy*: how to 'read' and 'write' *culture*."[59] Cultural literacy requires an ability to interpret the everyday context that surrounds our daily life, from the mundane nature of work and transportation to the pervasive social realities of mass media and *Zeitgeist*. However, exegeting these cultural phenomena theologically becomes difficult when "religion is the substance of culture and culture is the form of religion."[60] Further complications with reductionism, hermeneutics of suspicion,[61] and critical theory can make navigating the waters of cultural exegesis a whirlpool of circular motion.

Nevertheless, Vanhoozer proposes a method for theological reading of culture that emphasizes "the importance of hearing culture 'on its own terms'"[62] and the necessity of placing culture within the "biblical-theological framework of creation-fall-redemption."[63] On one level, while these two commitments could be seen as contradictory, holding them in tension is a fundamental task of cultural exegesis. Good interpreters of culture should never impose their own reading onto the cultural text, and yet, the very nature of theological interpretation is framed by a pre-existing narrative before it ever approaches the text of culture.

58. Vanhoozer defines cultural hermeneutics simply as "the art and science of interpretation . . . that treats cultural texts and trends as particular kinds of *discourse*: what someone says (or signs) to someone about something" (Vanhoozer et al., *Everyday Theology*, 36). Cultural Hermeneutics is a broad and diverse field with which I have chosen not to engage in an attempt to focus more specifically on approaches to cultural *exegesis*.

59. Ibid., 18.

60. Tillich and Kimball, *Theology of Culture*, 42.

61. With epistemological similarities to Nietzsche, Freud, and Marx, Paul Ricoeur recognizes that "the two major areas of hermeneutics, explanation and understanding" require a fundamentally "socio-critical suspicion" (Thiselton, *New Horizons in Hermeneutics*, 344).

62. Vanhoozer et al., *Everyday Theology*, 40.

63. Ibid., 48.

The best that cultural exegesis can do to mitigate the bias and agenda of Christian doctrine and tradition is to fully understand the nature of cultural discourse between the text and the world,[64] and to work toward an active and intentional awareness of the theological presuppositions that inform the reader's posture toward the text.

Given these considerations, it is important to remember that cultural exegesis is not an end unto itself; rather, it is a means to participate in the missional and redemptive agenda of the gospel in the world. Theological interpretation of culture does not provide a more "objective" or "exact" reading of cultural texts; what it *does* do is present a more *meaningful* and *multidimensional* reading of the fullness of culture as God intended. Any methodological precision in cultural exegesis must serve this purpose.

Therefore, cultural exegesis frames the task of cultural analysis with a theological commitment to evaluating the missional and redemptive implications of cultural texts. The exegetical questions posed in a particular cultural context then flow out of this core commitment. What could it look like to be sent incarnationally by a sending God into this culture? What aspects of this culture are reflective of the brokenness of the fall and how can a vision of shalom work redemptively to heal, rebuild, and restore? What local considerations must be taken into account when contextualizing these theological questions? Cultural exegesis examines these questions through a deep reading of a culture's content and context while also remaining conscious of the gospel's agenda to work redemptively within all cultures.

In the urban context—a setting characterized by density, diversity, and disparity—the challenge of embodying this gospel agenda in neglected, forgotten communities is pronounced. But in spite of these difficulties, evaluating a local culture missionally and redemptively uniquely shapes the process of interpreting the data that is collected in the observation phase of urban exegesis. While urban semiotics parses the context of an urban community into signs and symbols for textual analysis in order to better understand the built environment and its connotative meaning, cultural exegesis seeks to examine this semiotic

---

64. The world(s) *"behind, of,* and *in front of"* the text correspond to "the three moments in the general hermeneutics of culture that attend to the author/producer, text/product, and reader/consumer." See ibid.

data in consideration of its missional implications for the church and its redemptive value for the community.

In summary, urban exegesis, as a synthesis of observation through urban semiotics and interpretation through cultural exegesis, seeks to construct the cultural and theological meaning of the built environment in complex urban communities. Or in simpler terms, urban exegesis combines semiotic observation and cultural-exegetical interpretation to understand local context and develop local theology for particular communities in the city.

7

Observation: The Urban Context of Rainier Valley

THE RAINIER VALLEY IS both a geographic feature and a community of urban neighborhoods in southeast Seattle. Because of its unique identity as an area of distinct urban density, diversity, and disparity,[1] the Valley is an ideal context for semiotic observation. In order to understand the physical, social, and economic attributes of the Valley, the observation component of urban exegesis calls for an urban socio-semiotic analysis of the Valley's symbolic systems that signify density, diversity, and disparity in its various forms.

The process of observational analysis begins by locating urban sign objects within each domain, and then identifying their denotative and connotative meaning. Next, the form (signifier/object) and substance (signified/concept) of the signs are examined in cultural and historical context for any further symbolic meaning. Lastly, the sign is then "read" in its larger context of other signs in order to decipher any potential message or structure in the sign system. Its total meaning is constructed from these elements of semiotic analysis, which include both material (e.g., physical) and ideological (e.g., cultural) significance. To move toward an urban exegesis of the Rainier Valley community first requires an observational understanding of the multifaceted meaning of its built environment, social institutions, and economic indicators.

---

1. These three attributes of the urban context will be explained in more detail in Chapter 10.

SIGNS OF URBAN DENSITY: RAINIER COURT

Driving south on Rainier Avenue just past the intersection of Martin Luther King Jr. Way reveals a variety of urban conditions that represent a fairly typical commercial thoroughfare in southeast Seattle. On the right side of the street, a triangular commercial block is shared by Ace Cash Express, the Rainier Laundromat, and the Minute Mart. Their common parking lot often serves as a communal overflow area for the locals who gather at the National Pride Car Wash just behind the Minute Mart. Neon signs and vinyl banners read "checks cashed/payday loans" and "fried chicken and cold beer" as neighbors congregate between parked Cadillacs near the bus stop. The police frequently show up to make their presence known, but the flashing lights of a squad car or two have little effect at deterring the gatherings.

Continuing south on Rainier, groups of small, colorful storefronts—many with bars on their windows—are clustered together close to the sidewalks of the five-lane arterial. Most of the one or two story buildings are older structures in varied states of renewal or disrepair, from newly painted ethnic restaurants and markets to boarded-up industrial sites. Store signs that are written or printed in Vietnamese, Cambodian, Spanish, or Somali indicate the various immigrant populations present in the community. Despite this traditional urban landscape, each block is framed by a majestic collection of century-old trees that line the avenue in a curious contrast of gray concrete and dense greenery, a reminder of the thick forests that once surrounded the Rainier Valley.[2]

All of these urban objects are *signifiers*, structured vehicles of meaning lining the street like the trees that have seen more than a century of change in the Valley. Each object connects to the urban system of Rainier Avenue like branches on a tree, and together they shape the urban ecology of the community. As with any ecosystem, the urban cultural texts along Rainier are in a constant state of change as the life cycles of the city bring life, death, and rebirth in each season.

2. The Rainier Avenue corridor is a historic thoroughfare that was first cleared by a rail line intended to connect the growing urban core with the unsettled area surrounding the Valley. "The Seattle Renton & Southern Railway built King County's first true interurban railroad beginning in 1891, and spurred development of the then largely agricultural Rainier Valley" (Crowley, "Seattle Renton & Southern Railway").

Locating Sign Objects' Form and Substance

About five blocks south of the intersection with MLK, as Rainier Avenue curves further to the east, a large new development called Rainier Court emerges in the midst of a sea of abandoned concrete and used car lots. With looming profiles that rise above the trees, the newly constructed buildings seem strangely out of place in consideration of the scale of the surrounding area. Rainier Court, one of the clearest signs of urban density in the Rainier Valley, is a mixed-use residential development on seven acres of land with three primary structures, each with five to six stories of apartments and affordable senior housing built above street level retail and commercial space.

With over 500 units of housing and more than 10,000 square feet of commercial space, this large-scale project broke ground in 2003 and its fourth and final phase of construction was completed in 2010.[3] While the initial appearance of the physical structure of the buildings denotes an attractive, well-designed development of new construction housing, the actual type of housing on site conveys a very different connotative meaning to many in the community. Examining Rainier Court in its urban context reveals significant distance and dissonance between its form and substance.

Though Southeast Effective Development (SEED)[4] has marketed Rainier Court as "a marquee development that symbolizes progress and provides quality commercial space, affordable housing, pedestrian activity, and density for this community,"[5] for many in the neighborhood, the new housing facility's focus on "underserved"[6] populations is simply another symbol of the Rainier Valley's perpetual status as a dumping ground for the city. In this sense, Rainier Court as a sign of density may

3. These development specifications are based on the latest information available through SEED's printed media, press materials, and online information.

4. SEED is the largest not-for-profit community development corporation in the Rainier Valley and the primary partner in the Rainier Court redevelopment.

5. This project description was released in their initial marketing materials, and continues to be used for promotion of the development.

6. "Underserved" populations often include the elderly, "at-risk" youth, "special needs" groups, and low-income families. This designation is commonly used by the U.S. Department of Health and Human Services. Christian organizations like the Christian Community Development Association use terms like "under-resourced," which emphasizes a more positive focus on the root of the problem, as opposed to more traditional language like "at-risk."

have an attractive exterior, but new paint and tall buildings cannot hide the mentality behind the development. No amount of steel, glass, and masonry—regardless of its architectural combination—can disguise the intentional concentration of underserved populations in this particular place. Thus, as a physical signifier, the form of Rainier Court denotes the "progress" of new construction and community development, but as a social signified, the substance of Rainier Court connotes a relapse into old patterns that have long plagued the neighborhood.

Cultural and Historical Context

With nearly half of Rainier Court's total number of housing units dedicated to low-income senior housing managed by the large non-profit Senior Housing Assistance Group (SHAG), and another significant portion allocated for low-income renters of all ages, the presence and density of these particular populations signifies a burden on the social infrastructure of the surrounding neighborhood. With many additional low-income individuals and families living in close proximity to Rainier Court, the need for extensive support services becomes magnified in an area that is already saturated with high levels of concentrated poverty. With easily over two dozen distinct community-based organizations, social service agencies, and transitional housing facilities for populations with special needs within a one-mile radius of Rainier Court,[7] the surrounding area's overall density for these vulnerable groups is even more prominent.

Exploring the historical context of the land used in the development is indicative of a recurring problem of neglect. Prior to the Rainier Court redevelopment, the ground on which the site was built was designated as a brownfield[8] by the Environmental Protection Agency due to significant amounts of chemical contamination found in the soil. After decades of use as a landfill, which began in the 1930s, the site had also

---

7. A wide variety of social service agencies and non-profits are based in the Valley, from ethnic-specific counseling and job referral services to assisted living facilities for the blind, homeless, or those undergoing substance abuse rehabilitation.

8. Typically, brownfield land is designated as such by the EPA in order to target the site for environmental cleanup and redevelopment. This process often involves cooperation between federal funding, private developers, and local governmental officials. The EPA's Brownfields Program is an ongoing, national initiative.

been subject to illegal dumping of industrial waste, which was further blighted by criminal activity and a general disregard by authorities.

With at least two other brownfield redevelopment sites nearby, the pattern of serial dumping in the Valley was not unique to the Rainier Court location, though its site is the largest. The history of the ground being leveled with household garbage, along with the previous commercial use of the land as a mortuary, is symbolic of the death and decay that used to characterize its urban space. And though the formal dumping of waste has ended, the connotation of Rainier Court as a dumping ground of under-resourced populations continues to be a source of irony and tension in the community.

Coded Messages and Meaning

Another signifier of urban density in Rainier Court is the lack of open areas, courtyards, or green space for the large number of residents on site. Though residential density often forces personal interaction in the built environment, a lack of designated shared space can significantly limit opportunities for communal contact. This absence of available shared space is largely attributable to an open area in between the Rainier Court's massive buildings on Rainier Avenue that is currently occupied by an old, gravel lot filled with used cars and a dilapidated, portable structure surrounded by chain-link fencing. Repeated attempts by SEED to purchase and redevelop the land as a park for residents have been rejected by the owner, indicative of the cultural structures that reinforce the close coexistence of blight and new construction in Rainier Valley.

Despite these obstacles and setbacks, a concerted effort by a number of organizations, including SEED, SHAG, the EPA, King County, the City of Seattle, and the Environmental Coalition of Seattle brought about the cleanup and reconstruction of the Rainier Court site's infrastructure. The overall development, though still controversial to some, has also been recognized locally, nationally, and internationally as a model of livable urban density and successful commercial redevelopment.[9] For many outside observers not familiar with the immediate urban context of the Valley, the connotative meaning of Rainier Court as a dumping site may be harder to see.

9. Baerny, "Blight to All Right."

What messages do these signs of urban density communicate in the larger context of Rainier Valley? Reading an urban community for the significance of density does require a literacy of zoning codes and land use policy, but more important than the specific legality of urban planning is an intuitive sense of how healthy, sustainable density can facilitate personal interaction in a community. Intentionally designed shared spaces in the built environment can function as signs of communal values, from preservation and recreation to creativity and solidarity. These spaces, when properly constructed, can grow into powerful symbols of shared identity for a neighborhood. Though Rainier Court may currently connote more of the negative aspects of urban density, it is still under construction, and therefore a dynamic sign system in process.

SIGNS OF URBAN DIVERSITY: RAINIER VISTA

Less than a mile south of Rainier Court is a prominent sign of urban diversity in the Rainier Valley at the intersection of Martin Luther King Jr. Way and Columbian Way South. Highly representative of the socioeconomic, ethnic, and religious diversity that characterizes the whole of the Valley, Rainier Vista is a master-planned, mixed-used, mixed-income "garden community" redevelopment project of the Seattle Housing Authority.[10] Sometimes referred to as *New* Rainier Vista, the redevelopment is part of a massive restructuring of Seattle's many public housing projects.

At first glance, signs of diversity in Rainier Vista are readily apparent. Public art installations display the cultural stories of local communities, extended families span four generations in one household, multiple languages and dialects can be heard on the sidewalk, and recently resettled refugees live right next door to independently wealthy professionals. Therefore, the real challenge of locating signs of diversity in Rainier Vista is identifying and separating the signs that denote diversity but connote a false multicultural tokenism from the signs that denote *and* connote a more authentic diversity. In other words, some signs in the neighborhood represent the form but not the substance of diversity, while others are diverse in both form and substance.

10. The Seattle Housing Authority (SHA) is a public corporation that "provides long-term rental housing and rental assistance to more than 26,000 people in the city of Seattle. The agency owns and operates buildings of all shapes and sizes on more than 400 sites throughout the city" (SHA 2010).

Locating Sign Objects' Form and Substance

The "Rainier Vista Whirligigs" are kinetic, wind-powered sculptures that represent "whimsical expressions of important myths, legends, and stories of people from all over the world who make up Seattle's Columbia City neighborhood."[11] Designed by Seattle artist Carl Smool, these sculptures are illustrations of cultural stories that were installed on tall steel poles that line two blocks of the center landscaped area of Columbian Way. While the process of recording the cultural stories and commissioning the art publicly was a grassroots effort that involved a diverse community of individuals, the functional purpose of the Rainier Vista Whirligigs is largely ornamental. Despite their inherent cultural value as symbols of this "neighborhood of nations,"[12] the sculptures themselves often go unnoticed.

Thus, the small, spinning displays are signs of diversity in form, but in substance they are little more than a superficial tribute to a marketed ideal of multiculturalism in the neighborhood.[13] Though they signify a denotative message of diversity in the essence of the stories they describe, their signified connotation carries little cultural meaning. To a casual observer, they may improve the aesthetics of the street from the sidewalk, but it is unlikely that many residents of the community view the Whirligigs as representative symbols of genuine diversity in the neighborhood.[14]

11. This is a description from the artist's statement that was printed and distributed by the Seattle Housing Authority for the public dedication of the art project, which was installed on Columbian Way in July of 2006.

12. The Rainier Valley in general, and Columbia City in particular (the official Seattle neighborhood of which Rainier Vista is a part), has been nicknamed "Neighborhood of Nations" for its vast multicultural diversity. The Rainier Valley on the whole is one of the most diverse communities in the nation. See Woodward, *Rainier Valley Food Stories Cookbook.*

13. The Seattle Housing Authority, which funds much of the public art in the neighborhood, has worked hard to market the rich diversity of the community as a positive selling point for potential investors and home buyers. "Your front door to the world" is one of their common marketing slogans.

14. As a homeowner on Columbian Way with a Whirligig just feet from my window, this is my personal observation. However, I do value public art installations and believe that such efforts can be powerful signifiers when well designed and thoughtfully implemented. Unfortunately, the Rainier Vista Whirligigs have fallen short of expectations in the latter case.

In contrast to the Whirligigs, a sign of diversity in Rainier Vista that symbolizes the ideals of a diverse community in both form and substance is the Rainier Vista Multicultural Committee. Though the committee itself is not a constructed object of the built environment, its existence and influence in the neighborhood are signs of a local urban diversity that truly values building bridges for intercultural exchange. The group began in 2007 as a casual monthly meeting between neighbors at the suggestion of Tom Phillips, a local homeowner and former Catholic priest.

Tom's initial motivation for starting the group was rooted in the recognition that "differences in the neighborhood were so obvious . . . it would be too easy to segregate into isolated socioeconomic and cultural groups. 'Community' must be more than homeowners versus renters. Breaking down boundaries requires intentionality."[15] Despite growing up in an era of segregation, Tom always felt that people were inherently equal. During his second year of college, while on a road trip with friends through Jackson, Mississippi, Tom recounted the racism of his peers. "Their racial slurs infuriated me . . . it was just so hateful."[16]

After coming to faith through the charismatic Catholic movement in 1973, Tom got involved in a local parish in Las Vegas and felt the call to ministry. Once he completed seminary, he was ordained in 1985 and served as a parish priest for five years. Though Tom would later leave ordained ministry in the Catholic Church for personal reasons, he now worships with an emerging Episcopal congregation in Seattle. Tom admits that it is difficult to fully explain his concern for genuine diversity in the neighborhood; for him it is as much a natural inclination as it is a reflection of his faith. Nevertheless, in attempting to connect his faith to the context of the community, Tom simply says that "it's about Jesus; his life was remarkable . . . with that voice in the back of your head, you just can't hold the kind of prejudice that goes on in the world."[17]

Tom often facilitates the monthly meetings and has consistently encouraged the diverse cultural communities in the neighborhood to take ownership of the group. Seble Mesfin, a twenty-six-year-old Ethiopian mother of two, took Tom's advice and started a cross-cultural parenting group to encourage communication between different ethnic groups

15. Phillips, ethnographic interview.
16. Ibid.
17. Ibid.

about raising children and living in community. Naomi Chang, who works as a community builder for the Seattle Housing Authority, has also made numerous contributions, not least of which is serving as an administrative liaison to SHA and occasional translator for the many Chinese and Vietnamese seniors who live in the neighborhood. Each of these individuals is a signifier of a commitment to diversity in the community, and together the Multicultural Committee is advocating for this diversity in both form and substance.

The form of diversity in the committee is expressed in the various community projects undertaken by the group, from cultural presentations that provide opportunities to share about the unique history and social practices of particular ethnic groups, to more casual events like potluck meals and seasonal celebrations which involve the broader neighborhood. The group is currently in the process of compiling a "community scrapbook" project, which will combine a diverse collection of oral histories, favorite recipes, and stories of immigration from around the world to Rainier Vista. As Chinese, Vietnamese, Cambodian, Ethiopian, Somali, Eritrean, African-American, Asian-American, European, and Caucasian contributors work together on the project, accommodating signs of diversity is naturally a part of the process.

The substance of diversity in the Multicultural Committee is connected to its form, but the cultural complexities of the projects themselves have hardly been simple tasks to accomplish. After three years of meeting together, common courtesies like pronouncing different names correctly have been consistent challenges. Basic communication through five simultaneous translators can make group organization and project management a laborious process. Shifting the balance of power in the group from the English-speaking homeowners to a more diverse body of leadership that is representative of the whole neighborhood has been equally difficult. Each of these obstacles is a hindrance to understanding and experiencing the true substance of diversity, but small steps are being made in the right direction. When the many East African families who are practicing Muslims agreed to allow the Vietnamese seniors to bring food items cooked with pork to the community potluck, an informal type of interfaith dialogue began. Simply taking the time to label food with its ingredients and then placing dishes with pork on a separate table has created new opportunities for diverse groups to engage in the important cultural practice of sharing a meal together.

Cultural and Historical Context

Though some progress in multicultural diversity has been made, exploring the history of Rainier Vista reveals that diversity has long been a contentious issue in the neighborhood. The current balance of different income levels, ethnic groups, and their corresponding religious and cultural differences is carefully regulated by the codes and covenants of the Seattle Housing Authority.[18] Before the redevelopment plan that would transform Rainier Vista into a mixed-income community was implemented in 1999, the neighborhood was a public housing project comprised exclusively of low-income, government-subsidized housing. The local redevelopment was part of a national movement to recreate public housing as diverse, mixed-income communities, and the program was not without its vocal critics, at both local and national levels.[19] Local detractors like the Tenants Union of Washington State organized various protests against the inevitable displacement of low-income families, and some critics in Washington, DC, questioned the long-term viability of the government's financial investment in the redevelopment plan.

In the Rainier Valley, many community leaders and organizations decried what they perceived as a government-sanctioned form of forced gentrification, and the fact that allegedly unethical real estate developers in other cities profited at the expense of low-income families further fueled the public's outrage.[20] In 2002, a coalition of concerned neighbors and community members[21] sued SHA and its development partners over issues of density, environmental impact, and replacement housing for the displaced. In a reflection of Seattle's high level of social capital and commitment to community transparency in the process, the lawsuit

18. Details of the particular populations targeted in the redevelopment plan can be found through the SHA's redevelopment plans.

19. HOPE VI was a U.S. Department of Housing and Urban Development funding program that catalyzed the redevelopment of public housing projects into mixed-income communities all across the country. Needless to say, it was (and is) a controversial program aimed at making public housing more socially sustainable through placing diverse income levels in close proximity. See ABT Assoc. et al., "Historical and Baseline Assessment"; and U.S. General Accounting Office, "HUD's Oversight of Hope VI."

20. Housing projects funded by HOPE VI, like Chicago's Cabrini Green area, became infamous for their failed attempts at replacing affordable housing. See Bennett et al., *Where Are Poor People to Live?*

21. The parties involved as plaintiffs were the Friends of Rainier Vista, the Seattle Displacement Coalition and two Rainer Vista residents, Laurine Harris and Kathryn Smith. Details of the settlement terms can be found in the press releases of SHA in 2002.

halted demolition and was settled in late 2002 with a multilateral agreement on behalf of SHA to conduct a comprehensive feasibility study addressing the coalition's concerns in partnership with an independently appointed Citizen Review Committee.

Though Rainier Vista's master plan was later approved by the Seattle City Council in 2003 and the construction of new infrastructure in the neighborhood resumed in 2004, a residual suspicion of the long term benefits of mixed-income communities has left an ugly scar on the image of diversity that communities like Rainier Vista are seeking to promote. Additionally, the reality that the vast majority of homeowners who move in are white, while nearly all of the low-income residents are people of color, has not helped the situation. However, in spite of these challenges, many neighbors are making the best of it, and attempting to prove to outside critics that the social experiment of intentionally mixed-income communities can in fact be a healthy, sustainable way to redevelop the failed public housing policies of decades past.

Coded Messages and Meaning

Making sense of these varied signs of diversity in an urban context like Rainier Vista is a difficult task. Though some residents praise the progress that has been made, others in the community continue to see the neighborhood as a symbol of the gentrification and inequity that inevitably accompany "diversity." That the same signs can convey entirely different connotative meanings makes reading the diversity of the community an exercise in patience, community organizing, and consensus building. One of the messages that must be communicated in the face of opposing assessments of the neighborhood's diversity is that the shape and character of diversity always operates on a spectrum between the superficiality of the Whirligigs and the authentic relationships of the Multicultural Committee. These different forms of signifiers are not necessarily mutually exclusive and can coexist in spite of differing interpretations of their substance. In this sense, what is more important than reconciling different signs of diversity is attempting to move their denotative and connotative meanings in the same general direction.

Ultimately, in all of urban socio-semiotic analysis, the meaning of the sign object often depends heavily on the hermeneutic of the reader, and in the case of cultural diversity, a critical hermeneutic of suspicion must be balanced with a constructive hermeneutic of hope. Though the diversity of Rainier Vista is still very much a work in progress, the neighborhood continues to be a sign of a certain type of diversity in the Rainier Valley, and at the very least, it operates as an entry point into the dialogue about the true meaning of diversity in the urban context.

SIGNS OF URBAN DISPARITY: COLUMBIA PLAZA

Urban disparity is exemplified in the close proximity of people and institutions of differing backgrounds and social strata. Disparate socioeconomic circumstances that normally stratify urban communities come together in communities that are undergoing some form of large scale transition. Exploring these points of adhesion between contrasting signs of disparity reveals urban sign objects that coexist in a state of tension. Nowhere in the Rainier Valley is this more apparent than in Columbia City, where transition and gentrification have created overlapping and interlocking pockets of both wealth and poverty.

The Columbia City Landmark District is a four-block span of Rainier Avenue between South Alaska Street and South Hudson Street that has forty-five buildings constructed between 1891 and 1928 in a "cohesive urban mixed-use district which continues to convey Columbia City's economic, social, and developmental history."[22] The small-town feel of the turn-of-the-century storefronts and the restored brick pavers in the street match the period benches and light posts in the newly revitalized commercial areas. Along with the preservation and restoration that first popularized Columbia City as a trendy retail area has come a recent surge of economic development that has given the business district a strong local reputation for being completely gentrified. Though gentrification is an urban phenomenon that is difficult to measure quantitatively, the types of businesses in the Landmark District and the clientele they serve has certainly changed over the past few years.

Locating Sign Objects' Form and Substance

The clearest sign of urban disparity in the Columbia City neighborhood is the Columbia Plaza on Rainier Avenue, an old Tradewell Supermarket[23]

22. This description is an excerpt from the National Park Service documents that placed the Columbia City business district on the National Register of historic places in 1980. Original documents were sourced from the Rainier Valley Historical Society.

23. Tradewell Supermarkets operated locally in Seattle (in addition to stores in Oregon and California) from the 1950 to 70s. Though the Columbia City location

that was closed down during the community's rough years of decline in the early 1970s. It later reopened as an informal mini-mall of local vendors specializing in a variety of eclectic merchandise, from car audio and electronics accessories to bulk cigarettes and athletic apparel. Both its exterior and interior structures communicate a variety of messages about the form and substance of urban disparity.

The exterior structure of the Columbia Plaza is a sign of the stark economic disparity present in the business district. Across the street from the Plaza, in contrast to the attractive glass storefronts of renovated retail boutiques and cafes, the plain, brown exterior of the old Tradewell grocery store is faded and peeling. No identifiable markings on the face of the large building exist aside from the large, white capital letters that read "Columbia Plaza" above the front door. All of the front windows have been boarded up and covered crudely, leaving the interior without any natural light. Lastly, the building is set back from the street because of the front parking lot, which further isolates the Plaza as an anomaly of blight in an otherwise "up and coming" neighborhood.

Inside the Plaza, a mix of casually divided stalls and kiosks sell discounted apparel, pre-paid cell phones, and other seemingly random items like used car alarms and subwoofers. The whole place has the feel of a swap meet or flea market, as hand-written signs and unattended piles of merchandise clutter the space that has retained the vinyl floors and steel shelves of a 1970s grocery store. Though business was sustainable for the many years before the gentrification began in the late 1990s, recent years have seen a steady decline in customer traffic. On weekdays, the Plaza often feels like a ghost town with only a few vendors supervising the variety of different "stores" inside.

Thus the denotative form of the Plaza signifies an informal retail outlet where various "urban" goods and services can be purchased. Most consumers can identify these surface-level attributes of the Plaza's signs without much critical thought for interpretation. However, the connotative substance of the Plaza is highly dependent on the socioeconomic context of the reader; and as a sign of urban disparity, its meaning shifts according to the social position and economic status of the person or institution interacting with the Plaza's transition. While some local neighbors lament the decline of the Columbia Plaza because of what it

---

opened in 1958, the exact date of the closing is not known. Major decline in Columbia City hit bottom in the mid 70s. See Wilma, "Columbia Branch."

once represented about the community, other residents are celebrating its demise as they look forward to its eventual replacement.

Community advocates for the Plaza admit that its retail presence could use a significant makeover in the community, but many proponents of its future development want to ensure that the current clientele they serve will continue to be served by a revitalized Plaza. They see the Plaza as an unpretentious, everyday kind of place, where shoppers of different socioeconomic backgrounds can have access to a variety of affordable goods. In their eyes, the Plaza is a sign of inclusion and affordability in an otherwise gentrified business district that is becoming increasingly expensive as it moves upscale.

On the other hand, the many critics of the Plaza cannot wait to demolish the structure because they view its continued presence in the community as a sign of the old neighborhood that struggled with crime and prostitution for decades before the redevelopment of the 1990s. Local neighbors have long complained about gang activity and drug dealing at the Plaza, and a fatal shooting over a dice game in the parking lot in March of 2007 further reinforced its reputation as a trouble spot in the transitioning commercial area.[24] However, reported incidents of violence or criminal activity have been almost non-existent since then, though some continue to complain about the appearance of "suspicious" activities.[25] A few young African American men still occasionally park their SUVs, compare sound systems, and loiter in the Plaza's parking lot during the day, but today their presence is largely fading in numbers in Columbia City altogether. For those who consider the Plaza the last blighted property in the Landmark District, its redevelopment into an entirely new commercial site cannot come soon enough.

Cultural and Historical Context

In the summer of 1994, a group of urban youth working with the People of Color Against AIDS Network (POCAAN) were commissioned by the City of Seattle's Summer Youth Employment Program to paint a seventy-five-foot mural on the south side of the Columbia Plaza building's

24. Jamieson, "Violent Death in the Afternoon."

25. These claims are not entirely unsubstantiated. On several occasions, I have witnessed casual encounters behind the Plaza that resemble all the indicators of a quick exchange of controlled substances. Common knowledge in the neighborhood is that occasional drug transactions persist at several locations in or around the Plaza.

exterior wall. The public mural was designed by the youth as a tribute to their peers who had died from HIV/AIDS. With "vibrant colors and bold messages . . . the project allowed kids to pay homage to friends who had, as the mural puts it, 'Gone 2 Young.'"[26] However, not everyone in the neighborhood appreciated the art for its message of AIDS awareness and community solidarity.

In particular, Darla Morton, executive director of the Rainier Chamber of Commerce (RCC),[27] felt that the style and feel of the mural looked too much like graffiti. "'It looks like it's been defaced,' said Morton, who predicted the sanctioned spray-painting would inspire a rash of illegal 'taggers' in the business district."[28] But William Jones, a fifteen-year-old who helped to paint the mural, tried to explain that "for people who've left this earth, we're bringing them back in our own way. We've brought their souls back." Though many of the "youths likened their wall to the Vietnam Veterans Memorial,"[29] Morton was not swayed.

In addition to the cultural gap between Rainier Chamber of Commerce and POCAAN, it is possible that the RCC's reluctance to endorse the mural was connected to their desire to partner with the Neighborhood Farmers Market Alliance, a community-based organization that hosts neighborhood markets throughout the city of Seattle. In 1998, the Columbia City Farmers Market began meeting in the Columbia Plaza's parking lot—right in front of the contested mural—during the spring and summer months. The Farmers Market brings fresh, organic produce and other local vendors to the neighborhood, and though some efforts have been made to create an accessible and inclusive market, the price point of organic goods and specialty food items has largely appealed to the upwardly mobile professionals in the community. With steady growth in this sort of customer base over the past decade's gentrification, it is unlikely that many would understand or appreciate the public mural's history and value for those who simply wanted to honor the memories of their friends.

26. Goldsmith, "Mural's Beauty."

27. The RCC is the primary business association in the Landmark District, and has been a major player in the revitalization of the Columbia City commercial area along Rainier Avenue.

28. Goldsmith, "Mural's Beauty."

29. Ibid.

Ultimately, the final signifier of the impending socioeconomic change in the neighborhood was the 2007 purchase of the Columbia Plaza by HAL Real Estate Investments, a Seattle-based developer that specializes in mixed-use commercial and residential properties. With permitted plans for 330 underground parking spaces, over 8,000 square feet of street-level retail space, and six stories of over 300 units of new housing,[30] the proposed building will dwarf the old Plaza in both physical and social stature. Though an eventual replacement of the Plaza was inevitable, the sale of the Plaza for $6.6 million[31] was a symbolic closing chapter for one of the last "original" businesses of the old Columbia City. And as always, the redevelopment and transition has been welcomed by some but is bittersweet for many others.

Coded Messages and Meaning

Reading these signs of urban disparity in the context of Columbia City leads to an understanding that the most powerful codes structuring the change in the neighborhood are rooted in the patterns and regulatory practices of corporate-driven business economic development. The economic system of signs operates according to the flow of capital, and free market forces largely determine the outcome. When a signifier like the old Columbia Plaza does not fit within the prevailing economic system because of its "ghetto" connotations—expressed in either low-income retailers or what looks like graffiti to some—it is bound to be transformed into a signified that matches the economic codes of the structure in place.

The general pace and character of gentrification can be mitigated by a variety of factors, but no amount of community organization or political will can eliminate the economic tendency toward the poles of either gentrification or decline in communities where points of disparity are both visible and common. The very presence of urban disparity in a community—various signs of wealth and poverty in close coexistence—means that transition in one direction or the other is not far behind. Signs almost always naturally group with like signs in the urban context, and these ordered similarities create stratified structures in the city.

---

30. Cohen, "Columbia Plaza Environmental Review Approved."
31. Cohen, "Developer Buys Columbia City Plaza."

Whether it is affordable senior housing being built over former dumping sites, public housing projects that have been transformed into mixed-income neighborhoods, or low-income retailers that are being converted into condos, all of these urban phenomena are symbolic systems of meaning in the larger Rainier Valley community. These signs of density, diversity, and disparity in the urban context can seem disjointed and difficult to read at times, and a part of that difficulty rests in the dynamic nature of the systems that shape the urban context.

A neighborhood is a like a living text, and as it evolves over time, so do the signs and the codes that govern them. The system of "grammar" may change, shifting the denotative and connotative meaning of signifiers' form and substance. Signs that once represented positive aspects in a community can become negative, or negative signs can become neutral. But despite the perpetually shifting nature of urban neighborhoods, urban socio-semiotic analysis is still a relevant and effective method of locating, grouping, ordering, and interpreting signs in their immediate context. Like any language, becoming conversant with a broader vocabulary of signs, symbols, and codes (or words, ideas, and grammar) provides the reader with a more competent level of literacy and a more capable interpretive lens whenever the text, pseudo-text, or sign object changes.

8

Interpretation: A Local Urban Theology of Rainier Valley

CULTURAL EXEGESIS IS THE interpretation component of urban exegesis. The aim of this chapter is to examine and evaluate the culture of the Rainier Valley in order to develop a local, urban theology based on the socio-semiotic observations of density, diversity, and disparity explored through Rainier Court, Rainier Vista, and the Columbia Plaza. By focusing on the urban issues of place, neighbor, and community,[1] I will explore how a local theology can be rooted in both the culture of the Rainier Valley and the biblical narrative of the gospel, which offers a missional and redemptive perspective on the city. Additionally, I will incorporate the missional theology of cultural engagement that is outlined in part two as this exegetical consideration of the Valley takes on an embodied, prophetic, and subversive character through the themes of incarnation, confrontation, and imagination.

INCARNATIONAL PLACE-MAKING

To examine and evaluate the content and context of Rainier Court as a sign of density in the community is to wrestle with the missional implications of becoming creators and sustainers of a distinct sense of place in the face of urban isolation and anonymity. Therefore, a cultural exegesis of a place like Rainier Court requires a local *theology of place* that is both contextual to the urban density of Rainier Valley and accountable to the themes in the biblical narrative which call a pilgrim people to be *incarnational place-makers* in a culture of displacement and placeless-

1. Issues of place, neighbor, and community in the city will also be examined through the lens of contextual theology in chapter 11.

ness. If the people of God are characterized by an intentional, embodied presence in the city, then the task of engaging a lack of constructive place in the urban context requires a distinctly *placed* community.

Exegeting Density at Rainier Court

The content of Rainier Court is reflective of a design movement that seeks to push the limits of urban density on a parcel of land that already faces physical, geographic limitations which constrain its residential capacity. This maximization of urban density at the potential cost of the community's infrastructure is often motivated by increased potential for revenue generation in an area that would otherwise have a lower occupancy. At Rainier Court, the size of the development's footprint, the height of its structures, and the needs of its population are at risk of overwhelming the surrounding neighborhood.

The debate over whether its presence is creating a place for seniors and low-income renters or essentially dumping another social service facility on an already overtaxed community is a familiar conversation in the context of Rainier Valley. Though the redeveloped Rainier Court is certainly an improvement over the environmentally contaminated dumping ground it once was, many neighbors are left wondering why the Valley is so often the recipient of these kinds of redevelopment projects. Should not other parts of the city share equally in the burden of supporting under-resourced populations? With hundreds of seniors corralled into its towers and little opportunity for shared open space, at what point does the congestion of human need outweigh the ability to create a place for community?

Urban density in Rainier Valley is a complex social reality because it facilitates a double movement toward both interaction and isolation. A balanced level of density that holds both proximity and privacy in tension can facilitate healthy interaction where people's dwelling places overlap in designated shared spaces. On the other hand, too much density creates an overcrowding, which leads to a sense of isolation in congested areas. At Rainier Court, where the high level of density exceeds the livability of the available space, there is an inherent anonymity in the large population on site that hinders the potential for community building interaction.

In a place where personal space is limited and privacy is in short supply, conflict is an inevitable byproduct of proximity. And more often than not, when people who are crowded together also have pronounced physical, social, and economic needs, density is more likely to lead to confrontation than relationship. Unfortunately, a lack of a common sense of place in this context further exacerbates this problem. Individuals who share *space* but not *place* cannot resolve conflict or invest in community, and the result of this arrangement is a collective of broken and lonely individuals who merely occupy the same physical area.

Cultivating a genuine sense of place requires more than spatial cohesion, and a group of people in the same place does not automatically create a community. Rather, creating *place* necessitates an intentional effort to consciously inhabit the space in which we find ourselves. This is true in both the residential layout of an apartment complex and the arrangement of buildings on a city block. If Rainier Court is to become more than a place of urban density for dumping, then a community of people committed to the potentially redemptive *placiality*[2] of its space will have to invest in its renewal.

Making Place in the Valley

Rainier Court is but one example of unsustainable density in the Rainier Valley that reiterates the challenges of cultivating place in the city. Wendell Berry argues that so many of the urban realities that hinder a local development of place are often characterized by "a rootless and placeless monoculture of commercial expectations and products,"[3] and that this modern urban culture "is inherently a culture of displacement, of homelessness."[4] It is not only the homeless, *Beyond Homelessness* contends, who suffer from a sense of being displaced.

Urban density in the Valley is further complicated by the anonymity and isolation that continually accompanies this displacement. In "the marginality of the poor in the inner city . . . there is a profound sense that we are all strangers. And that estrangement . . . that culture-wide sense of displacement, is fundamentally a feature of our migrancy."[5] Migrancy in this regard is not limited to a physical transiency; rather, "the migrant's sense of being rootless, of living between worlds, between a lost past and

---

2. A place's unique character, or the "personality" of a place (e.g., a place of density, diversity, and disparity).

3. Berry, *Sex, Economy, Freedom, and Community*, 151.

4. Bouma-Prediger and Walsh, *Beyond Homelessness*, 6.

5. Ibid., 8.

a non-integrated present, is perhaps the most fitting metaphor of this (post)modern condition."[6] Many residents of the Valley do not need to geographically relocate to feel rootless; their marginalization as the poor has already robbed them of their sense of place.

In this culture of displacement and placelessness that arises from urban density, cultural exegesis calls the people of God to be creators and sustainers of place in the city. Amidst a pervasive sense of "homelessness," the church must become a community of hospitable "homemakers," who are created in the image of "a homemaking God who creates a world for inhabitation. This God is a primordial homemaker, and creation is a home for all creatures."[7] In the urban context where merely sufficient *housing* often falls short of a safe and healthy *home*, the need for a place where people can truly be at home is accentuated. While the Valley could certainly use more quality, affordable housing, the need for genuinely loving homes of hospitality is much greater. Homemaking through compassionate, incarnational hospitality is a way of making a place for the poor and overcrowded masses of the city.[8]

Making a place for understanding the concept of *home* theologically is best situated in the story of the people of God and their longing for a home both *for* and *with* YHWH. Rooted in the biblical narrative of exile and homecoming,[9] the Christian story is one of migrancy and loss that always culminates in a return to a distinct place of being home, whether that home is in the tabernacle, the Promised Land, or the reconstruction of the temple in Jerusalem.[10] This pattern of going away but coming back again repeats itself throughout the narrative, and uniquely equips Christians who identify with this story to wrestle with the tension of being simultaneously at home in the present, but not yet *fully* at

6. Chambers, *Migrancy, Culture, Identity*, 27.

7. Bouma-Prediger and Walsh, *Beyond Homelessness*, 14.

8. Notably, the Catholic Worker movement's emphasis on hospitality houses for the poor and marginalized has embodied this ethic of "homemaking/place-making" in the urban context. See Murray, *Do Not Neglect Hospitality*; and Ellis, *Year at the Catholic Worker*.

9. "Exile and Homecoming" are core biblical motifs that have been noted by numerous theologians in both academic and popular work. See Brueggemann, *Commentary on Jeremiah*; and Wright, *Simply Christian*, 76.

10. Though God cannot be "domesticated" within the physical space of a "home" (see Isa 66:1), there is a sense in which the biblical narrative is always wrestling with finding a place to be "at home" with YHWH, both theologically and geographically.

home. The already but not yet reality of the kingdom of God means that Christians, as a pilgrim people, must be place-makers wherever they are, including the urban context. For Christians to be fully present in the city will require an intentional investment in urban communities like the Rainier Valley.

Ultimately, biblical homecoming is not about *us* finding *our* place; it is about God coming to dwell with us. From the pillar of cloud or fire outside the tabernacle to the first chapter of John's Gospel, God is insistent about making his presence known among his people, and the incarnation is the ultimate expression of this ministry of presence that refused distance. God makes himself at home in the human flesh of Jesus of Nazareth, and then invites all of Israel to embrace this incarnational ethic of relocation from a place of esteem and prestige to the eventual humiliation of the cross. This downwardly mobile *cursus pudorum*[11] is what enables the eschatological homecoming in Revelation 21.

John's vision of the New Jerusalem descending to earth out of heaven echoes the eschatological vision at the end of Isaiah 66 of a new heaven and a new earth.

> Revelation 21: The New Heaven and the New Earth
>
> [1] Then I saw a new heaven and a new earth; for the first heaven and the first earth had passed away, and the sea was no more. [2] And I saw the holy city, the new Jerusalem, coming down out of heaven from God, prepared as a bride adorned for her husband. [3] And I heard a loud voice from the throne saying,
>
> "See, the home of God is among mortals.
> He will dwell with them;
> they will be his peoples,
> and God himself will be with them;
> [4] he will wipe every tear from their eyes.
> Death will be no more;
> mourning and crying and pain will be no more,
> for the first things have passed away."
>
> [5] And the one who was seated on the throne said, "See, I am making all things new."

This final place that shapes the trajectory of the biblical narrative is a picture of the incarnation. In verse 3, it is the *skēnē*, or tabernacle,

---

11. Latin for "course of humiliation." See the section on "Downward Mobility" in the third chapter for an expansion of this idea.

of God that takes up habitation among people and God will *skēnōo* (en-camp, reside) with them in the same way that the Word became flesh and made his dwelling among us. The incarnation is the singularly *placed* re-ality that marks the identity of a *placed* people as the community of God.

A local theology of incarnational place-making in a context of urban density and displacement must locate itself in this story of home-coming if the people of God are indeed called to be creators and sustain-ers of place in the city. Thus, the church as a community of incarnational place-makers must understand exile and homecoming as a lived nar-rative in the midst of homemaking that can transform the density and marginalization of Rainier Court into a place of hospitality and presence in the neighborhood.

PROPHETIC NEIGHBORLY JUSTICE

A cultural exegesis of Rainier Vista as a sign of diversity in the com-munity calls those who are seeking a more genuine diversity to become neighbors that share in a common sense of responsibility to work toward a *prophetic, neighborly justice*[12] in the community. This local theology of neighborliness that is contextual to the diversity of the Rainer Valley and rooted in a reconciling gospel must be committed to cultivating a people of both courage and humility in their pursuit of diversity for its capacity to create a community that cares for the "orphan, widow, and stranger"[13] with "steadfast love, justice, and righteousness."[14]

Obstructing Neighborly Justice

The primary obstacle that challenges this commitment to a deeper un-derstanding of diversity in Rainier Vista is similar in many ways to the superficiality of the Rainier Vista Whirligigs. The Whirligigs represent a tangible expression of the reality that many neighbors in the commu-nity prefer the form and appearance of an abstract diversity over the substance and praxis of a more concrete diversity. Many residents of the neighborhood, particularly the homeowners who moved to Rainier Vista by choice, may enjoy the idea of public art that represents other cultures,

12. See the fourth chapter's section on "Prophetic Justice" for a more detailed dis-cussion of the character of justice in the Old Testament prophetic tradition.

13. Deut 10:18.

14. Jer 9:24.

but very few are interested in making a relatively small investment in the praxis of diversity by actually serving on the Multicultural Committee.[15] Most neighbors appear to appreciate a more detached ideal of diversity in word but not deed, and at a safe, comfortable distance.

In a community like the Rainier Valley that is often praised and celebrated for its diversity,[16] the concept of diversity can also be a cipher for other agendas. Real estate developers working with the Seattle Housing Authority have to market a carefully calculated image of diversity as a desirable attribute of the neighborhood in order to attract home buyers. This often reduces diversity to various forms of tokenism, like subtle suggestions that experiencing ethnic restaurants and seeing children of color actually leads to deeper cultural understanding. Also, many gentrifiers who live in the Rainier Valley often feel compelled to flaunt the diversity of the community to other people of privilege who live in more homogeneous communities and are therefore assumed to be less "cultured" in the ways of "urban living." In this way, diversity becomes more of a "lifestyle" issue than about actual relationships. These distortions of diversity serve the agenda of those who stand to profit—economically or socially—from false conceptions of diversity.

Love of God and Neighbor

To reflect missionally about the possibility of substantive relationships between diverse neighbors in this context of manufactured and ornamental diversity is the task of a local theology of prophetic, neighborly justice. Throughout the biblical narrative, love of God and love of neighbor are held together with profound implications; these two inseparable ideals are upheld as the greatest commandment with utmost importance, a supreme imperative on which "all the law and the prophets"[17] are hung. Though this oft-quoted commandment is frequently paid tribute as a central but generic commitment of Christianity, the essential interde-

15. While there has been consistent (albeit distanced) support for the committee from various neighbors and the homeowners association, the simple task of recruiting volunteers for community events has consistently relied on the same handful of individuals in a neighborhood of hundreds of residents.

16. Professor Sheryll Cashin identifies southeast Seattle as a "racially integrated community" and "multicultural island" that is "bucking the trend" of urban segregation. Nevertheless, many problems related to integration remain. See Cashin, *Failures of Integration*, 52–54.

17. Matt 22:40.

pendence between love of God and love of neighbor suggests a radical and prophetic theology of neighborliness in the urban context.

In a community like the Rainier Valley, where high levels of cultural, ethnic, and socioeconomic diversity often result in the segregation and stratification of the city, the level of Christian commitment to building relationships and coalitions between diverse neighbors is a reflection of the church's faithfulness to the greatest commandment. Simply put, if loving God presupposes love of neighbor, then a lack of genuine relationships with these diverse neighbors reveals a deficiency in love for God. To claim to love at a distance denies the incarnational ethic of presence as a prerequisite to demonstrations of love.

Practically speaking, a casual love of neighbor often implicitly presumes similarity, and loving those who share in the assumptions of our social location, cultural background, and economic status is certainly easier than seeking to love neighbors across the boundaries that are created when those assumptions are not shared. But in the urban context, the abstraction of the orphan, widow, and foreigner becomes the common reality of the fatherless, the single mother, and the immigrant or refugee. And building relationships with people in these particular situations requires much more than a common social interest or an ability to dole out charity. Rather, what is needed is a commitment to seeking justice (in steadfast love and righteousness) alongside these diverse neighbors.

This commitment to become a community in which the burdens of some are truly shared by all requires a thoroughly Christocentric understanding of how Jesus has reconciled formerly divided groups across ethnic and cultural barriers. The Apostle Paul speaks of the necessity of grasping this essential spiritual unity to the diverse community of faith in Ephesus.

Ephesians 2: One in Christ

[11] So then, remember that at one time you Gentiles by birth, called "the uncircumcision" by those who are called 'the circumcision'—a physical circumcision made in the flesh by human hands— [12] remember that you were at that time without Christ, being aliens from the commonwealth of Israel, and strangers to the covenants of promise, having no hope and without God in the world. [13] But now in Christ Jesus you who once were far off have been brought near by the blood of Christ. [14] For he is our peace; in his flesh he

has made both groups into one and has broken down the dividing wall, that is, the hostility between us. [15] He has abolished the law with its commandments and ordinances, so that he might create in himself one new humanity in place of the two, thus making peace, [16] and might reconcile both groups to God in one body through the cross, thus putting to death that hostility through it. [17] So he came and proclaimed peace to you who were far off and peace to those who were near; [18] for through him both of us have access in one Spirit to the Father. [19] So then you are no longer strangers and aliens, but you are citizens with the saints and also members of the household of God, [20] built upon the foundation of the apostles and prophets, with Christ Jesus himself as the cornerstone. [21] In him the whole structure is joined together and grows into a holy temple in the Lord; [22] in whom you also are built together spiritually into a dwelling-place for God.

With Christ at the center of this process of reconciliation between Jews and Gentiles, "Christ himself (note the emphatic *autos*) is our peace (v. 14). It does not say that he gives peace but rather that he is our peace. . . . By this Paul means that Christ himself in his own person and death is the destroyer of all hostilities between Jew and Gentile. He has made of the two peoples one new person. A unity has been created where previously there had been no such unity."[18] That the catalyst for this new creation of peace and unity in the place of hostility and separation is the destruction of the *phragmos*, or dividing barrier, is a sign of the necessity of dismantling the structural forces that enable segregation. Further, it is also a reminder that the process of working to remove "the dividing wall(s) of hostility" is a costly one, for it is only in the flesh and blood of Christ's broken body that "one new humanity" (v. 15) can be created.

To be transformed from "strangers and aliens" to joint "members of the household of God" (v. 19) in a diverse community like the Rainier Valley will require the costly sacrifice of many people who are willing to stand in prophetic contradistinction against the status quo of urban stratification. In this way, a genuine love of neighbor must go beyond the cordiality of social platitudes toward the family ethics of the divine *oikos* (household). When one family member suffers, the whole family is affected. Thus, when some neighbors in the urban context are excluded, marginalized, and oppressed, it is the shared responsibility of the neighborhood to alleviate suffering and work toward structural change. The

---

18. Witherington, *Letters to Philemon, the Colossians*, 259.

church must be this reconciled and reconciling community of a new humanity in the city.

Ultimately, this commitment to cultivating a prophetic, neighborly justice cannot rest on a desire to serve others or a conviction rooted in an ideal of the "common good." Instead, it must be framed by the value of communal Christian solidarity. Theologian James Cone, in *God of the Oppressed*, explains:

> The Christian community, therefore, is that community that freely becomes oppressed, because they know that Christ himself has defined humanity's liberation in the context of what happens to the little ones. Christians join in the cause of the oppressed in the fight for justice not because of some philosophical principle of "the Good" or because of a religious feeling of sympathy for people in prison. Sympathy does not change the structures of injustice. The authentic identity of Christians with the poor is found in the claim which the Christ-encounter lays upon their own lifestyle, a claim that connects the word "Christian" with the liberation of the poor. Christians fight not for humanity in general but for themselves and out of their love for concrete human beings.[19]

To stand in solidarity with the poor and oppressed is to connect "the authentic identity of Christians with the poor" in such a way that the inherent definition of a Christian is one who loves and liberates the poor in order to live in God's new community of people who are reconciled in Christ. Therefore, a good neighbor in the urban context of diversity is one who seeks to plant and nurture seeds of solidarity between diverse neighbors out of Christian love and prophetic conviction. A local theology of neighborliness in the Rainier Valley must remain steadfast in this work of peace and justice for all.

IMAGINATIVE COMMUNITIES OF REDISTRIBUTION

Finally, to understand the culture of Columbia Plaza as a sign of disparity in the neighborhood requires an exploration of the missional implications of socioeconomic redistribution in the context of gentrification. A cultural exegesis of Columbia Plaza examines and evaluates a theology of community that is both contextual to the urban disparity of the Rainier Valley and faithful to the biblical narrative which calls the

19. Cone, *God of the Oppressed*, 136.

people of God to be an imaginative community of redistribution in a society that disproportionately allocates resources.

Gentrification with Justice

The Plaza is just one among many signs of disparity and gentrification in the Rainier Valley. Its scheduled redevelopment is symbolic of the final domino to fall in what has been a long line of businesses that have steadily turned over in the Columbia City business district. For many poorer residents in the community, debating the strategies of contextual economic development in tension with unbridled gentrification is a moot point because it is difficult for them to imagine how the area could become any *more* gentrified. However, there are others who are working to preserve the few remaining locally owned businesses that have a long history in the Landmark District, holding on to hope that Columbia City can retain its diverse character and unique history. Still others— many with the economic resources to support new development—are aggressively pushing for widespread business "revitalization"[20] in the area because of the recognition that the potential for commercial growth among untapped consumer bases is strong.

Though it is quite clear that the reality of recent gentrification has significantly impacted the community in numerous ways, many well-intentioned people on all sides of the debate continue to disagree over the costs and benefits of gentrification for the Rainier Valley as a whole. Unfortunately (but predictably), the inherent socioeconomic disparity that stratifies groups in the urban context also segregates their respective understandings of change and development in the community. Regardless of whether gentrification is perceived as a potential tool in developing "a market with a conscience,"[21] or merely the "new urban colonialism,"[22] what is needed in this broader conversation is a willingness to explore creative options that allow for the market realities of urban redevelopment while also taking into account the importance of

20. Community "revitalization," frequently used as a friendlier or more palatable term than "gentrification," is often viewed with suspicion as a code word for development with the intent to displace "unwanted" populations. See Palen and London, *Gentrification, Displacement*.

21. Lutpon, "Gentrification with Justice."

22. Atkinson and Bridge, *Gentrification in a Global Context*.

retaining and investing in the existing social fabric of communities that are likely candidates for targeted gentrification.[23]

"Gentrification with justice" is one such idea. As a compromise between the unregulated development of real estate and the urban isolation that inevitably leads to blight and deterioration, gentrification with justice suggests that while gentrification cannot be stopped (nor should it), its most damaging effects can be mitigated by an intentional process of inclusion that seeks to care for the long-term sustainability of the poor.

> "Gentrification with justice"—that's what is needed to restore health to our urban neighborhoods. Needed are gentry with vision who have compassionate hearts as well as real estate acumen. We need gentry whose understanding of community includes the less-advantaged, who will use their competencies and connections to ensure that their lower-income neighbors share a stake in their revitalizing neighborhood. The city needs land-owning residents who are also faith-motivated, who yield to the tenets of their faith in the inevitable tension between value of neighbor over value of property. That is why gentrification needs a theology to guide it.[24]

A theology of gentrification in the context of urban disparity must hold social, economic, and theological concerns together in order to pursue a potentially holistic understanding of gentrification as a complex urban phenomenon. Ultimately, if gentrification is going to be connected to these multiple dimensions of justice, then it must function in such a way as to ensure that socioeconomic capital can be distributed fairly, generously, and with a particular concern for the fatherless, the single mothers, and the immigrants in the urban context. In cities where stark disparities so often dominate the urban landscape, this kind of distributive justice will inevitably be a *re*-distribution of resources.

Thinking about gentrification in these terms requires a theology that grasps the social and economic dimensions of redistribution, but also sees the theological capacity of redistribution as a redemptive communal practice. If gentrification is seen as primarily an economic issue,

---

23. It has been my continual assertion that searching for signs and symbols of urban disparity provides some of the clearest signifiers for change in communities undergoing transition.

24. Lupton, *Gentrification with Justice*.

then redistribution of economic capital will simply be perceived as a form of punitive taxation on the upwardly mobile. On the other hand, if gentrification is seen only as a social issue, then redistribution of social capital will not be able to address the structural economic systems that perpetuate urban disparity. However, if a theology of gentrification binds both social and economic concerns together with a commitment to the biblical concept of Jubilee justice, then forms and practices of socioeconomic redistribution have the potential to be redemptive activities for the benefit of the whole community.

An Urban Jubilee Community

The year of Jubilee as described in Leviticus 25 is framed within in the broader Levitical context of the communal holiness of Israel. To practice Jubilee was not merely a social and economic restructuring of society; first and foremost, this was a spiritual and religious commitment that grew out of the covenant with YHWH. "The priestly traditions view this as a community-wide enactment of release and freedom. The pragmatics of such an institution are, at best, difficult and complex, and the evidence for its practice is scant."[25] However, regardless of how Jubilee was either idealized or implemented, "theologically, it remains an important aspect of the priestly vision of the Israelite community as the holy people of Yahweh."[26]

> Leviticus 25: The Year of Jubilee
>
> [8] You shall count off seven weeks of years, seven times seven years, so that the period of seven weeks of years gives forty-nine years. [9] Then you shall have the trumpet sounded loud; on the tenth day of the seventh month—on the day of atonement—you shall have the trumpet sounded throughout all your land. [10] And you shall hallow the fiftieth year and you shall proclaim liberty throughout the land to all its inhabitants. It shall be a jubilee for you: you shall return, every one of you, to your property and every one of you to your family. [11] That fiftieth year shall be a jubilee for you: you shall not sow, or reap the aftergrowth, or harvest the unpruned vines. [12] For it is a jubilee; it shall be holy to you: you shall eat only what the field itself produces. [13] In this year of jubilee you shall return, every one of you, to your property. [14] When you make a

25. Gorman, *Divine Presence and Community*, 138.
26. Ibid.

sale to your neighbor or buy from your neighbor, you shall not cheat one another. [15] When you buy from your neighbor, you shall pay only for the number of years since the jubilee; the seller shall charge you only for the remaining crop-years. [16] If the years are more, you shall increase the price, and if the years are fewer, you shall diminish the price; for it is a certain number of harvests that are being sold to you. [17] You shall not cheat one another, but you shall fear your God; for I am the LORD your God.

Celebrated as a Sabbath of Sabbaths, Jubilee begins on the Day of Atonement (v. 9), which is a communal marker for penitence and forgiveness of the sins of the people. In this way, the social and economic ordinances that define the practice of Jubilee are rooted in a spiritual conviction that the redistribution of land, labor, and resources is an act of obedience to the holiness code that reconciles the community to God. The repeated imperatives that apply to "every one of you" (vv. 10, 13) indicate the wide scope of this communal vision, and the layers of connection between rest, return, and financial integrity link generosity and simplicity with holiness and redemption.

However, it is important to remember that even though the root metaphor is the atonement of a holy covenant community, the economic implications of redistribution remain salient and essential to the practice of Jubilee. "The jubilee was intended to prevent the accumulation of the wealth of the nation in the hands of a very few . . . the biblical law is opposed to the monopolistic tendencies of unbridled capitalism."[27] In the cultural context of Israel's society, "this text represents an attempt to modify a contemporary economic praxis that was leading to the progressive economic deterioration of significant portions of the population."[28] Thus, the recognition of the importance of Jubilee is intimately connected with the reality of economic disparities that needed to be reconciled through redistribution.

Jubilee also reminds the people of God that they are stewards—and not owners—of the land, labor, and resources with which they have been entrusted. These assets of the material economy were gifts to be managed for their flourishing, not commodities to be exploited. Treating workers fairly, setting slaves free, lending without interest, welcoming foreigners, and freely redistributing wealth are each reflections of an alternative

27. Wenham, *Book of Leviticus*, 323.
28. Gerstenberger, *Leviticus*, 398.

economy in which YHWH is the arbiter of justice and righteousness. In the Jubilee economy, the culmination of Sabbath rest, is the institution of this rhythm of communal justice in the life of the people Israel. Establishing Jubilee as a natural, recurring equalizer protected the poor and encouraged societal generosity as Israel sought to remember that all things truly do belong to God.

To contextualize Jubilee ethics in the present era of capitalism and consumerism is no simple task. But to live as a Jubilee community in the urban context is not just a solution to the free market forces that create disparity and gentrification; more importantly, it is a prophetic act of worship and submission to an alternative vision for society. Jesus was captured by this same vision in his proclamation of the good news in Luke's Gospel.

Luke 4: The Beginning of the Galilean Ministry

[14] Then Jesus, filled with the power of the Spirit, returned to Galilee, and a report about him spread through all the surrounding country. [15] He began to teach in their synagogues and was praised by everyone. [16] When he came to Nazareth, where he had been brought up, he went to the synagogue on the Sabbath day, as was his custom. He stood up to read, [17] and the scroll of the prophet Isaiah was given to him. He unrolled the scroll and found the place where it was written:

[18] "The Spirit of the Lord is upon me,
because he has anointed me
to bring good news to the poor.
He has sent me to proclaim release to the captives
and recovery of sight to the blind,
to let the oppressed go free,
[19] to proclaim the year of the Lord's favor."

[20] And he rolled up the scroll, gave it back to the attendant, and sat down. The eyes of all in the synagogue were fixed on him. [21] Then he began to say to them, "Today this scripture has been fulfilled in your hearing."

The prophetic imagination of Isaiah 61 is what enlivens Jesus' proclamation of the fulfillment of the "year of the Lord's favor." As Jesus begins his public ministry with a declaration of Jubilee justice, he is announcing that the arrival of the Kingdom of God coincides with both the freedom and redistribution of Leviticus 25 and the hope and restoration of Isaiah 61. The reign that Jesus inaugurates casts an imaginative vision of beauty, strength, and redemption in the face of an oppressive empire that had all but crushed the longings of many who dreamt of a restored holy city on the Temple Mount. Directly after Jesus' quotation of Isaiah 61:1–2 in Luke 4:18–19, the prophetic text continues:

> ³ to provide for those who mourn in Zion—
> to give them a garland instead of ashes,
> the oil of gladness instead of mourning,
> the mantle of praise instead of a faint spirit.
> They will be called oaks of righteousness,
> the planting of the LORD, to display his glory.
> ⁴ They shall build up the ancient ruins,
> they shall raise up the former devastations;
> they shall repair the ruined cities,
> the devastations of many generations.

In the same way that Isaiah sees a restoration of the urban devastation that has brought despair to so many generations, Jesus connects the good news of Jubilee with the rebuilding of the city. Just as "Isaiah links God's new day for the poor with the promise of urban recovery,"[29] Jesus' gospel is one of renewal for those who are so often marginalized in the city. This renewed urban context is a place where the poor can share in the wealth of the rich, the captives can be released in the streets, the blind can see in a community of inclusion, and the oppressed are liberated by the justice of God. The faithful imagination of Isaiah that empowers Jesus' ministry in Galilee must also capture the hearts and minds of Christ-followers in today's cities.

Ultimately, a local theology of community in an urban context of disparity must shape the people of God into creative advocates of Jubilee justice and imaginative agents of redistribution. Redistribution in the diverse and stratified neighborhoods of the Rainier Valley may not look exactly like the Jubilee practices of Leviticus 25, but if a local theology of community can begin to challenge the inevitability of a gentrification that "tramples on the heads of the poor"[30] through displacement and exclusion, then finding ways of creatively redistributing land, wealth, and access to equal opportunities should be the next step in the process. And while it is always important to be developing practical tools for

29. Gornik, *Live in Peace*, 28.
30. Amos 2:7.

implementation and engagement in the community, [31] John Perkins also reminds those who are seeking to embody Jubilee ethics that "in the final analysis, *there is no redistribution without relocation.* The most important thing we have to redistribute is ourselves. Justice cannot be achieved by long distance . . . only after people are redistributed can we employ money in ways that produce development rather than dependency."[32] By linking redistribution with relocation, Perkins brings this missional theology of cultural engagement full circle in a return to the incarnational ethics of *kenosis* and downward mobility. These dialectical tasks are embodied, prophetic, and subversive expressions of a called and sent community in the city.

THE VALLEY AND THE CORNER REVISITED

As an interdisciplinary method of observing and interpreting urban communities, urban exegesis synthesizes the symbolic systems of *urban semiotics* and the missional theology of *cultural exegesis* in order to draw out the multifaceted meaning of complex environments in the city. With a particular emphasis on neighborhood-level analysis, urban exegesis offers a unique perspective on the urban context that facilitates critical interaction between the built environment and a local urban theology.

Through the observational analysis of urban socio-semiotics, the Rainier Valley is described as a place of distinct structures, pluralities, and contrasts. The density of Rainier Court, the diversity of Rainier Vista, and the disparity of Columbia Plaza exemplify these urban characteristics. Each attribute of the community—through the form and substance of its urban signs objects in cultural and historical context—communicates coded messages and meaning.

Subsequently, the interpretive analysis of cultural exegesis examines and evaluates the culture of the Rainier Valley in order to develop a local, urban theology based on the semiotic observations of density, diversity, and disparity. This local theology engages in incarnational place-making in a context of density and displacement, prophetic neighborly justice amidst the oppressed in diversity, and advocacy for imaginative communities of redistribution in economic disparity. All of these prac-

31. John Perkins and the CCDA provide a wealth of accessible resources for developing practices that cultivate socioeconomic redistribution in under-resourced communities. See Perkins, *Restoring At-Risk Communities* and *With Justice for All.*

32. Perkins, *With Justice for All,* 192.

tices are contextual expressions of missional theology in the culture of the Rainier Valley.

Though the lens of urban exegesis focuses primarily on the locality of the city, the particular character of the Valley's street signs also provide a hermeneutic for examining the universality of the Corner in urban attributes like density, diversity, and disparity, and important issues like place, neighbor, and community. In other words, while the Valley's unique history and physical environment has undoubtedly shaped its contemporary situation, there is also a sense in which its urban context represents several common patterns that emerge on streets and corners in every city.

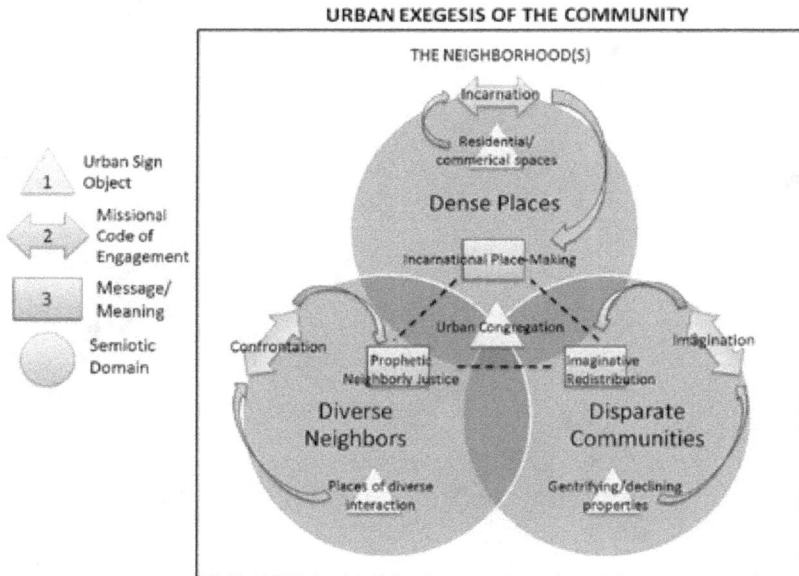

FIGURE 1: Urban Exegesis of the Community[33]

---

33. The basic structure of this initial Venn diagram serves as a template for the remaining two diagrams, which represent an urban semiotic model of the city and an urban contextual theology. Though the diagram identifies only one urban sign object per semiotic domain, there are many simultaneous sign objects in overlapping domains that move through a regulatory code to create meaning in the urban context.

PART 4

An Urban Contextual Theology

There is no such thing as "theology"; there is only *contextual* theology: *feminist* theology, *black* theology, *liberation* theology, *Filipino* theology, *Asian-American* theology, *African* theology, and so forth. Doing theology contextually is not an option, nor is it something that should only interest people from the Third World, missionaries who work there, or ethnic communities within dominant cultures. The contextualization of theology—the attempt to understand Christian faith in terms of a particular context—is really a theological imperative. As we have come to understand theology today, it is a process that is part of the very nature of theology itself.

—Stephen Bevans, *Models of Contextual Theology*, 2002

A s THE LAST TRANSITION from the lens of urban exegesis to the lens of contextual theology begins, this process facilitates the conceptual shift from the locality of the Valley to the universality of the Corner. In order to move from the specific perspective of urban exegesis to the broader contours of an urban contextual theology, a thorough understanding of the process of contextualization and the nature of the city is essential.

Thus, part 4 will examine the urban context from both a cultural and theological perspective in order to construct an urban contextual theology. Chapter 9 will explore the process of contextualization by defining contextual theology and "culture." Applying what Catholic missiologist Robert Schreiter calls "semiotic description of culture"[1] will then be presented as a preferred method of cultural analysis. Chapter 10 will then look specifically at the urban context as a place characterized by density, diversity, and disparity. Each of these aspects of the city's environment will be examined for its semiotic meaning and significance.

---

1. Schreiter, *Constructing Local Theologies*, 61.

Lastly, chapter 11 will synthesize the cultural analysis with theological reflection on the city in order to develop an urban contextual theology of place, neighbor, and community.

9

Contextualization as Process

A s the first two chapters repeatedly affirmed, a crucial component of contextualization is the necessity of developing a critical
understanding of particular cultural settings. Unfortunately, for many,
the faith and culture dialogue has been discussed primarily in a Western
context in which "culture" has been defined more broadly as representative of the whole of society. Much like its usage in H. Richard Niebuhr's
five typologies, culture is simply "that total process of human activity
and that total result of such activity to which now the name culture, now
the name civilization, is applied in common speech."[1] Niebuhr goes on
to insist that "a theologian's definition of the term must, in the nature of
the case, be a layman's definition, since he cannot presume to enter into
the issues raised by professional anthropologists . . . a Christian of the
West cannot think about the problem save in Western terms."[2]

This "layman's" definition of culture as interchangeable with "civilization" may be suitable for a kind of ethical and theological discourse
within the bounds of a monolithic Western culture, but the problem is
that many of its assumptions about the nature of culture itself remain
unexamined. This is precisely where "discipline-oriented approaches" to
faith and culture that are rooted in the social sciences have a wealth of
resources to employ in a more systematic and analytical investigation of
the complexities of culture. Contextual theology aims to tap into these
resources in the process of cultural analysis, and in doing so it proposes
an important theological imperative that is intimately connected to, as
Bevans states so succinctly, "the very nature of theology itself."[3]

1. Niebuhr, *Christ and Culture*, 32.
2. Ibid., 30–31.
3. Bevans, *Models of Contextual Theology*, 3.

UNDERSTANDING CONTEXTUAL THEOLOGY

The necessity of doing theology "contextually," that is, with a particular concern for the local setting of Christian faith and practice, is obviously not a "new" suggestion. As the second chapter's discussion of faith and culture established, the most basic nature of the task of theology has always been a contextual endeavor. To understand theology is to understand its context: historical, political, social, ethnic, economic, religious, and so on. However, this simple recognition that theology is always done contextually in a broad, general sense does not necessarily require a critical examination of common, tacit cultural presuppositions, like individualism or collectivism, socially embedded expectations of gender roles, or any other number of cultural predispositions.[4]

Particularly in the modern era, an *implicit* awareness of the importance of context has not at all prevented a fairly egregious list of errors and offenses connected to the modern projects of colonialism and paternalism, or various forms of cultural imperialism within the church.[5] Any cursory review of the history of Christian mission reveals the challenges of contextualization when confronted with the vast disparities of cultural, economic, and geopolitical distance in the world. And in a rapidly globalizing society, these disparities are confronting the church not only "abroad," but increasingly "at home." How, then, can contextual theology reconcile such cultural distance while remaining faithful to the orthodox commitments of the Christian faith, which are always situated within a particular set of contexts?

In the variety of ways that contextual theology seeks to make sense of this plurality of cultural contexts, one consistent value is expressed in the priority given to an *explicit*, intentional investigation of cultural context, and an equally critical evaluation of the process of theology. This dual emphasis takes seriously the essential task of doing theology with a careful consideration of all the unique facets that define, create, and sustain "culture" in society, as well as the distinct convictions that

---

4. These values, along with power distance, uncertainty avoidance, and time orientation are common cultural characteristics used to distinguish between national and/or ethnic cultural categories. See Hofstede, *Cultures and Organizations*.

5. Notably, the church was not alone in committing these errors, nor were the offenses of the church any more egregious than its counterparts in the state or any other societal institution. This acknowledgment is merely a recognition that contextualization, when done poorly, has consistently had unfortunate outcomes.

shape theology as it interacts with tradition, the Christian Scriptures, and human experience.[6]When theology as an abstraction[7] confronts tangible human reality, it inevitably becomes inculturated,[8] or adopted and adapted into a particular cultural context. This process of theological inculturation is the most basic reality of contextual theology, and one of the central theological affirmations of contextual theology is the inherently contextual nature of the inculturated gospel itself.

> One thing must be made clear from the beginning in relation to the process of inculturation. It must always be borne in mind that, strictly speaking, Christian proclaimers of the gospel anywhere do not preach "the Gospel," or "the message of Christ," or "revelation," or whatever other expression may be used to explain this task. The gospel as proclaimed is not a disembodied reality, a pure emanation from God. It is essentially a cultural reality. What Christian missionaries do, rather, is to transmit to their listeners their own understanding of the gospel.[9]

African theologian Laurenti Magesa, in referring to the faith-culture encounter that leads to inculturation,[10] identifies the epistemological and existential limitations[11] of every gospel proclamation. There is no such thing as a culture-free gospel; rather, there is only the gospel that is understood from a personal vantage point, trapped within the

6. For sustaining this essential task, contextual theology is deeply indebted to the plethora of research from missiologists and Christian anthropologists cited in the second chapter. Unfortunately, due to limitations of scope, I have intentionally chosen a smaller number of interlocutors for this section, despite the significant contributions of Kraft, Hiebert, and the many others who established the field.

7. I recognize that "theology in the abstract" is a bit of a contradiction in terms if indeed all theology is essentially contextual. If the false dichotomy can be allowed temporarily, I am working toward deconstructing the myth of an epistemologically "pure" theology.

8. At this preliminary point, I am using the language of "inculturation" somewhat synonymously with "contextualization," though the particular nuances of both will be examined in the following section.

9. Magesa, *Anatomy of Inculturation*, 6.

10. Magesa defines inculturation "from the Christian theological perspective" as "understood to be the process whereby the faith already embodied in one culture encounters another culture. In this encounter, the faith becomes part and parcel of this new culture" (Magesa, *Anatomy of Inculturation*, 5).

11. Magesa declares the proclaimed gospel a "cultural reality," not a "pure emanation"; hence the epistemological limitation is rooted in its cultural conditioning, and its existential limitation is rooted in its ontological inaccessibility.

boundaries of linguistic comprehension, and limited by the plausibility structures[12] constructed in society, which determine the shape and character of what is reasonable and credible.

Newbigin also affirms this recognition that even the most basic communication of the gospel through language is intricately entangled with our cultural worldview.

> Neither at the beginning, nor at any subsequent time, is there or can there be a gospel that is not embodied in a culturally conditioned form of words. The idea that one can or could at any time separate out by some process of distillation a pure gospel unadulterated by any cultural accretions is an illusion. It is, in fact, an abandonment of the gospel, for the gospel is about the word made flesh. Every statement of the gospel in words is conditioned by the culture of which those words are a part, and every style of life that claims to embody the gospel is a culturally conditioned style of life.[13]

This fundamentally contextual nature of the gospel is not a license for baseless cultural relativism, nor is it an obstacle to understanding the particular characteristics of the gospel. Rather, the gospel as an essentially embodied reality is representative of the significance of the incarnation, and an invitation to consider the rich plurality of ways that an incarnate faith witnesses to the God of all cultures.

There is a dynamic challenge in this cultural plurality, one that constantly has to balance what Bevans calls an adherence to either the "contextual experience of the present" or the "traditional experience of the past."[14] In the present context, the significance of anthropological factors like identity formation, social change, and social location are weighted heavily. These immediate cultural realities must be taken into account when contextualizing theological propositions and practices.

---

12. Sociologist Peter Berger describes plausibility structures in the context of "society as subjective reality." He suggests that "subjective reality is thus always dependent upon specific plausibility structures, that is, the specific social base and social processes required for . . . the particular suspension of doubt without which the definition of reality in question cannot be maintained in consciousness" (Berger and Luckmann, *Social Construction of Reality*, 154–55). Newbigin builds on Berger's definition as he speaks extensively about the role of plausibility structures in limiting our understanding of culture (Newbigin, *Gospel in a Pluralist Society*).

13. Newbigin, *Foolishness to the Greeks*, 4.

14. Bevans, *Models of Contextual Theology*, 32.

On the other side of the spectrum is the experience of the past, which places emphasis on theological issues like the interpretation of scripture, established church traditions, and historical precedent. Contextual theology seeks to find a balance between these two poles, a compromise of theological inculturation.

Thus, the whole of contextual theology is not only a theological imperative, but also an ongoing dialectic that continually challenges the theologian—practical, academic, amateur, or otherwise—to think and then rethink, try and then retry, develop and then redevelop theological approaches to culture that are both authentically situated in the context of a local setting and deeply rooted in the orthodox Christian tradition. Skillfully navigating this dialectical exchange is a complicated process,[15] but its necessity is both crucial and urgent in our contemporary cultural context.

Ultimately, contextual theology is needed to move from the "political correctness"[16] of cultural *sensitivities* to truly *intercultural competency*[17] in a global marketplace of diverse ideologies. Contextual theology motivated by promoting a more sensitive, palatable accommodation of diverse cultures will never engage the substantive interaction between faith and culture that occurs in true contextualization. Instead, it will only domesticate other ideologies within its own self-understanding. But contextual theology that is seeking a mutually transformative encounter between faith and culture will equip the church with the ability

15. Bevans's six models (anthropological, transcendental, praxis, synthetic, translation, and countercultural) are each distinct in their methodology and metaphors with unique emphases on context, Scripture, tradition, and revelation.

16. A "politically correct" understanding of cultural sensitivity often merely glosses the surface of the real issues in intercultural communication. Political science professor Michael Cummings defines political correctness as "an ideological narrowing, intolerance, and silencing of dissent, commonly attributed to the left by the right" (Cummings, *Beyond Political Correctness*, 315). More important, however, is his argument that the movement and language of political correctness in the contemporary U.S. context has actually hindered genuine political discourse about social transformation in its inadvertent avoidance of sensitive issues.

17. The term "intercultural competency" is often used alongside organizational theory in corporate settings to promote managerial effectiveness in international contexts as in Hofstede's *Cultures and Organizations*. However, I think there is value in adapting the idea to contextual theology in a global "marketplace" of cultural and religious pluralism.

to enter into unique intercultural contexts with a credibility that facilitates genuine opportunities to embody the gospel.

From Indigenization to Contextualization

In order to more fully grasp how the process of contextualization has developed within contextual theology over time, a perspective on earlier forms of contextualization reveals how contextual theology has evolved in its methods, language, and emphases. In particular, by examining the strengths and weaknesses of *indigenization, adaptation,* and *inculturation,* the benefits of contextualization as a specific correction to those models become clear.

Indigenization is a term that was commonly used to convey the anthropological necessity of allowing cultural context to take primary precedence in the process of communicating the gospel cross-culturally. Through discouraging missionaries from importing their own theological assumptions into the receiving culture, indigenization cultivated a more organic process in which the gospel could only be grown with deep roots in the local soil. This viewpoint sees the inherent value in cultural context and looks for signs of the gospel already present in the culture. However, in placing such emphasis on the importance of the local culture, some leaders in indigenous churches began to feel that the process "focused purely on the cultural dimensions of human experience,"[18] much of which "tended to relate the Christian message to the traditional cultural forms—forms that belonged to the past and from which young people were turning away under the pervasive influence of 'modernization.'"[19] Similarly, in recent years, others have "regarded indigenization as past-oriented and domesticating"[20] with a distinctly colonialist connotation. Though contemporary missiology still emphasizes the importance of indigenous leadership development and indigenous church planting movements, the particular language of *indigenization* in reference to the whole process has been largely replaced by other terms.

Adaptation is another approach to faith and culture that differs methodologically from indigenization primarily because of its emphasis on translation. Rather than viewing the local culture as a seedbed for

18. Bevans, *Models of Contextual Theology*, 26.
19. Newbigin, *Foolishness to the Greeks*, 2.
20. De Mesa, *Why Theology Is Never Far*, 27.

indigenous theology, adaptation approaches the receptor culture with a gospel message that simply needs to be translated into the relevant vernacular. By adapting theological propositions to the local context, the gospel can be understood as long as it is translated properly. Often referred to as the "kernel and husk model," the external husk or appearance of the communication may adapt, but the core of the gospel in the kernel remains unchanged.[21] While adaptation values the integrity of scripture and tradition in the gospel message, the problem was that "it tended to obscure the fact that the gospel as embodied in the missionary's preaching and practice was already an adapted gospel, shaped by his or her own culture."[22] This simplistic notion of a pure gospel imbues adaptation approaches with a certain theological naiveté.

Ideologically situated in between indigenization and adaptation, the concept of *inculturation* developed primarily in the Roman Catholic Church as a term that merged the theological doctrine of the *incarnation* and the process of *acculturation* from the social sciences in which people take on the cultural characteristics of another group. Still in common usage in missiology, inculturation is a process that occurs when an embodied faith of one culture encounters another, and that faith "fuses with the new culture and simultaneously transforms it into a novel religious-cultural reality. In practical terms, this process involves the interaction of mutual critique and affirmation. It entails acceptance or rejection of thought forms, symbolic and linguistic expressions and attitudes between the faith-cultures in question. This process is usually primarily instinctive and popular, without much systematic planning and arrangement to it. But it can also be promoted and enhanced by institutional study and direction."[23] In describing the efficacy of the encounter between faith and culture, Magesa highlights the dialectical exchange of "mutual critique and affirmation." As a corrective to the colonial connotations of indigenization and the reductionist approach of adaptation, inculturation recognizes the importance of both speaker and hearer. Through the encounter, change confronts the transmitting culture and the receptor culture with varied forms of acceptance and rejection.

21. Bevans, *Models of Contextual Theology*, 40.
22. Newbigin, *Foolishness to the Greeks*, 2.
23. Magesa, *Anatomy of Inculturation*, 5.

Magesa also emphasizes the "instinctive" nature of inculturation that accounts for the flexible and organic fashion in which the process typically unfolds. This concession to the often mysterious and tacit ways that cultures change provides a crucial balance to empirical methods of understanding culture. In other words, "when we talk about the process of inculturation, we must always keep in mind that it is first of all and fundamentally an intuitive process of finding one's faith and religious identity in the context of one's cultural world. At the very least, it is not as logical as it is often made out to be."[24] This continual tension between intuition and logic is an issue that permeates the process of cultural analysis.

Finally, *contextualization* is a umbrella term that includes the whole of the spectrum between indigenization and adaptation, and though it is closely related to inculturation, contextualization "broadens the understanding of culture to include social, political, and economic questions."[25] It does not connote the imperialistic implications of indigenization nor does it reduce the process of adaptation to simplistic translation. Instead, contextualization takes seriously both the anthropological context of cultural experience and the theological context of scripture and tradition. "Contextualization points to the fact that theology needs to interact and dialogue not only with traditional cultural value, but with social change, new ethnic identities, and the conflicts that are present as the contemporary phenomenon of globalization encounters the various peoples of the world."[26] This contextual flexibility regarding the process of contextualization is what allows different models of contextual theology to critically engage the complexities of culture.

DEFINING CULTURE

If contextualization is the primary process at work within contextual theology, and this process requires a careful balance of critical understandings of both faith and culture, then the particular "facets that define, create, and sustain culture in society"[27] still remain to be explored. Though "culture" on the whole as synonymous with "civilization" is too

24. Ibid., 153.

25. Bevans, *Models of Contextual Theology*, 26.

26. Ibid., 27.

27. A phrase I used at the beginning of the chapter to emphasize contextual theology's interest in a critical understanding of cultural context.

broad to be examined in depth, an interdisciplinary definition of culture that draws on some broad themes in anthropology, sociology, and cultural studies will provide an ideological foundation for evaluating specific methods of cultural analysis.

Countless analogies and metaphors attempt to encapsulate the meaning of culture, but most are deficient in one way or another. As an academic concept, culture is simply a slippery term. The more certain disciplines work to systematize its definition, the more the ineffable essence of culture is seemingly lost. Conversely, relegating the process of defining culture to the realm of intuition or popular understandings of tacit assumptions precludes constructive engagement with issues of cultural identity and social change. Regardless of where one lands on the spectrum between rigid, systematic models and fluid, flexible characterizations, some definition—however inadequate—is necessary.

Unfortunately, the main obstacle to arriving at a definition is that "culture is one of the two or three most complicated words in the English language. This is so partly because of its intricate historical development . . . but mainly because it has now come to be used for important concepts in several distinct intellectual disciplines and in several distinct and incompatible systems of thought."[28] The interdisciplinary scholar Raymond Williams, whose academic work in literary theory would eventually become foundational in cultural studies,[29] identifies that one of the most basic difficulties in defining culture is its variety of competing (and sometimes conflicting) definitions in disparate fields of study. Different academic disciplines each take a unique approach to defining culture, and while many are in general agreement on the broad, colloquial understanding of culture as civilization, the particular disciplinary details of these fields are distinct. Anthropology, sociology, and cultural studies each approach the study of culture from a certain specialized perspective.[30]

28. Williams, *Keywords*, 76–77.

29. Williams was a prolific scholar who published in political science, literature, media studies, critical theory, and sociology. He taught at both Cambridge and Stanford, and is well known for his research in cultural materialism, which would become foundational in the development of cultural studies. See Williams, *Culture and Society*; and Higgins, *Raymond Williams*.

30. I certainly recognize that the brief disciplinary synopses that follow are barely scratching the surface of each field's diverse expressions. My intent is to merely highlight some simple, fundamental distinctives that differentiate academic explorations of "culture."

Anthropology was one of the first modern academic disciplines to propose the study of human culture as a central theme.[31] Today, cultural anthropologists conduct research about culture primarily through observing and interpreting the holistic behavior of people.[32] In this sense, a basic definition of culture from modern ethnography is "knowledge that is learned and shared that people use to generate behavior and interpret experience."[33] Culture is a kind of communal knowing that guides personal actions and makes sense of the world in the process. In anthropology, understanding culture is a dynamic process of discovery in which cultural knowledge is propagated through the everyday human environment.

Another key social scientific perspective on culture comes from sociology, which is centered on the concept of society and tends to focus on societal structures and systems. Sociological approaches to culture examine the interactions between these social structures, and the processes and networks at work therein. One sociological definition of culture based on consensus theory[34] separates society into "four sub-systems: economic, political, kinship, and cultural . . . culture includes roles, statuses, values and norms, all of which help to produce social order. Through socialization individuals learn to adopt the value consensus."[35] This particular sociological perspective emphasizes the structural role that systems play in society; each aspect of culture works together to construct the whole.

Lastly, cultural studies is a newer, emerging field[36] that takes an interdisciplinary approach to understanding culture. While engaging

31. British anthropologist Edward Tylor exemplifies this proposition in his early work *Anthropology: An Introduction to the Study of Man and Civilization*.

32. "Behavior" is being used in a very broad sense here; it includes the whole of cultural knowledge and practices, as well as the issues in worldview formation that shape such cultural values. Common anthropological research methods include ethnography, participant observation, interviewing, and other types of fieldwork.

33. McCurdy, *Cultural Experience*, 5.

34. Sociological consensus theory is a part of structural functionalism, with its origin in both positivism and structuralism. Emile Durkheim emphasized the role of consensus in maintaining social order. Consensus theory differs from other sociological approaches, like conflict theory in Marxism or symbolic interactionism. See Parsons, *Theories of Society*.

35. Lawson et al., *Advanced Sociology through Diagrams*, 3.

36. Some credit the establishment of the University of Birmingham's Centre for Contemporary Cultural Studies in 1964 as the academic origin of the field. Others sug-

with the fields of cultural anthropology and sociology, its many subdisciplines also include critical theory, political science, popular culture, philosophy, literary theory, media and communication studies, linguistics, gender studies, and other associated fields. With a heavy emphasis on critical theory, this multifaceted approach to studying culture often tends to focus on issues of power, class, social inequity, and ethnic studies. In this context, the meaning of culture is as broad as the range of disciplines in the field. By necessity, therefore, "cultural studies works with an inclusive definition of culture . . . it is the practices and processes of making shared meanings . . . in this way, then, cultures are made from the production, circulation, and consumption of meanings."[37] These shared meanings are the elemental building blocks of society by which culture is constructed.

In this vast field of academic inquiry on culture, missionaries and missiologists, some of whom were the earliest cultural anthropologists in certain foreign contexts by default, have frequently drawn from a variety of disciplines and traditions in their understanding of culture.[38] Though anthropological perspectives have been essential in the cross-cultural communication of the gospel, as *Christian* anthropologists, personal faith and theological propositions have always altered the academic discipline to some degree. For example, ethnography as a research method becomes a means and not just an end; interpretation of culture serves both academic and theological purposes. Thus, the task of defining culture for the purpose of developing a critical understanding of context in the faith and culture dialogue must always be an interdisciplinary effort. Any definition of culture that is domesticated within a single discipline (including theology) will inevitably be co-opted by the biases, assumptions, and agenda of that discipline. That is to say, a *theological* definition of culture must engage the breadth of the social sciences as well as the diversity of cultural studies if it is to take seriously the claims of contextual theology.

---

gest that the interdisciplinary approach of cultural studies preceded its founding. See Hoggart, *Contemporary Cultural Studies*.

37. Storey, *Cultural Studies and Popular Culture*, 3.

38. Anthropology is probably the most dominant perspective, but many missiologists have embraced other disciplines as well. For example, Lesslie Newbigin describes culture as having three main elements: language (central to the three), story (unifying narratives), and transmission (shared knowledge). Newbigin's focus on sociology and epistemology also demonstrates his interdisciplinary interests.

Additionally, an academic definition of culture does not need to be inaccessible to the non-academic. In a popular understanding of the term, it is often the case that "culture is used to name a reality that we all vaguely know something about, but cannot really explain."[39] Disciplinary terminology cannot dispel this tacit knowledge, nor should it. Defining culture is not an "either/or" of academic versus popular notions of the term. By definition, culture is "both-and," a social reality and an intellectual concept, an everyday given and a complex phenomenon requiring critical discourse.

How, then, can defining culture across disciplines—and in both academic and popular terms—establish a working definition of this most fundamental human reality? Taking all this into account, and in an effort to synthesize the variety of cultural perspectives that have been briefly explored, a working definition of culture for the purpose of this research is a hybrid combination of many of the aforementioned terms and ideas. Culture is *a **dynamic, contextual process** of sharing learned practices that shape and **make meaning** of personal experience and social structures in the world around us.* Key emphases in this definition are on *process* and *meaning.* Capturing the dynamic nature of culture is essential because the "knowledge that is learned and shared"[40] in society is always evolving and adapting. The Latin root of culture means "to cultivate," which explains why historically, "culture in all its early uses was a noun of process: the tending of something."[41] Culture is only culture when it is actively *cultivating* people, ideas, and values in society. Additionally, the contextual nature of culture as process points to the importance of locality. The reality of the immediate setting always shapes the process of learning and sharing. *Meaning* is equally important because humans are fundamentally *homo significans,* or meaning-making creatures. Humans are self-aware, rational beings that naturally engage in acts of creativity and transcendent contemplation.[42] This existential consciousness is of great consequence from a theological standpoint; part of this definition

---

39. Dietterich, *Cultivating Missional Communities,* 3.

40. McCurdy, *Cultural Experience,* 5

41. Williams, *Keywords,* 77.

42. Philosophically speaking, this unique ability to contemplate both the *self* and the *other* is "the distinctive capacity of the human." See Hutchison, *Living Options in World Philosophy,* 81.

of culture captures the inherent human longing for purpose and significance in the world.

Finally, it is also essential to recognize that the boundaries that define "culture" are not merely geographic; several layers of cultural categorization exist. Traditionally, the most common designation of a single culture has to do with either national or ethnic boundaries; thus people speak of "Brazilian culture" or "Chinese culture" or "Western culture." These macro-level cultural categories are familiar and can be relevant on a large scale, but they are not the only types of cultures to consider. At the meso level, there are also countless *sub*cultures, many of which have superseded the influence of macro-cultures in the wake of globalization's blurring of national and political boundaries.[43] A subculture differs from a macro-culture in that its boundaries are not geopolitical, but it still encompasses a holistic way of life. Hence we can identify the "urban subculture" or the "hip-hop subculture" or the "Asian American subculture." Lastly, there are also micro-cultures to consider; these are unique cultural contexts created in particular settings that have all the signifiers of a distinct culture (shared language, practices, social structures), but the values may not encompass "a whole way of life."[44] For example, people may mention the organizational culture of Starbucks, the popular culture of "hipsters," or the suburban culture of "soccer moms." Each of these cultural categories—macro, meso, and micro—are individual "cultures" with soft boundaries that shape the knowledge, practices, experiences, and values of people in the world, and each must be considered on its own terms.

With this proposed definition of culture in consideration, a more critical understanding of the role of culture in contextual theology is beginning to take shape. And with a working definition of culture in place, the next step in understanding the process of contextualization requires an exploration of different approaches to cultural analysis.

---

43. For example, university students from different countries who are part of an "international student subculture" may have far more in common with one another than with people of their own national culture who are not university students in the same context. In this sense, subcultural values can supersede macro-cultural values, or a non-geographically defined set of cultural values can exceed the cultural influence of the nation-state in defining identity and shaping social change.

44. McCurdy, *Cultural Experience*, 15–17.

Approaches to Cultural Analysis

Cultural analysis is the process by which the dynamic, contextual nature of culture is unpacked and examined for the purpose of interpretation. Because culture itself is in process, analytical tools and methods are needed to provide the structure in which cultural understanding can take place. The "methods" explored here are not specific research methods like participant observation or case studies; rather, they are general themes and approaches that provide the process of cultural analysis with some guiding principles for effective interpretation of cultural contexts.

Filipino theologian Jose De Mesa describes cultural analysis broadly as an approach to unpacking integrated systems of meaning. "Cultural analysis is a systematic process of bringing into explicit awareness and orderly categorization (i.e., to thematize) the implicit cultural meanings arising from a tradition of experiences which are embodied in specific cultural elements or aspects within the framework of culture as an integrated system."[45] At the most basic level, cultural analysis derives meaning from embodied experiences and then categorizes these cultural meanings into an explicit system. This process of transforming implicit, integrated meaning into explicit categories is intended to enable cultural outsiders to understand what the insiders already know tacitly. Unfortunately, this "systematic process" is often much more complicated and organic than it sounds. Rarely is there a checklist or step-by-step model by which the framework of entrenched cultural traditions can be separated from the culture itself. Nevertheless, De Mesa, along with Robert Schreiter, does make several suggestions.

First, there is the importance of listening to and learning from a culture, which ideally is given priority *before* the process of cultural analysis begins. Too often, paternalistic attitudes have precluded a true posture of listening, and unintentional cultural imperialism is usually the result. Schreiter asserts that "there must be a clear commitment to listening as a point of departure for constructing local theologies, and a commitment to continue to listen; indeed, to develop . . . a 'listening heart.'"[46] This kind of listening must be patient, sensitive to ethnocentricity, and holistic in its emphasis to consider all aspects of a culture.

---

45. De Mesa, *Why Theology Is Never Far*, 127.
46. Schreiter, *Constructing Local Theologies*, 40.

Second, "any approach to culture must be able to address the forces that shape *identity* in a culture," which "often center around two considerations: group-boundary formation and world-view formation."[47] Group boundaries are formed to essentially differentiate between "us" and "them." These anthropological and existential boundaries, which at some level are universal to all human cultures, determine how difference creates social categories. Designations of basic cultural characteristics like male and female, young and old, rich and poor, and other identifiers can define the roles and expectations of individuals based on their perceived social status. Particular sets of attributes like gender, age, or status then work together to reinforce a concept of cultural identity within certain structural guidelines.[48] These group boundaries, once established, then work in conjunction with worldview formation, which is the complex process by which cultural identity shapes values, perception, and interpretation of the world.[49]

For example, the Amish are a cultural group with a highly differentiated set of boundaries that define their cultural identity; their worldview is subsequently subject to the particular aspects of this group-boundary formation. Thus, any attempt at cultural analysis of the Amish context must take into account the forces and factors that determine this understanding of their collective identity. How do simplicity, the tenets of Mennonites and Anabaptism, and the practices of nonviolence work together to shape Amish identity? How does a cultural practice like *rumspringa*[50] serve the purpose of reinforcing the group boundaries and worldview of Amish adolescents? These questions explore the cultivation of Amish culture through the lens of identity development. Put simply, in effective cultural analysis, "the approach to a culture must

47. Ibid., 44.

48. Though some cultural groups have highly differentiated boundaries and others are much more ambiguously defined (e.g., "small agricultural societies vs. "urban-industrial cultures"). See Schreiter, *Constructing Local Theologies*, 44.

49. "Worldview" as the German concept *weltanschauung* will not be explored in depth; the use of "worldview" in "worldview formation" is a more basic understanding of the fundamental framework or lens in place by which individuals perceive the world.

50. *Rumspringa* is a Pennsylvania Dutch word that means "running around." Its use in Amish communities refers to a period of adolescence during which Amish youth are given the choice to leave the Amish community and experience the outside "English" world. For some, this is a particular rite of passage, but for others, it is a general time of relaxed cultural norms or a season to search for a marriage partner. See Shachtman, *Rumspringa*.

be able to attend to these twin dimensions of identity formation: group-boundary and world-view."[51]

Lastly, cultural analysis must have the capacity to consider and confront the challenge of *social change*.[52] Social change is in part a perpetual reality for culture defined as a dynamic process, but it is also a particular phenomenon that arises when significant alteration of social structures occurs. The challenge, then, is being able to "distinguish between that which is, in a sense, continuously 'changing' (and which, in another sense, remains relatively unchanged) and that which constitutes 'change.'"[53] Seminal sociologist Talcott Parsons called this distinction change *within* the system or change *of* the system,[54] or in a more detailed sense, the "orderly processes of ongoing change within the boundaries of a system, as opposed to the processes resulting in changes of the structure of the system under consideration."[55] This latter type of change which emphasizes fundamental structural rearrangement is the kind of social change which cultural analysis must address.

The most obvious examples of social change in particular cultural contexts are often connected to large scale shifts in societal structures that occur in cultural phenomena like modernization and industrialization. Historically, these kinds of changes have often been catalyzed by imperialism and colonialism, which have implemented these changes in the name of "civilization" or "development." When Christopher Columbus "discovered" the "New World" in 1492, the social changes that immediately occurred for the indigenous peoples of the Americas were not the sort of ongoing internal changes that had been occurring in cycles for generations prior. Rather, the arrival of Europeans and their colonial ideology forever altered the societal structure of local cultures, whether through socioeconomic arrangements like slavery or the religious imperialism of the Christian church.[56] And though our con-

---

51. Schreiter, *Constructing Local Theologies*, 44.

52. Social change is a foundational concept in sociology that encompasses a wide array of social theory addressing issues of change in social order and structure, from structuralism and Marxism to paradigm and economic theory. See Sztompka, *Sociology of Social Change;* and Noble, *Social Theory and Social Change.*

53. Strasser, *Introduction to Theories of Social Change*, 12.

54. Parsons, *Social System*, 480.

55. Strasser, *Introduction to Theories of Social Change*, 12.

56. Zinn, *People's History of the United States*, 5.

temporary context is largely postcolonial in a geopolitical sense, global forces like industrialization are continuing to confront formerly agrarian cultures in a way that leaves indelible social change in its wake. It is estimated that anywhere between thirty-five and fifty thousand people migrate from rural China into the country's city centers every day,[57] and this massive influx of migrant laborers is altering the social and economic structures of Chinese culture at an unprecedented rate. This type of large scale social change is indicative of the dynamic challenge that methods of cultural analysis must engage.

Thus, approaches to cultural analysis in the process of contextualization must be committed to these three values. First, there is the importance of holistic listening; only an attentive humility before the whole of a culture can create the space for genuine "mutual critique and affirmation"[58] between faith and culture. Second, there is the necessity of addressing identity formation through understanding group boundaries and worldview; this commitment explores the development of cultural identifiers. Third, there is the crucial requirement of attending to social change; this value examines not only the inherent nature of culture as process, but also the structural changes that occur as culture inevitably confronts the changing world. Cultural analysis in contextual theology is guided by these principles.

SEMIOTIC DESCRIPTION OF CULTURE

In order to understand cultural context according to these guiding principles of cultural analysis, specific interpretive methods must be employed in the analytical process. And just as different academic disciplines operate with varying definitions of culture, so do the analytical methods vary. Cultural anthropology suggests that ethnographic research methods are the best tools to examine cultural data; participant observers get "up close and personal" with the experience of cultural context. Sociology takes a different approach to interpreting culture, one that seeks to order social systems according to particular theoretical

---

57. Though it is difficult to be precise with these large numbers, most internal metrics (e.g., the National Bureau of Statistics in China) indicate an urban migrant laborer population of 150–200 million people, much of which has grown predominantly in the last decade. See Zhang, *China's Poor Regions;* and Fan, *China on the Move.*

58. Magesa, *Anatomy of Inculturation*, 5.

models.[59] Cultural studies utilizes a plurality of interpretive methods, from the systems theory of political science to the literary methods of critical theory. Each of these approaches has strengths and weaknesses,[60] and no one approach is inherently more effective at interpreting culture than another. However, given the interdisciplinary definition of culture that has already been constructed for this research, a similarly interdisciplinary interpretive method is suitable. Semiotics provides such a method.

Broadly speaking, semiotics[61] is a diverse, interdisciplinary field that studies how signs and symbols create meaning in contexts ranging from linguistics and anthropology to biology and computer science.[62] Its fundamental inquiry has to do with the nature of the sign, and its function in the realm of meaning, with all the dimensions of complexity therein. With the sign as a basic building block of meaning, Swiss linguist Ferdinand de Saussure (1857–1913) established that "the linguistic sign is, then, a two-sided psychological entity . . . a sign is the combination of a concept and a sound pattern. We propose . . . to replace *concept* and *sound pattern* respectively by signification and signal."[63] This recognition of the dual nature of signs would eventually become a foundational principle in semiotics, though the terms would evolve slightly.

American semiotician Thomas Sebeok, tracing the history of Saussure's terminology, identifies the sign characteristics that are now well established in semiotics. The sign is "made up (1) of something physical—sounds, letters, gestures, etc.—which he termed the *signifier*;

---

59. For example, Schreiter briefly examines *functionalist* (society is comprised of interrelated parts of a cultural whole), *ecological/materialist* (culture is shaped by "earthly existence" and/or the environment), and *structuralist* (tacit structures create cultural patterns) approaches to culture before proposing semiotic methods. See Schreiter, *Constructing Local Theologies*, 45–48.

60. Given the working definition of culture I have already developed with an interdisciplinary emphasis, I did not see the necessity of repeating a step-by-step analysis of the strengths and weaknesses of each field's interpretive methodology for cultural analysis.

61. Stemming from the Greek word *semeion*, meaning "sign."

62. The field of semiotics breaks down into (at least) three primary areas: syntactics (defined sets of relationships, like grammar), semantics (the content or meaning of the message), and pragmatics (the rules that govern the communication). Cultural semiotics, which is the specific topic of interest for this research, touches on all three areas. See Eco, *Theory of Semiotics;* and Sebeok, *Signs.*

63. Saussure, *Course in General Linguistics*, 67.

and (2) of the image or concept to which the signifier refers—which he called the *signified*. He then called the relation that holds between the two *signification*."[64] The example Saussure used to illustrate these terms was a tree. The actual word "tree" is the *signifier*, while the concept, or mental image of a tree as a large, leafy plant is the *signified*. The significance of parsing the nature of signs lies in the complex ways that people are able to move from signification to cultural meaning. Culture provides the framework for distinguishing between (and thereby making sense of) the countless signs that create meaning in society.

Hence, *cultural* semiotics is a branch of semiotic analysis that "sees culture as a vast communication network, whereby both verbal and nonverbal messages are circulated along elaborate, interconnected pathways, which, together, create the systems of meaning."[65] Seeing culture through the lens of semiotics transforms every facet of society into a sign or symbol, and as an interpretive method, semiotic description of culture then explains the *dynamic, contextual process* of culture in terms of these signs and symbols.

In the same way that symbols (letters, for example) in language combine to form verbal or textual messages, so do cultural signs come together to create cultural messages. The whole process is governed by codes that order and regulate signs in relationship with each other, and in context, these messages generate meaning. Semiotic description of culture can be separated into four main areas: *location, definition, interpretation,* and *categorization*. As with most methods of cultural analysis, these areas are interrelated *tasks* and not necessarily sequential *steps*. And though each area will be explored conceptually in sequence, the process in practice is just as organic as it is logical.

Location of Cultural Texts

In the process of developing a semiotic description of culture, the first area involves *locating* "cultural texts,"[66] which represent the most basic units of semiotic analysis. They are called "texts" (or sometimes pseudo-texts) simply because these building blocks of culture communicate meaning that requires interpretation. "Cultural texts are hu-

64. Sebeok, *Signs*, 6.
65. Schreiter, *Constructing Local Theologies*, 49.
66. Or "culture texts" as Schreiter refers to them.

man actions, events, and material works that embody meanings that are widely shared,"[67] and these texts function as signs and symbols that "can be verbal and nonverbal, visual, auditory, and tactile, simple and highly complex."[68] Theologian Kevin Vanhoozer, in his essay "Toward a Theory of Cultural Interpretation," argues that cultural texts have four primary purposes: they *communicate* (create hermeneutics), *orient* (provide order and direction), *reproduce* (spread and self-perpetuate), and *cultivate* (grow the human spirit).[69] Each of these functions points to the multidimensionality of cultural texts. Cultural texts do not merely convey cold, rational data in a mode of intellectual discourse. Rather, they communicate with all the richness and variety of culture itself.

An important method in locating cultural texts is connected to the guiding principles in cultural analysis; namely, that cultural texts ought to be selected based on their ability to "speak" about issues of identity formation and social change. For example, distinctive social characteristics, communal celebrations, traditional rites of passage, and methods of conflict resolution can all function as cultural texts that convey meaning about group boundaries, worldview, and the process of adapting to change. Breaking down the complex cultural systems of society by choosing basic textual units for analysis is the initial task in developing a semiotic description of culture.

Definition of Signs

Once cultural texts have been located, the second area involves *defining* each text through identifying the dual nature of its sign(s) as signifier and signified. Sebeok describes the structural properties of signs as having two basic types of characteristics.

> Most human signs have the capacity to encode two primary kinds of referents,[70] *denotative* and *connotative* . . . *denotation* is the initial referent a sign *intends* to capture. But the denoted referent, or *denotatum*, is not something specific in the world, but rather a prototypical *category* of something . . . in human semiosis a sign can be *extended* freely to encompass other kinds of referents that appear, by association or analogy, to have something in common

67. Romanowski, *Eyes Wide Open*, 57.

68. Schreiter, *Constructing Local Theologies*, 62.

69. Vanhoozer et al., *Everyday Theology*, 29–31.

70. A "referent" is a concept or object to which a sign refers.

with the denotatum. This *extensional* process is known as *connotation,* and the new referents are known as *connotata.*[71]

Defining a sign in a cultural text requires an understanding of both its denotation and connotation in order to capture both its explicit and implicit meaning—meaning that conveys the content of its engagement with issues of identity formation and social change. It is important to note that the relationship between signs and cultural texts is complicated in part because a cultural text can be both a sign and a combination of signs, but regardless of whether the cultural text being defined is a singular sign or a set of signs, the dual nature of both the sign and the cultural text still applies.

Interpretation of Contextual Messages

The third area in semiotic description of culture involves *interpreting* or "reading" the cultural text(s), which requires the combination of multiple signs and texts into messages that produce meaning. And in order to construct the meaning of these messages, it is necessary to understand signs in their coded context. "Signs need to be identified in culture texts. To discern the messages involved will depend upon the codes in which the signs are embedded . . . codes provide the basic rules for the exercise of the sign function. They are, so to speak, the 'grammar' of culture texts."[72]

Much like the highly contextual nature of culture itself, the messages of cultural texts are dependent on the rules of the context. For example, waving an American flag at a Fourth of July celebration conveys a very different message from folding an American flag at a military funeral. The denotation of the flag as a cultural text is in one sense the same in each context, but the connotative meaning of the sign is quite distinct in each setting because of the inherent interpretive rules specific to each context. Thus, the signs in cultural texts, when understood in the

71. Sebeok, *Signs,* 7. The example that Sebeok cites in this description of denotation and connotation is the word (or sign) "cat." In this case, the denotatum is not necessarily a specific cat, but rather a descriptive category of "catness" that denotes a relatively small, four-legged, furry mammal with pointy ears and perhaps whiskers. The signifier "cat" also has connotative potential to signify other "feline qualities," for instance through its usage in phrases "cat fight" or "cool cat." The sign is both the denotatum and the connotata.

72. Schreiter, *Constructing Local Theologies,* 67.

code of "cultural grammar," work together to convey a message, which ultimately carries the meaning of cultural texts.

Categorization of Meaning

Lastly, the fourth and final area in the overall process of developing a semiotic description of culture involves *categorizing* the messages cultural texts into *semiotic domains* of meaning. One of the crucial tools that catalyzes this categorization is the use of metaphors, which link signs together into sign systems. When a "complex sign, code, message, and metaphoric process spreads itself over an area of culture and brings it together as a constellation of meaning, we have a *semiotic domain*. A semiotic domain could be considered an assemblage of culture texts relating to one set of activities in culture (economic, political, familiar), which are organized together by a single set of messages and metaphoric signs."[73] Multiple culture texts conveying a plurality of connected messages create these semiotic domains, or systematic categories of meaning, whether religious, economic, social, or political. Each domain may be governed by unique metaphors which frame or root the sign systems in particular kinds of meaning. For example, a central metaphor in the religious domain of Christianity is marriage. Israel is the bride of YHWH, the church is the bride of Christ, and culture texts and messages in this semiotic domain revolve around this metaphor. Language of courtship, fidelity, and intimacy communicate meaning through the signs of the bride and groom, the wedding ceremony, and so forth. Holistic semiotic description of a singular culture (macro, meso, or micro) occurs when multiple semiotic domains are linked together in some common fashion.

These four areas—(1) the *location* of cultural texts, (2) the *definition* of their dual-natured signs, (3) the *interpretation* of their messages in context, and (4) the *categorization* of their meaning into domains— encompass a systematic analytical method for semiotic description of culture. But what does this semiotic description of culture look like when it is actually described? Often times, the end product of this analytical method appears far more narrative and flexible than rigid and systematic.

---

73. Schreiter, *Constructing Local Theologies*, 69.

Thick Description

American anthropologist Clifford Geertz, who became a prominent proponent of symbolic anthropology at the University of Chicago from the 1970s onward, was an advocate for semiotic description of culture in his seminal work, *The Interpretation of Cultures*. "The concept of culture I espouse . . . is essentially a semiotic one. Believing, with Max Weber, that man is an animal suspended in webs of significance he himself has spun, I take culture to be those webs, and the analysis of it to be therefore not an experimental science in search of law but an interpretive one in search of meaning."[74] Once again, the centrality of meaning in defining and understanding culture is emphasized. Meaning is not structured and proven empirically; it is created and discovered organically—as natural of a process as a spider spinning its web. In his discussion of the highly symbolic nature of these cultural webs, Geertz goes on to insist that "the aim of anthropology is the enlargement of the universe of human discourse . . . it is an aim to which a semiotic concept of culture is peculiarly well adapted. As interworked systems of construable signs, culture is not a power, something to which social events, behaviors, institutions, or processes can be casually attributed; it is a context, something within which they can be intelligibly—that is, thickly—described."[75] Believing that semiotics frames cultural interpretation appropriately as a context and not a monolithic entity to which all of culture is attached, Geertz is perhaps most well known for his usage of "thick description,"[76] an ethnographic method that focuses heavily on the context of signs in communication, as opposed to "thin description," which focuses more narrowly on phenomena and behavior without taking cultural symbolism into account.[77] Geertz contends that thick description "shows the wealth and randomness of human behavior"[78] in a way that systematic semiotic theory cannot.

In his well known essay "Deep Play: Notes on the Balinese Cockfight," Geertz outlines, with layers of precise details, the deeply symbolic

74. Geertz, *Interpretation of Cultures*, 5.

75. Ibid., 14.

76. The language of "thick description" is a concept Geertz admittedly borrows from British philosopher Gilbert Ryle. See Ryle, *Collected Papers*.

77. Geertz's essay "Deep Play: Notes on the Balinese Cockfight" is often upheld as his best model of thick description (Geertz, *Interpretation of Cultures*, 412–51).

78. Schreiter, *Constructing Local Theologies*, 53.

nature of this seemingly "ordinary" cultural occurrence in Bali. By defining the signs, roles, and messages of cocks, men, and all the vibrant innuendo present in this primal competition, Geertz captures the meaning of this cultural text with meticulous care.

> What makes Balinese cockfighting deep is . . . the migration of the Balinese status hierarchy into the body of the cockfight . . . the cocks may be surrogates for their owners' personalities, animal mirrors of psychic form, but the cockfight is—or more exactly, deliberately is made to be—a simulation of the social matrix . . . and as prestige, the necessity to affirm it, defend it, celebrate it, justify it, and just plain bask in it is perhaps the central driving force in the society, so also—ambulatory penises, blood sacrifices, and monetary exchanges aside—is it of the cockfight . . . the cockfight, and especially the deep cockfight, is fundamentally a dramatization of status concerns.[79]

Much of Geertz's semiotic description of culture reads in a similar fashion to this passage, and curiously absent from his lengthy and exhaustive narrative of this cultural text are rigid forms of systematic semiotic analysis. No explicit mention is made of denotatum or connotata, little attention is paid to the technicality of linguistic signification, and no step-by-step process of categorizing semiotic domains can be found. And yet, the thick description that is present throughout the essay is more than sufficient for effectively parsing the symbols and codes of these Balinese cultural texts. Geertz goes to great lengths to define the messages and meaning behind the cockfight,[80] and though the sign systems may not be articulated in an overtly methodical manner, the semiotic meaning is constructed cogently nonetheless.

Ultimately, a balanced method of semiotic description of culture must hold rigid, systematic analysis and fluid, narrative depiction in tension with the central pursuit of constructing meaning.[81] As Schreiter

79. Geertz, *Interpretation of Cultures*, 436–37.

80. For example, on more than one occasion in the essay, Geertz engages the idiosyncrasies of the multiple phallic metaphors head-on, perhaps as a sign of his fluency in the cultural text itself.

81. It should be noted that the particular four part model of semiotic description of culture that I have developed here and the narrative approach of Geertz's thick description are not the only two semiotic approaches to cultural analysis to be reconciled; they are merely the two that I have chosen to compare and contrast. Numerous semiotic variants exist in the field, not least of which are Louis Hjelmslev's formal linguistic approach, Umberto Eco's literary approach, and the Moscow-Tartu school (rooted in

interprets the methodology of thick description, he claims that Geertz's "primary interest in the semiotics of culture has to do with interpretation or explanation of meaning: the messages and the signs that bear them. He is not so interested in elaborating the codes or sets of rules. He is interested in how the messages are understood rather than the structures that make intelligibility possible. He is not looking for a unified theory of semiotics; he is concerned more with the interpretation of the prolixity of human life in its concrete settings."[82] Thick description as a method of semiotic analysis navigates this tension by seeking to sort significant cultural texts into meaningful cultural structures so that the messages can be "decoded" from embedded systems. An emphasis on metaphor and narrative allows thick description to decipher meaning in a way that retains the richness of story and the heart of cultural experience.

Overall, a semiotic description of culture, when applied to a particular context and understood missiologically, should create a "kind of richly textured local theology."[83] It must be kept in mind, particularly given the potential complexity of semiotic analysis, that the end goal of utilizing semiotic description of culture for this particular research is not necessarily theoretical coherence, or even cultural meaning. Rather, the primary purpose of employing semiotic description of culture as an interpretive method is to aid in the process of theological contextualization. Applying semiotic description of culture to the urban context is part and parcel of developing an urban contextual theology.

---

the Prague Linguistic Circle). See Noth, *Handbook of Semiotics;* and Eco, *Semiotics and the Philosophy of Language.*

82. Schreiter, *Constructing Local Theologies,* 54.

83. Ibid., 61.

10

The Urban Context

A S A SOCIETAL FIXTURE of the modern world, defining the urban context is both simple and difficult; simple because of its ubiquity and yet difficult because of its layers of meaning. In the same way that "culture" is a slippery term, as a specific cultural phenomenon, the urban context is equally "a reality that we all vaguely know something about, but cannot really explain."[1] Our inability to be explicit in our description of the urban context stems primarily from our inattentiveness to the urban environment in general.

We may know that cities often have tall buildings and concrete highways and civic institutions, but we also know implicitly that a city is not defined by its built environment alone. This challenge is further complicated by the fact that "scholarship devoted to the city has yet to find a commonly accepted definition of either *a* city or *the* city.[2] The diversity of cities makes such a question extremely difficult."[3] Is a city defined by its geographic size, its systems of infrastructure, its population demographics, its political status, or its cultural influence? All of these urban attributes (and many others) work together to inform the contours of the city, but they do not provide a definitive center by which

1. Dietterich, *Cultivating Missional Communities*, 3.

2. This distinction between *a* and *the* city is a good example of the semiotic nature of the signifier "city." Its denotatum is not a specific geographic location of *a* city, but rather is a semantic category encompassing many aspects of *the* city. Its corresponding connotata then spans the range of "city-ness," from aspects of the built environment to the "urban lifestyle."

3. Conn and Ortiz, *Urban Ministry*, 157. I am frequently using the terms "city" and "urban context" interchangeably, but they are not identical concepts. Whereas a city always has an urban context, the urban context is not necessarily a city *per se*. The urban context, though functioning as an *object* of analysis, is also *adjectival* with relationship to the city.

other "non-cities" can be identified. This complexity (not ambiguity) is a result of the reality that—particularly for the semiotic purposes of this research—the city is fundamentally a system of signs.[4]

Thus, even though this section will not work toward a systematic definition of the city, it will address some of the primary attributes that are signified in the urban context. This examination of the city as a cultural text takes a semiotic approach to describe and decipher the urban context by identifying prominent signs, codes, and messages in urban communities.[5] The urban characteristics of *density, diversity,* and *disparity* function as distinct yet overlapping semiotic domains for *physical, social,* and *economic* systems of meaning that shape issues of identity formation and social change in the urban context.

It is important to note that the *theoretical* method of "location, definition, interpretation, and categorization" looks slightly different in this *application* of semiotic description because the areas are not as clearly defined or sequentially structured. First, location and definition tend to blend together (in part because of their common emphasis on identity formation and social change), and second, *categorization* has been implicitly[6] moved to the front end of the process and *interpretation* to the tail end. This shift enables a more organized presentation of the semiotic domains and reflects the *results* of a semiotic description of the urban context as much as the *process.*[7] These small but significant changes re-

4. The sixth chapter's section on "Urban Semiotics as Observation" attempts to quantify this affirmation.

5. The specific type of urban context I am focusing on is found most commonly in North American cities, though some principles certainly have areas of application in global contexts.

6. The categorization of the urban context into physical, social, and economic domains is a function of the preassigned urban attributes of density, diversity, and disparity. Hence, the process of categorization is implied and not explicit. Nevertheless, the characteristics of density, diversity, and disparity are not rooted in random, preconceived notions of the city; rather, they are reflections of years of study of the urban context. Unfortunately, the scope of this research will not allow for a full discussion of why those attributes were chosen over others, and so a window into that particular process will have to remain implied for now.

7. Basically, in a *developmental* model of semiotic description of culture, categorization should be closer the end of the process because it is important that the categories (semiotic domains) arise from the data (i.e., grounded theory) rather than the other way around. If preconceived categories are imposed prematurely on the context, then they may force the cultural texts (and hence their meanings) to conform to the tacit assumptions of the researcher. However, because I am now presenting an *application*

flect both the narrative flexibility of thick description, and the value of *meaning* in the urban context over systematic methods of analysis.

URBAN DENSITY

Urban density in the physical dimensions of settlement space is one of the defining attributes of a city.[8] In fact, the occurrence of high levels of density in either *population* demographics or the *built environment* is one of the most common identifiers that distinguishes urban areas from rural and—in most generally urbanized Western contexts—suburban areas as well.[9] Density can also define the boundaries of urban contexts. Urbanized areas are frequently identified as "continuously built-up regions" or *agglomerations* with a particular population density.[10] In a political definition, to live within a particular urban setting is to be bounded by the specific jurisdiction of a municipality. These boundaries are typically defined physically by roads, freeways, or natural geographic delineations. To be a citizen of a city or a distinct urban neighborhood is to live within these types of boundaries, and these physical locations are factors that shape identity, both individual and collective. To be *from* a *certain* place[11] is often an identification with physical space and its aspects of density, or lack thereof.

---

of the model (though parts of the process are implicit), I decided it would be more productive to start with the semiotic domains. There did not seem to be any way to effectively articulate the process of sorting out countless types of signs and cultural texts in the urban context without any categorical identifiers to frame the presentation.

8. Urban density has become a particularly pressing issue as environmental sustainability has become a larger priority in urban studies. Fields like geography, political science, urban planning, and architecture have all refocused on the sustainable aspects of urban density. See Baofu, *The Future of Post-Human Urban Planning* and Farr, *Sustainable Urbanism*.

9. In much of global urban studies, suburban areas are often implicitly included in the urban context because they are not rural. However, in much of Western urban studies, the focus is often more explicitly preoccupied with "inner-city"/urban core types of areas. Regardless, density in planning and zoning is one of the large distinctions between suburban and urban contexts. See Friedman, *Sustainable Residential Development*.

10. The defining characteristics that distinguish between a town, city, municipality, urbanized area, metropolitan area, conurbation, and so on depend on the context, but density—again in either the built environment or population—is a common metric used to categorize the different types and sizes of urban developments.

11. The colloquial question "Where are you from?" is more than just conversational small talk; rather, it is a reflection of our distinctly human association with *place*. This dynamic will be explored further in the following section.

Locating and Defining Signs of Density

Basic cultural texts that operate as physical signs of urban density are varied and abundant, and locating the texts that communicate messages concerning identity formation and social change requires an understanding of the physical structures that house and reflect density within the city. These structures are typically expressed in two forms according to the two primary types of urban density, namely in *population* or the *built environment*. Naturally, these forms of density are intimately connected because a dense population necessitates the creation of a dense built environment; people organically shape their surroundings to support their needs. Nevertheless, the distinction is made because the wide variety of cultural texts in this setting communicates through specific signs of both *human* density and physical, human-*made* density.

Thus, a fundamental sign of human density in the urban context is the physical congregation of people in a particular constructed place. For example, at the 2008 Summer Olympics in Beijing, China, more than ninety-one thousand people gathered for the opening ceremonies in Beijing National Stadium, also known as the "Bird's Nest."[12] And while much larger or higher density gatherings have occurred in various contexts, what makes this particular form of density *urban* is its connection to a *physical, structural expression* of human density in the material construction of the stadium itself. The presence of people alone does not constitute urban density (though the stadium alone could be considered an urban cultural text in this regard); rather, it is the combination of, and connection between, the people and the place that makes the gathered crowds in the Bird's Nest a cultural text that signifies urban density.

Further, the Beijing National Stadium also functions as an urban cultural text because it speaks about the formation of the Chinese national identity in a context of massive social and economic change. As the largest steel structure ever constructed, the award-winning architecture of the Bird's Nest is an evocative symbol of national pride and accomplishment. The coveted and prestigious Lubetkin Prize, an international recognition of the "most outstanding work of architecture outside the European Union," confirmed that "the National Stadium in Beijing will for a long time to come, and around the world, remain amongst the most memorable emblems of 2008 and of the resurgence of

12. DesignBuild-Network, "Beijing National Stadium."

China as a global power. For a single work of architecture to hold such a charge is extremely rare, and at the same time to flawlessly accommodate a very complex set of functions makes the feat still more extraordinary."[13] This colossal urban stadium seeks "to embody everything from China's muscle-flexing nationalism to a newfound cultural sophistication . . . it is also an aesthetic triumph that should cement the nation's reputation as a place where bold, creative gambles are unfolding every day."[14]

Ultimately though, a definitive aspect of the Bird's Nest as a cultural text is its signification of "a nation that, despite its outward confidence, is struggling to forge a new identity out of a maelstrom of inner conflict."[15] In the wake of rapid urban growth (and its inevitable forms of increased structural density) in both the city of Beijing and the nation as a whole, questions of ethical labor laws, environmental standards, and fair treatment of the poor swirled around the construction of the National Stadium. Thus its signification, while denoting newfound national successes in one sense, also carries the connotations of a China that is struggling to maintain face[16] in a season of monumental change.

Interpreting Codes and Messages of Density

Many other types of cultural texts that operate as signs of urban density are at work in the city; reading them in context requires an understanding of the codes that control and regulate density. Codes like zoning[17] and occupancy regulations, which function as forms of "urban grammar" in the planning process of city, aim to organize the wide variety of cultural texts present in the urban context. For example, in many types of residential communities, signs of density span the socioeconomic spectrum, from luxurious skyscraper condominiums in the downtown

13. Waite, "Beijing 'Bird's Nest' Stadium."

14. Ouroussoff, "Olympic Stadium with a Design to Remember."

15. Ibid.

16. "Face" is an important sociological concept common in Eastern cultures that refers to the roles of honor, respect, and prestige in maintaining cultural dignity (in contrast to shame). For a contemporary political perspective on the issue, see Gries, *China's New Nationalism.*

17. Zoning in North American cities is commonly categorized according to several different designations of land types: residential (single family, multifamily, etc.), commercial, industrial, and many variants in between. See Punter, *Design Guidelines in American Cities.*

business core to dilapidated brick towers[18] in the government housing projects.

At first glance, reading these cultural texts requires little urban literacy as even uninitiated visitors to a city can easily recognize the difference between these two types of dwellings. Tourists in Rio de Janeiro would never mistake a five-star hotel on the beach for the shanty town *favelas*[19] in the hills overlooking the water. However, as multiple types of housing coexist in close proximity in the city, reading the particular context of these dwellings becomes a prerequisite to understanding their organization, which is distributed in set patterns. This type of patterned density is regulated according to a body of zoning legislation and occupancy controls, which often restrict certain types of development in order to control urban growth or mitigate changes to levels of density. The codes also allocate signs of urban density into homogenous groups so that similar signs are clustered together in the urban context.[20] While these codes are usually intended to ensure well-designed communities, they can also be used to segregate or standardize urban areas.

The messages communicated in this regulation of density are as varied as the cultural texts themselves. Wealthy "gated communities"[21] are zoned with minimal density to maintain privacy and anonymity. Security fences, armed guards, and large homes set far back from the street often convey a sense of privilege and elitism. On the other hand, in many public housing projects, families may be crammed into spaces where bedrooms can hardly hold a bed, and "living rooms" are comparable in size to a suburban walk-in closet. In these kinds of spaces,

18. Many of these "brick towers" were built after WWII concurrently with the construction of the suburbs. However, the public housing projects were designated for the urban poor in the limited space of the city, and hence were sometimes called "vertical ghettos." See Moore, *Vertical Ghetto.*

19. A *favela* is type of Brazilian settlement that translates roughly into "slum." In the urban context of Rio, many *favelas* and wealthy tourist areas often share adjacent urban space in relatively close proximity. See Perlman, *Myth of Marginality.*

20. For example, most urban zoning set and coordinates the height limits of structures so that uniformity in appearance and function can remain consistent. This is why you will never find a skyscraper in a residential neighborhood zoned for single family homes.

21. Gated communities are an area of interest for social commentators and residential planners alike. On the whole, the upper-class stigma of gated communities has made them a consistent target of cultural critique. See Blakely and Snyder, *Fortress America;* and Ehrenreich, *This Land Is Their Land.*

any semblance of privacy or anonymity is simply not an option. Urban density can also create competition over scarce resources when too many people are corralled into tight spaces. High levels of density in ghettos (where loose regulation of occupancy codes can create slum-like conditions) can lead to turf wars, gang violence, and other forms of social conflict simply because physical space is so limited. When "space to breath" is in short supply, forms of conflict resolution may become more confrontational than constructive.

However, density can also convey positive messages in an urban community. Using open space for shared, walkable areas instead of parking can encourage personal mobility and interaction instead of automobile-dependence. In contrast to most suburban areas that are designed around individual cars as the basic cultural texts, urban areas with higher density are scaled around people as the basic cultural texts.[22] Design with "human scale" (as opposed to automotive scale, for example) in mind is said to actually *humanize* the city. Multiple sole proprietorships in place of retail "big box stores" make the process of consumerism less sterile.[23] Beautiful parks in the center of a central business district can disrupt abrasive commercial density with inviting, open green space. But how can *meaning* be constructed from these varied messages?

Density (or lack thereof) as a physical characteristic of the urban context carries multiple meanings, depending, of course, on the particular setting. The values of privacy, security, and economic status are contrasted with issues of anonymity, congestion, and loneliness. Some of these seemingly contradictory messages highlight another urban reality catalyzed by density: pluralism and paradox. The urban context may be saturated with countless people from all walks of life, and yet a distinct sense of isolation—hopelessness, even—often pervades the marginalization of many urban neighborhoods. Ironically, urban density and social

22. Numerous works critiquing suburban planning address the lack of density in sprawl. See Kunstler, *Geography of Nowhere;* and Duany et al., *Suburban Nation.*

23. Increased retail density (e.g., many small produce vendors in one area) humanizes the market because it increases personal interaction and attention to the consumption process while also reducing the need for transportation. In contrast to this model, one big-box store "mega-retailer" per community makes transportation central to buying, and mechanizes much of the interaction in the process. See Mitchell, *Big-Box Swindle.*

loneliness sometimes go hand-in-hand.[24] Therefore, understanding the meaning of density in the city requires a balanced engagement with this paradox. Not enough urban density can promote the sort of hyper-individualism that fragments communities through isolation, but too much density can lead to conflict, scarcity, and similar forms of isolation.

A semiotic description of urban density seeks to reconcile these varied messages while also maintaining space for sign systems that seem to work in opposite directions. Thus, density in the city—represented by a plurality of cultural texts that are organized according to multiple urban codes—creates multifaceted meaning in urban space. Ultimately, this richly textured meaning only makes sense when it interacts with other semiotic domains. In this way, physical density in the urban context is also connected to the other two primary urban attributes: *diversity* and *disparity*.

URBAN DIVERSITY

The vast implications of urban diversity have far more than merely *social* dimensions, but for the sake of remaining in one semiotic domain of meaning, social (or sociological) diversity is the focus in this description. That the city is a sociologically diverse place is simply a given in our contemporary urban context. Recent immigrants, established professionals, working-class families, and marginalized transients—along with children, students, and retirees of every color and creed—work and play side by side in the city, often sitting together on a bus or passing each other on the sidewalk. This presence of diversity highlights the confluence of these many different ethnic, religious, and socioeconomic backgrounds. But this widespread existence of urban diversity has not led to the commonly held "melting pot" mentality that many Americans once upheld as a social ideal.[25] Sociology and cultural studies now largely refer to the diverse urban context as much more of a "tossed salad"[26]

24. Some studies have shown a high correlation between high density urban areas and a social sense of personal detachment. See Savage et al., *Urban Sociology, Capitalism and Modernity*.

25. Israel Zangwill's 1908 play *The Melting Pot* coined the term, but its conceptual intent was a reference to the melding of various "white" European "races" into a new, singular American identity. Not surprisingly, this combination excluded Blacks, Asians, Latinos, and Native Americans. See Jacoby, *Reinventing the Melting Pot*.

26. The homogenization of diverse cultures is now largely dismissed in favor of a multiculturalism in which distinct cultures partially assimilate and yet still maintain

than a melding of "races."[27] Regardless of what metaphor for diversity is used, the prominent social reality of urban diversity is a setting in which numerous cultural texts address issues of identity formation and social change.

Locating and Defining Signs of Diversity

The location of cultural texts that signify urban diversity requires a critical understanding of the social context of the city. Particular aspects of this social context may be unique to a specific urban neighborhood or consistent across the structural patterns of the whole city. Because the identification of signs of diversity is highly contextual, any cultural text that is selected must be defined in its immediate environment with careful attention given to its local meaning.

In the city of Seattle, Martin Luther King Jr. is symbolic of many different social ideals of diversity. As a political symbol, a black and white image of King's face is the official logo of King County,[28] of which Seattle is the county seat. With political aspirations that evoke the memory of King's legacy of advocacy for civil rights, Seattle's local government seeks to cultivate a political climate in which diverse leadership and constituencies can create equitable policies for all. However, despite this appearance of progressive diversity, Martin Luther King Jr. does not always symbolize tolerance and equality in the city. Quite to the contrary, *Martin Luther King Jr. Way*, a major thoroughfare that runs through southeast Seattle, connotes a very different kind of message about urban diversity.

Originally named Empire Way in 1913 in honor "'Empire builder' James J. Hill, who built the transcontinental railroad to Seattle,"[29] the street was designed as an urban expressway with the functional purpose

their unique identities. See Sullivan, *Living Across and Through Skins.*

27. "Race" as a concept is a constellation of sociocultural, political, and biological factors. See Banks, *Ethnicity*; Gates, *Cultural and Literary Critiques*; Gergen, *Invitation to Social Construction*; and Rosenblum and Travis, *Meaning of Difference.*

28. Originally named after William R. King, the thirteenth vice president of the U.S., the first logo of King County was a royal crown, and this symbol persisted until 2007, when governor Christine Gregoire officially renamed the county in Dr. King's honor and county council member Larry Gossett, a well-known community organizer and former Black Panther, helped advocate for a change of the county's official logo from a royal crown to an image of Dr. King's face.

29. Davila, "MLK Way."

of alleviating traffic flow from Rainier Avenue, a more established commercial thoroughfare that ran roughly parallel to Empire Way. And with that purpose in mind, little thought or attention was given to aesthetics, planning, zoning, or neighborhood design. Instead, the street became a somewhat haphazard combination of "service stations, fuel companies, garages and used-car lots that sold vehicles to people with all kinds of credit: little, bad and none. There were taverns, groceries and retail stores . . . the street was also the backbone of a thriving residential community, folks who couldn't or wouldn't be accommodated elsewhere. When the city needed homes for defense-contract workers, it built low-cost housing projects Rainier Vista and Holly Park. When racial covenants kept blacks out of other parts of the city, they moved here, too."[30] Community activist Eddie Rye Jr., who first petitioned the city to rename Empire Way to Martin Luther King Jr. Way, traces the idea back to Stevie Wonder and Jesse Jackson, who he claims suggested the idea. "The Norwegians, Italians, Germans and Japanese who had populated the valley in the early 1900s had given way to Filipino, Chinese, African Americans and Vietnamese by the 1970s. That so many different people had found a place here, Rye figured, made Empire Way an obvious choice to salute King. The local businessman and, at the time, radio talk-show host, collected some 4,000 signatures and submitted a petition to rename the street."[31] Despite some initial opposition, the name change was approved by the city council in 1981, and Empire Way was officially christened Martin Luther King Jr. Way.

However, the change in name was hardly a transformative moment for the street which had come to represent a kind of urban diversity that some felt was unsafe, unattractive, or altogether unappealing. While the eclectic nature of having corner stores, used car lots, modest ethnic restaurants, and low-income housing in close proximity was endearing for some—and indeed "home" for many—the perception of MLK Way remained blighted. As the south Seattle hip-hop group Blue Scholars articulate in one of their songs, Martin Luther King Jr. Way "looks a lot like his legacy: permanently under construction."[32]

30. Ibid.

31. Ibid.

32. Blue Scholars is a south-Seattle-based conscious hip-hop duo that is active in the urban community. This excerpt comes from their song "Back Home," from their 2007 album *Bayani*.

As a cultural text, Martin Luther King Jr. is an obvious sign of urban diversity, but as this local context attests, the symbolism is complex. As a signifier, Martin Luther King Jr. denotes a man whose work as an African American Baptist preacher, civil rights leader, and Nobel Peace Prize laureate influenced many. But the signified connotation of MLK varies greatly as one moves from the broad ideological context of Seattle's political climate to the local, concrete setting of southeast Seattle, where the actual rubber meets the road. The former connotes the symbolic memory of King's legacy of social justice, whereas the latter connotes the tangible reality of the injustices that remain in certain contexts of social diversity. This is the inherent dualism of the sign in cultural semiotics: a county logo on a courthouse stands for justice and equality while the same name on a street sign represents the ugliness of the ghetto.

Thus, Martin Luther King Jr. shapes the social and political identity of Seattle and King county, and in an entirely different way, forms the group boundaries of one of the city's most diverse urban neighborhoods. Further, the adoption of King's image for the city's leadership is representative of social change, even if only on a symbolic level, while naming Empire Way after MLK does very little to change the social fabric of the community. Understanding these kinds of local dynamics of the sign systems at work in the city is an essential step in defining cultural texts.

Other prominent cultural texts that operate as signs of social diversity in the city are found in public schools, social services, and the arts. The social demographics of public schools are most often the clearest indicators of its immediate residential context. A socially diverse neighborhood will have a socially diverse school, and vice versa. Reading a public school's demographic profile, which includes statistics on ethnic composition, academic achievement, and socioeconomic status[33] is a good indicator of the level of diversity in the surrounding community. Similarly, the presence of social services in the urban context represent what types of populations they serve. The Boys and Girls Club, Neighborhood House, Union Gospel Mission, Horn of Africa Services, Technology Access Foundation, Asian Counseling and Referral Services,

---

33. A key socioeconomic indicator in public schools is the number of students who qualify for free or reduced lunch, a federal mandate of the National School Lunch Program that subsidizes meal costs for low-income families. Most public schools also track other social indicators like ethnicity, family structure, how many parents are in the home, and what languages are spoken. In Washington State, this information is available through the Office of the Superintendent of Public Instruction.

Somali Community Services, and Refugee Women's Alliance[34] each work with distinct populations with unique needs. Surveying the variety of non-profit agencies and organizations in an urban context reveals the particular types of social diversity in the area. The arts community is another culture text that symbolizes diversity in the city. What voices and stories are represented in public art? How do local poetry slams, art and history museums, independent live music, cultural festivals, and publicly commissioned murals each reveal the social context of people with different ethnicities and backgrounds? What religious traditions and philosophical worldviews are espoused in the local arts scene? Reading these signs in context speaks to the diverse identities of both individuals and groups in the city.

Interpreting Codes and Messages of Diversity

Many different codes dictate how these diverse cultural texts interact, but some of the most dominant and influential are the implicit and explicit rules of housing[35] and real estate. Finding a place to live often appears to be a personal decision based on preferences and choices, but identifying the urban codes that regulate social diversity reveals many implicit rules at work behind that decision making process . Explicitly, residential and commercial real estate trends and practices work in conjunction with large economic forces to segregate different ethnicities and social classes into different parts of the city. In her explanation of America's "Institutionalized Separatism," professor Sheryll Cashin argues that separatism as a "shared cultural value" points to how "the geographic separation of the classes in America has become pronounced. In any given metropolitan area there is a hierarchy of neighborhoods that roughly approximates the American income scale and the varying social classes. Racial differentiation is also very much a part of this sorting of the populace."[36] Racial and economic segregation between neighbor-

34. All of these organizations operate on (or within several blocks of) a two-mile stretch of MLK Way.

35. It would be difficult to overstate the role of housing in shaping social diversity in the urban context. Sheryll Cashin puts it this way: "Housing—where we live—is fundamental in explaining American separatism. Housing was the last plank in the civil rights revolution, and it is the realm in which we have experienced the fewest integration gains. When it comes to integration, housing is also the realm in which Americans most seem to agree that separation is acceptable" (Cashin, *Failures of Integration*, 3).

36. Cashin, *Failures of Integration*, 84–85.

hoods is an urban reality, nearly without exception, that still exists as a reminder of the unfinished legacy of a post–civil rights era.[37]

Two examples of these regulatory codes are *racial steering* and *redlining*, both of which significantly shaped (and are shaping) the character of social diversity in the urban context. Racial steering is a common real estate practice that involves either intentional or unintentional "behavior that directs a customer toward neighborhoods in which people of his or her racial or ethnic group are concentrated."[38] Regardless of where a potential home buyer wants to live, the practice of racial steering directs people to areas that match their ethnicity. The occurrence of this discriminatory housing practice in the urban context is well documented.[39] The other code at work is redlining, a neighborhood rating system devised by the Home Owners' Loan Corporation of the Federal Housing Administration in the 1930s. This system assigned color values to residential areas based on their racial composition, which was then correlated to financial risk. Neighborhoods with higher concentrations of people of color were given the lowest rating—the color red—and thus denied federal funding for home mortgage loans.[40] Though both of these practices are now illegal and thus no longer officially practiced by the real estate industry or the federal government, the problems they created and the implicit, underlying cultural values—much like institutionalized separatism—persist today.[41]

37. As cited earlier in the first chapter, urban segregation in various forms is a well-established reality of the city. Many studies from disciplinary perspectives have been published, particularly in urban sociology. See Massey and Denton, *American Apartheid* and Cashin, *The Failures of Integration.*

38. Yinger, *Closed Doors, Opportunities Lost*, 51.

39. The most substantial body of research is the nationwide, federally-funded Housing Discrimination Study of 1989 and 2000. This research examined thousands of case studies in dozens of regions and urban areas and demonstrated conclusively that housing discrimination is alive and well in the U.S. For more detailed findings, see De Souza Briggs, *Geography of Opportunity.*

40. "The HOLC's rating procedures thus systematically undervalued older central city neighborhoods that were racially or ethnically mixed" (Massey and Denton, *American Apartheid*, 51). Redlining, perhaps more than any other federal housing practice, has indelibly racialized urban society in coordination with economic stratification.

41. More than forty years after all the Fair Housing legislation that came on the heels of the civil rights movement, residential segregation is as persistent and homogenized as ever, especially in the urban context. Many scholars continue to point to racial steering, redlining, and other similar practices as the phenomena that established the patterns of segregation that persist in our cities today. Legal scholar John A. Powell

As the dominant regulatory codes in the urban context, the contemporary legacy of racial steering and redlining controls the growth and distribution of the cultural texts that signify social diversity in the city. Diversity does not occur at random in some sporadic manner; rather, there are large, structural forces at work determining how and where diversity will exist. In this sense, cultural texts are intentionally arranged according to agenda of these discriminatory policies. These codes, in cooperation with market realities, largely determine who lives where. In turn, the rules of housing and real estate distribute the culture texts of public schools, social services, and their corresponding arts communities along the segregated lines that define our cities.

What messages are conveyed by these signs of diversity under this system and what is the social meaning of it all? First, ethnic or racial diversity consistently has a high correlation with socioeconomic diversity, or in other words, people of color are disproportionately represented among the lower social classes. Second, people of a particular class status or ethnic identity are socially conditioned to segregate in accordance with the structures and codes that already enforce urban segregation. Thus, the social segregation already inherent in the urban system further perpetuates itself. Third, the structures themselves can lead to identity shifts that facilitate cultural phenomena like self-segregation and internalized oppression.[42] As like signs group with other like signs, the culture texts that represent "diversity" only do so because they contrast with groups outside of their social boundaries. Ultimately, as social, ethnic,

---

says: "At one point, we had explicit laws that said 'whites are on top and blacks are on the bottom.' Today we have many of the same practices without the explicit language. And those practices are largely inscribed in geography. So geography does the work of Jim Crow laws. Many people are confused—why after 50 years of civil rights are our schools, housing markets, and jobs still segregated? A lot of this is a function of how we've re-inscribed the racial-geographic space in the United States. That structure is still what we're living in today" (Adelman, "Race—the Power of an Illusion").

42. An example of the internalized oppression that is common in the urban context is how marginalized groups tend to otherize/oppress more marginalized groups (or even themselves) in the same way that they have been discriminated against. For example, African American communities may segregate themselves from East African immigrants and the immigrant communities in turn may internalize this marginalization by viewing themselves as deserving of lesser status. In the city, this dynamic is present in schools, neighborhoods, and housing. See Greene and Blitz, *Racism and Racial Identity*.

and economic signs are linked, a new urban reality arises: most often, diversity in the urban context also means disparity.

URBAN DISPARITY

Just as urban diversity is more than a social reality, so is urban disparity more than merely an economic domain of meaning. But economic disparity in the urban context is the most apparent form of inequity, and is therefore the focal point of this third and final analysis of urban attributes. Disparity goes hand-in-hand with diversity, and like its partner, is accepted as a given in the urban context. The "haves" and "have-nots" coexist in stark contrasts that we rarely find ironic or unusual; that the pan-handler and wealthy executive share space on the sidewalk is merely an everyday reality of the city. Urban dwellers are socially conditioned by the ubiquity of such contrasts to overlook economic disparity; few are even consciously aware of the ways that urban cultural texts boldly display the gaping chasm between the rich and the poor. Because signs of disparity tend to blend into the urban landscape, locating cultural texts, identifying their codes in context, and interpreting their messages and meaning is an important process in developing a more critical understanding of urban communities.

Locating and Defining Signs of Disparity

Cultural texts that signify urban disparity do so on the basis of their ability to exist in between economic extremes. Neither the "wealthy" nor the "poor"[43] can symbolize disparity independent of one another; rather, cultural texts of disparity display the contrast(s) between the rich and poor. In this sense, the text itself can be both the *combination* of the extremes and the *space between* extremes. Obviously, varying degrees of both poverty and wealth are present in the urban context, but the key

---

43. Both of these classifications are very general economic categories, as class stratification is often a complex system of at least five to seven different nested taxonomies of social and economic indicators. Rather than parse the details of class theory, my use of "wealthy/rich" and "poor" will be more contextual, as in rich or poor in contrast to the surrounding community. For example, relative measurements of wealth/poverty often use proportional assessments as opposed to absolute; people at 30/50/80 percent above or below median incomes are deemed rich or poor in relative amounts. See Grusky, *Social Stratification.*

to reading the signs of economic disparity involves locating the symbols that reveal how and where these different groups live in tension.

The northern property boundary of Parnell's Mini Mart, an urban point of interest in the first chapter, is a cultural text that signifies economic disparity because it separates the edge of Parnell's parking lot from a new, mixed-use development project of *Pb Elemental*, an architectural firm that designs and builds "innovative, iconic buildings and dynamic urban environments."[44] Parnell's faded street sign is literally just inches from the foundational concrete of Pb Elemental's strikingly modern work-live urban lofts, and the contrast between these two distinct cultural texts has created a new sign of disparity in the narrow space that exists in these inches. Just as Parnell's represents the character of the old neighborhood, so do the new, urban *Dearborn Lofts* symbolize the imminent transition on the horizon. Thus the combination of these texts signifies the economic disparity that is commonplace in the city.

The appearance of Parnell's humble exterior is characteristic of convenience stores; aesthetics take a back seat to function, and no amount of pretense is needed to dress up the purpose of the mini-mart. A satellite dish is haphazardly bolted to the corner of the roof, and towing signs threaten loiterers. Numerous vinyl banners advertising for the Washington state lottery adorn the faded exterior, and a red donation bin that reads "clothes & shoes" sits in the corner of the parking lot. These kinds of economic indicators—even in small ways—shape the identity formation of those who patronize Parnell's regularly, and as signs of their social context, they reinforce the group boundaries that define what it means to be a consumer at the corner store.[45] And in this immediate context, one of those boundaries is now the northern threshold of the parking lot, which symbolizes the end of old neighborhood and the beginning of yet another gentrified property.

44. This brief marketing excerpt is from their promotional literature. As one of the most prominent regional firms that specializes in environmentally sustainable, ultramodern architecture, their target market is well suited to the urban context of Seattle.

45. Lotto advertisements and clothing donation bins alone do not significantly shape identity; however, the cumulative effect of a retail environment like Parnell's does arguably define a particular type of consumer, one that is accustomed to the signs of urban convenience stores. In this regard, Parnell's establishes group boundaries that distinguish between different types of consumers. Regular shoppers at the local, organic farmers' market will not likely be found at Parnell's, and vice versa.

The Dearborn Lofts could not be more different from the ordinary appearance of Parnell's. The sharp lines, boxy design, and abundance of glass and unique exterior surfaces accentuate the modern architectural statement of these dramatic town homes built above new commercial space. On the southern edge of the property that connects to Parnell's parking lot, an enormous, thrity-five-foot-tall solid wall, painted bright, glossy orange and towering over Parnell's roof, shoots straight up from the concrete, demarcating the boundary with an emphatic plane of separation. Interestingly, on the lowest ten feet of the wall which is accessible at street-level from Parnell's parking lot, a bright orange mural was painted preemptively, perhaps because the builders instinctively knew that it would be the target of graffiti. When Pb Elemental released the pricing for the first 1,500 square foot loft, the value was set at $649,000. The potential home buyers for the Dearborn Lofts are likely young professionals, probably without children, who want to be close to the city core but also want to make a lifestyle statement through their stylish urban loft. The identity formation of this demographic is often shaped by expensive purchases, and their presence at the intersection of 23rd Avenue and Dearborn Street is a major signifier of social change in the neighborhood.

Like Parnell's, the dual-natured signification of the Dearborn Lofts is informed primarily by local context. For longtime residents of the Judkins Park neighborhood, the presence of Pb Elemental is merely another economic indicator of the rampant gentrification that overran the community years ago. The connotation from this perspective is primarily one of inevitability and economic change. But for more recent transplants to the area who are taking advantage of new opportunities for development, the denotation and connotation are more closely linked and positive in nature. Language of "cleaning up the neighborhood" and "restoring blighted properties" is used to reference the changes in the community. On either side of the boundary between Parnell's and the Dearborn Lofts, the connotations are diametrically opposed, and reconciling these disparate sign structures in a changing system is not a simple task.

Diverse communities that are in some form of transition, either a neighborhood that is gentrifying or an area that is in economic decline, are cultural texts that highlight the tension of social change. Also found in these transitional communities are many additional types of cultural texts of disparity, from the predatory lending of payday loans stores alongside commercial banks to the curb appeal of high-end residential construction that is adjacent to an abandoned property. The reality that these kinds of contrasting urban fixtures can coexist in such close proximity communicates a wealth of messages about how disparity is dealt with in a community.

Interpreting Codes and Messages of Disparity

The codes and patterns that regulate economic disparity in transitional communities largely determine the pace and scope of either gentrification or decline. Governed predominantly by an informal mediation process between private investment and community-based organizations,[46] a pendulum often swings between economic development and social resistance to change. In a manner that reflects the connections between density, diversity, and disparity, other codes like zoning laws and real estate practices also heavily influence the process. For example, commercial real estate developers may want to build a large mixed-use structure with condominiums and retail space, but community organizations may band together to negotiate for the importance of environmental impact studies and livable scale being taken into account. In other cases, contracts with land owners and city officials may require quotas of affordable housing or rent ceilings. These types of negotiations can favor gentrification when social capital in the community is lacking, or they can halt the process of development when agreements cannot be made between parties.

Making sense of urban disparity requires an understanding of the economic messages that drive the tension in transitional communities. In a culture of rampant consumerism, for some, signs of disparity are the ever-present reminders of the challenge of "keeping up with the Joneses." The perpetual accumulation of consumer goods and experiences fuels the human appetite for upward mobility, and in some cases, this causes a systemic bias against cultural texts that connote lower-income signs like Parnell's. For sign systems on the upwardly mobile side of a cultural text of urban disparity, the signs of lesser economic status are to be slowly transformed into the likeness of the other side. For example,

46. Community-based organizations that regulate the kind of private development that often leads to gentrification may be neighborhood coalitions, local business associations, or other similarly oriented non-profits.

from the rooftop decks of the Dearborn Lofts, the dingy parking lot and somewhat dilapidated building of Parnell's Mini Mart appear to be signs of lesser economic status that should be "cleaned up," or better yet, torn down and replaced with more "innovative, iconic buildings" from Pb Elemental.

Ultimately, the introduction of new signs in the built environment of the city always alters the system, and the transformation of surrounding cultural texts always moves in the same direction as the flow of economic capital. When financial investment in a community introduces new signs of upward mobility, the impact of that investment can have a ripple effect through the community that transforms cultural texts of disparity into signs of economic equality. And in reverse fashion, when a lack of financial investment in a community causes new signs of downward mobility, the impact of that divestment can influence the degradation of cultural texts of disparity into signs of economic poverty.

For many in transitional communities, most often those on the margins of social change, they view economic disparity with disdain as it foreshadows cultural transformation on the horizon that will not include them. Gentrification is a social and economic phenomenon that inherently displaces people, and many see disparity as the precursor to their inevitable forced relocation. If the existence of economic disparity in the urban context communicates anything, it is the inevitability of social change. And while for some, this change is welcomed, for many, it means starting over or being left behind.

In summary, locating cultural texts, defining their dual-natured signs, interpreting their messages in context, and categorizing their meaning into domains is a method of semiotic description of the urban context that breaks down the complex sign systems of the city into meaningful structures of urban significance. And while it is not a systematic approach to constructing an analytical model for examining every facet of the urban context, it is a descriptive method that seeks to explain cultural texts with depth and clarity in regard to their signification about identity formation and social change.

Urban density, diversity, and disparity are core themes that shape our understanding of physical, social, and economic meaning in the urban context, and interpreting the city in this way is designed to uncover the key cultural themes that make constructing an urban contextual theology possible. The next chapter aims to engage the urban culture explored here with a transformative contextual theology that is both situated in the reality of the city and faithful to the process of contextualizing the gospel.

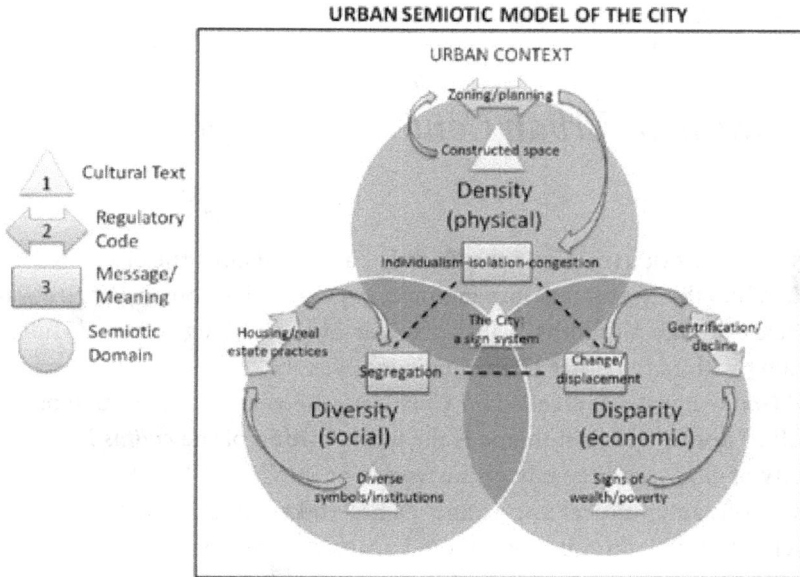

FIGURE 2: Urban Semiotic Model of the City[47]

47. Using the same patterns, in this second diagram that broadens the scope to the urban context of the city, the "cultural text" replaces the "urban sign object" as the basic unit of analysis. Subsequently, the "regulatory code" replaces the "missional code of engagement" in the first diagram's model of urban exegesis.

11

Toward an Urban Contextual Theology

IN THE YEAR 410, Alaric the Goth led a siege against the city of Rome. When this seemingly impenetrable capital of the Roman Empire was sacked by the Visigoths, a fifty-six-year-old Saint Augustine of Hippo, along with many other Roman citizens, was shaken to the core.[1] In *City of God*, Augustine's treatise on Christian philosophy in the wake of the fall of Rome, a central theme is the juxtaposition of the *civitas Dei*—the City of God—and the city of the world (or the City of Man) in a time of religious and political uncertainty. "I have taken upon myself the task of defending the glorious City of God against those who prefer their own gods to the Founder of that City . . . the task is long and arduous, but God is our helper. . . . Therefore I cannot refrain from speaking about the city of this world, a city which aims at dominion, which holds nations in enslavement, but is itself dominated by that very lust of domination. I must consider this city as far as the scheme of this work demands and as occasion serves."[2] The City of God, like the eschatological New Jerusalem it represents, is the spiritual victory of heaven that the church is called to pursue in all its earthly aspirations. On the other hand, the City of Man is overrun with pagans[3] who "prefer their own gods" to the one true God. Thus, the city that controlled an empire and had conquered the known world had itself been conquered. This urban context of Rome, and the reality of its uncertain future, prompted Augustine to

---

1. Augustine, *Concerning the City of God against the Pagans*, ix.

2. Ibid., 5–6.

3. Interestingly, the word "pagan" stems from the Latin word *paganus*, which originally meant "rural" or "from the country." By inference, it is apparently the urban dwellers who were deemed more theistic.

reject the false ideologies and materialism of the worldly city in favor of the spiritual triumph of the heavenly city.[4]

In a sharply contrasting modern perspective on the city, Harvard theologian Harvey Cox published *The Secular City* in 1965, a book whose international success would eventually leave a definitive mark on his scholarship and research. The central thesis of *The Secular City* is that "secularization—if it is not permitted to calcify into an ideology (which I called "secular-*ism*")—is not everywhere and always an evil."[5] Rather, secularization has constructive influence in society: it "prevents powerful religions from acting on their theocratic pretensions. It allows people to choose among a wider range of worldviews."[6] For Cox, the City of God and the City of Man are not diametrically opposed; instead, he proposes a different biblical metaphor. "We already live in the world-city and there is no return. God has placed us in this urban exile, and is teaching us a more mature faith, for it is a quality of unfaith to have to flee from complexity and disruption, or to scurry around trying to relate every segment of experience to some comforting inclusive whole, as though the universe might implode unless we hold it together with our own conceptualization."[7] Here Cox frames the urban context as exilic and therefore beneficial because of its potential to deepen the faith of the church by embracing the uncertainty of the city. The future of the city may indeed be further secularization, but perhaps there is some providential certainty at work in that urban future.

Despite their opposing views, neither Augustine nor Cox is solely correct in their theological assessment of the city; both perspectives are rooted in their local cultural context[8] and representative of the need for different approaches to the city in varying circumstances. At times, a call to reject the worldliness of the urban context is completely merited; the people of God must live into a different spiritual and eschatological reality.[9] And yet, on other occasions, the church must embrace the

4. This is hardly a sufficient summary of this massive theological work of Augustine; my intent in this introduction is merely to provide a snapshot of one representative approach to the question of the urban context and the role of the city.

5. Cox, "Secular City 25 Years Later."

6. Ibid.

7. Ibid.

8. Augustine's immediate context is the fall of Rome, and Cox's is the shifting religious and philosophical mores of the 1960s.

9. Hence the need for "confrontation as the prophetic task" in missional engagement with culture.

compromise of the secular city, particularly as it wrestles with its in-carnational vocation. The reality of understanding the urban context is that the practice of contextualization in the city is often somewhere in between Augustine and Cox, and draws on both perspectives of contra-distinction and inculturation.

Having examined the process of contextual theology, evaluated different approaches to cultural analysis, and applied semiotic description to the urban context, the final task is to construct the foundational components of an urban contextual theology. The specific character of an urban contextual theology is always shaped by both the *everyday experience* of density, diversity, and disparity and the *theological reflection* that grows out of those contexts. If the urban context is indeed definitively characterized by the symbolic systems and structural expressions of physical density, social diversity, and economic disparity, then an urban contextual theology must engage these domains of meaning with a local theology of *place, neighbor,* and *community* in the city.

PLACE IN THE CITY

A theology of *place* in the urban context must see the multifaceted nature of place as more than just theologically neutral territory. The full dimensionality of place is more than a geographical location, more than a sense of environment, and more than just a physical state of being in a specific space.[10] Unfortunately, the concept of place in the frenetic urban environment of Western society is largely a functional, consumer-driven idea often motivated by little more than comfort or convenience. Where we live, where we work, where we worship, and how we feel about these specific places may be just an incidental reality that we are often too rushed to consider more carefully.

But for those willing to engage in a more critical examination of place, the challenges are complex. Like the word "*culture,*" "'Place' is one of the trickiest words in the English language, a suitcase so overfilled one can never shut the lid. It carries the resonance of homestead, location,

---

10. The concept of "place" in place studies is closely connected to the interdisciplinary structure of cultural studies; thus its dimensions vary in literary, anthropological, architectural, geographical, and sociological perspectives. My interaction with place will tend to focus on theological perspectives, though theology has naturally drawn on the broad research of place studies to inform its reflection. See Inge, *Christian Theology of Place*; and Gorringe, *Theology of the Built Environment*.

and open space in the city as well as a position in a social hierarchy."[11] Thus we can speak of physically "going to this or that place" and socially "knowing your place" in a relational context and existentially "understanding our place in the world" all in the same sentence. How, then, does a critical understanding of place relate to the urban context? *Density, shalom,* and *being human* each inform the theological character of place in the city.

Place and Density

Particularly in the density of the urban context, understanding place is especially difficult when so many different kinds of places and spaces[12] coexist and overlap in the city. Added to this complexity is the physical congestion and overcrowding of urban density (and its subsequent encounters with urban diversity and disparity), and it is not surprising that cities are sometimes perceived as less than desirable places. But as semiotic description of the urban context demonstrates, these "undesirable" attributes do not randomly develop in cities without cause or control. Quite to the contrary, the presence of physical density in urban communities is in many ways the direct result of codes and laws that arrange cultural texts and their signs into particular recurring patterns. And if this process is a given in the urban context, how can the reality of density in the city be evaluated theologically?

Because density is a fundamental attribute of the urban context, any theological analysis of the city as a particular place must come to terms with the long-standing anti-urban bias[13] in theology of the city.[14] Even though the arc of the biblical narrative moves "from Eden to Jerusalem, from a garden to a city,"[15] the city has long been seen as a place character-

11. Hayden, *Power of Place*, 15.

12. "Space" and "place" are distinct terms that carry unique connotations in place studies. In general, *space* is a more generic, abstract concept (e.g., "outer space") and *place* is a more local, particular arrangement of space. However, though places exist in space according to this definition, it is also true that particular kinds of spaces (from a design perspective) can exist in one particular place. See Tuan, *Space and Place*.

13. This anti-urban bias in theology is largely influenced by the broader anti-urban bias that developed in literature and the social sciences along with the onset of industrialization. Urban anthropology and sociology document this phenomenon fairly well. See Hannerz, *Exploring the City*.

14. Dyrness and Kärkkäinen, *Global Dictionary of Theology*, 187–88.

15. Ellul, *Meaning of the City*, 173.

ized by an "inherent diabolism."[16] In his description of the first city as an urban archetype, Ellul explains that "the city is the direct consequence of Cain's murderous act and of his refusal to accept God's protection. Cain has built a city. For God's Eden he substitutes his own, for the goal given to his life by God, he substitutes a goal chosen by himself . . . such is the act by which Cain takes his destiny on his own shoulders, refusing the hand of God in his life."[17] Banished from the idyllic rolling hills of Eden's lush garden, part of Cain's curse is to establish the first city, a place that is constructed in stark opposition to the rural paradise of Eden as a result of Cain's rejection of God. Though this harsh urban metaphor is softened by other images of the city in scripture, the historical emphasis in the church has tended to focus more on negative portrayals of places like Babel, Sodom, Gomorrah, Babylon, and Rome.[18] Unfortunately, the explosive urban density that characterized the industrial revolution—and the slums and squalor that accompanied it—merely served to reinforce this anti-urban bias in both the church and society at large.[19]

Density in the city continues to be a point of contention in contemporary Western theology; only in the past few decades have constructive perspectives on urban theology sought to portray the city as a potentially redemptive place instead of just a mission field to be "saved."[20] And though the importance of the city in the process of theology is increasingly being recognized[21] as urbanization (and hence urbanism) continues to pervade our cultural context, many challenges remain.

The most basic reality about places of density in the North American context is that they stand in opposition to one of the most highly prized cultural values in the U.S.: individualism.[22] Density confronts the cul-

16. Ibid., xi.

17. Ibid., 5.

18. Urban missiologist Harvie Conn has singled out evangelicals in particular in his statement that "the history of the evangelical church in the American city has been liberally sprinkled with a cultural pessimism toward things urban" (Conn, *American City and the Evangelical Church*, 194).

19. Conn outlines the anti-urban debate more exhaustively in a section titled "The City: Enemy or Ally?" in *Urban Ministry*, 85–89.

20. Bakke, *Theology as Big as the City*, 22–24.

21. Orsi, *Gods of the City*.

22. In the vast international research that Hofstede conducted on intercultural communication, the U.S. ranked highest, above all other countries surveyed, on his scale of individualism versus collectivism. See Hofstede, *Cultures and Organizations*.

tural norm to desire our own "personal space" and in the context of the city, Christians live and work in close proximity to people of other faiths and backgrounds. Pluralism is removed from the realm of abstraction and *placed* on the doorstep of an urban stoop. This kind of religious and philosophical environment forces a kind of theological formation that is equipped to encounter pluralism graciously without retreating into a privatized relativism. Additionally, dense places challenge the necessity of individualism by thinking theologically about privacy, isolation, and loneliness. If the city is a place of density where people hide behind anonymity, then a theology of place in the urban context must address the inherent costs of individualism that arise from urban isolation. Ultimately, density is merely one of the placial indicators that defines the need for a particular kind of theological reflection in the city.

Place and Shalom

The combined influence of density, diversity, and disparity on the urban context points to the reality of the city as a difficult place for contextualizing a gospel of inclusion, equality, and community. Therefore, in addition to addressing issues of pluralism and individualism, a theology of place in the city must also be committed to engaging these "difficult places" (where extremes of density, diversity, and disparity are signified) for the purpose of seeking the *shalom* of the city.

The particular substance of *shalom* is intimately connected to justice, but is also the product of "right, harmonious relationships" between people, God, and creation that are rooted in "an ethical, responsible community."[23] Far more than merely the absence of hostility or conflict, the peace of shalom is a web of multilayered interdependencies which cultivate the flourishing of the created order. The pursuit of this shalom in difficult places has always been a central task of the people of the *missio Dei*.

As the prophet Jeremiah sent a letter from Jerusalem to the community of exiles in Babylon, he gave this advice:

> Thus says the LORD of hosts, the God of Israel, to all the exiles whom I have sent into exile from Jerusalem to Babylon: Build houses and live in them; plant gardens and eat what they produce. Take wives and have sons and daughters; take wives for your sons, and give your daughters in marriage, that they may

23. Wolterstorff, *Until Justice and Peace Embrace*, 69–72.

bear sons and daughters; multiply there, and do not decrease. But seek the welfare of the city where I have sent you into exile, and pray to the LORD on its behalf, for in its welfare you will find your welfare.[24]

As a place of defeat and abandonment, Babylon signified the despair of being far from home and subjected to foreign authority. But the repeated commands to build, plant, eat, marry, and multiply tasked the exiles with pursuing the peace and wholeness of the very place that represented their oppression. "The imperative bestows upon this vulnerable, small community a large missional responsibility. In this way, the community is invited into the larger public process of the empire. Such a horizon prevents the exilic community from withdrawing into its own safe, sectarian existence, and gives it work to do and responsibility for the larger community."[25] Rather than retreating into an enclave of protection, seeking the shalom of the city always involves the *whole* of the city, which includes its places of density, diversity, and disparity. The city is only at peace when shalom is shared by both the privileged and the marginalized; in this sense, it must be equally accessible to the inner city ghetto, the urban neighborhood, and the suburban community.

Seeking the peace and prosperity of *place* in the urban context will require a radical commitment to seek out these "hard places," rather than retreating from them. Furthermore, part and parcel of this quest for urban restoration also requires the conviction to challenge the status quo arrangement of upward mobility and social stratification that segregates communities into of places of disparity. Historically, the tragic legacies of "white flight" and "brain drain"[26] have decimated urban neighborhoods, and too often the church in its complacency and isolation has failed to act on behalf of these hard places.

24. Jer 29:4–7. This preamble to the oft-quoted verses 11–13 is an essential element of understanding the narrative in context.

25. Brueggemann, *Commentary on Jeremiah*, 257–58.

26. "White flight" is the mass exodus of whites from communities with transitioning demographics toward ethnic and socioeconomic diversity, and "brain drain" is the common sociological phenomenon that occurs when the best and brightest escape marginalized communities and never return, leaving the fabric of the culture and the infrastructure to the fate of the "lowest common denominator." For a contemporary example of these urban issues, see Birch and Wachter, *Rebuilding Urban Places after Disaster*.

For the past two decades, we have been abandoning our strategic locations within city cores and traditional neighborhoods, and we have tried to create for ourselves a new kind of society in the form of suburban megachurches. And as individual Christians, we have marched right along with the rest of our culture and moved our homes outside of the urban core into the sanitized world of the suburbs. Even when we have not participated directly in this radical shift, we have come to view the particularities of functioning in the midst of the city (restricted parking, unsympathetic neighbors, and pushy transients) as inconveniences rather than as opportunities for ministry . . .

Unfortunately, if we were to take a hard look at how Christians in this country have come to view their cities, we would have to conclude that our views have not necessarily been shaped by the Bible, prayer, or meaningful discussions among fellow Christians. It might be more accurate to say that the fear of cities, or the fear of one another, or possibly the love of convenience has been the actual basis of much of our current perceptions about the city.[27]

Jacobsen levels a serious accusation at the church in his argument that fear and comfort have superseded any theological convictions about the urban context. Viewed as a place of inconvenience, crime, and general immorality, the city has become a place to avoid, not a place to *incarnate*.

And while it is not necessarily the responsibility of a particularly enlightened or self-sacrificing few to take the mantle of solving urban problems on their shoulders by "moving to the ghetto" to "rescue the poor people" from their distress,[28] an urban contextual theology of place must understand the physical, social, and economic dynamics that influence identity formation and social change in the city as a distinct place. Particular places shape people in unique ways, and a distinctly urban *placiality*[29] leaves an indelible mark on the lives, stories, and values of the people who dwell there. Only a deeper, holistic understanding of these placial dynamics in theological context will be able to alter our negative perceptions of the city as an undesirable place. If the church is

27. Jacobsen, *Sidewalks in the Kingdom*, 17.

28. Nor is there some specific theological mandate for the entire church to engage in John Perkins's model of Christian community development that requires relocation, reconciliation, and redistribution. However, I do believe that there is theological justification for the whole Church to adopt a more prophetic and compassionate posture toward the whole city.

29. A place's unique character, or the "personality" of a place (e.g., a place of density, diversity, and disparity).

unwilling or unable to respond to the injustices and inequities of these hard places, then their self-perpetuating circumstances will merely continue. Whenever the church neglects its prophetic vocation to stand in solidarity with those who are marginalized in urban places, it ceases to be the church.[30]

Place and Being Human

Regardless of how Christians choose to respond to the specific placiality of the urban context, an understanding of the theological significance of place must also be integrated with our basic understanding of what it means to be human. "To be human is to be placed: to be born in this house, hospital, stable . . . it is to live in this council house, semi-detached, tower block, farmhouse, mansion. It is to go to school through these streets or lanes, to play in this alley, park, garden . . . these facts are banal, but they form the fabric of our everyday lives, structuring our memories, determining our attitudes."[31] This fundamental connection between humanity and place is also affirmed by the recognition that "the places in a person's world are more than entities which provide the physical stage for life's drama. Some are profound centers of meanings and symbols of experience. As such, they lie at the core of human existence."[32] Incidental geography cannot capture the meaning of place because its significance is wrapped up in the human story.

If part of what it means to be human is to be placed, and to be Christian is to place our humanity in the biblical narrative, then reimagining the biblical narrative of "creation, fall, and redemption" as being "placed, displaced, and re-placed"[33] is a task of a contextualizing the human story in a theology of place. With its continual emphasis on covenant and the significance of land, place is a central theme in the biblical narrative, from the particular hope of the Promised Land in the Exodus to the specific location of Zion on the Temple Mount. These

---

30. Space will not allow for a full theological justification of this statement, but the prophetic vocation of the church, as outlined in the fourth chapter, is committed to criticizing and energizing in the urban context that seeks to embody steadfast love, justice, and righteousness for the orphan, the widow, and the foreigner (or the fatherless, the single mother, and the immigrant).

31. Gorringe, *Theology of the Built Environment*, 1.

32. Relph, *Rational Landscapes and Humanistic Geography*, 174.

33. Bouma-Prediger and Walsh, *Beyond Homelessness*, 28.

places are integral to the trajectory of God's story that interacts with creation, which consistently calls people to inhabit the particularity of these sacred places.

Speaking of sacred places, poet (and many would say, prophet) Wendell Berry, in his poem "How to Be a Poet"[34] reminds the reader to:

> Breathe with unconditional breath
> the unconditioned air.
> Shun electric wire.
> Communicate slowly. Live
> a three-dimensioned life;
> stay away from screens.
> Stay away from anything
> that obscures the place it is in.
> There are no unsacred places;
> there are only sacred places
> and desecrated places.

In response to Berry's insistence that an intentional attentiveness to place is inherently sacred, theologian Ellen Davis says that "here we have come to an area of mass insensitivity for urban Western Christians. The secularity of place is part of our cultural mindset . . . for most of us, place is little more than real estate, wherever we happen to be paying rent or a mortgage at any given time. Therefore the biblical insistence that God can invest hopes and dreams in a particular place, can even make a kind of home on this earth, is incomprehensible and often offensive."[35] If the city at large is not a secular place, is the urban context a *sacred* place or a *desecrated* place? What hopes and dreams has God invested in the gutters, street corners, and public housing projects of the city?

Only by recovering a sense of the inherent theological value of place as intimately connected with the whole of human experience will the church be able to find its voice to speak about the holistic nature of a gospel that seeks the transformation and redemption of the urban context. If the city is an ordinary place, just like every other geographic space that is settled and occupied by humans, then the arrangement of its systems and structures is little more than a function of its signs and cultural texts taking their natural course toward density, diversity, and disparity. However, if the city is a particular place of both sacred and

---

34. Berry, *Given.*
35. Davis, "Holiness of Place."

desecrated spaces, each deserving of *shalom* because the parts and the whole share a common accountability to one another, then the unique opportunity of a theology of place in the urban context is to facilitate this relationship for the sake of those who call the city their home.

NEIGHBORING IN THE CITY

"The Word became flesh and blood, and moved into the neighborhood."[36] Eugene Peterson's well known paraphrase of this memorable introduction in the first chapter of John's Gospel is more than just a clever rewording of this incarnational doctrine. That God chooses to dwell among us and essentially become our neighbor is a powerful biblical metaphor that should shape and inform our understanding of what it means to love our neighbors as ourselves, especially those in our urban neighborhoods.

An urban contextual theology of neighbor(ing) in the city must engage the primary semiotic domains of meaning in the urban context. Physical *density* means that neighbors live near us, may invade our privacy, or on occasion, come "too close for comfort," violating the all important social principles of individualism and personal space. Social *diversity* means that we encounter neighbors who are quite different from us; their backgrounds, lifestyles, values, and religious worldviews may not mesh with our own. Economic *disparity* means that the needs of our neighbors are at times quite tangible and may "cost" us, in terms of time, money, or other resources. Thus, an urban contextual theology of neighboring seeks to know those who are near, embrace those who are "other," and serve those who are in need. Though "neighbor" is traditionally a more static category of people, this theological concept of "neighboring" in the city is a dynamic verb of action and engagement.

And Who Is My Neighbor?

Luke 10: The Parable of the Good Samaritan

[25] Just then a lawyer stood up to test Jesus. 'Teacher,' he said, 'what must I do to inherit eternal life?' [26] He said to him, 'What is written in the law? What do you read there?' [27] He answered, 'You shall love the Lord your God with all your heart, and with all your soul, and with all your strength, and with all your mind;

36. Peterson, *The Message.*

and your neighbor as yourself.' [28] And he said to him, 'You have given the right answer; do this, and you will live.'

[29] But wanting to justify himself, he asked Jesus, 'And who is my neighbor?' [30] Jesus replied, 'A man was going down from Jerusalem to Jericho, and fell into the hands of robbers, who stripped him, beat him, and went away, leaving him half dead. [31] Now by chance a priest was going down that road; and when he saw him, he passed by on the other side. [32] So likewise a Levite, when he came to the place and saw him, passed by on the other side. [33] But a Samaritan while travelling came near him; and when he saw him, he was moved with pity. [34] He went to him and bandaged his wounds, having poured oil and wine on them. Then he put him on his own animal, brought him to an inn, and took care of him. [35] The next day he took out two denarii, gave them to the innkeeper, and said, "Take care of him; and when I come back, I will repay you whatever more you spend." [36] Which of these three, do you think, was a neighbor to the man who fell into the hands of the robbers?' [37] He said, 'The one who showed him mercy.' Jesus said to him, 'Go and do likewise.'

In the parable of the Good Samaritan, the passage opens with an abrupt interaction between Jesus and an expert in the law about what must be *done* to inherit eternal life. It is important to recognize that the qualification of faithfulness to the *shema* (Deuteronomy 6:4–9) that is outlined by the lawyer and affirmed by Jesus is portrayed in an intentionally *active* light. The discussion is not merely theological and propositional; it is by definition connected to the concrete reality of neighboring in the world. "That the practice of God's word is the central issue in this narrative unit is obvious from the repetition and placement of the verb 'to do' . . . in this way the first segment of this unit (vv 25–28) is bound together with references to *praxis*."[37]

The defensive question "And who is my neighbor?" that the lawyer poses to Jesus is one of justification and avoidance. But Jesus replies with a radical narrative of countercultural neighboring, one in which traditional cultural categories were shattered in favor of a different definition of neighbor. After the priest and the Levite had failed to intervene on behalf of the beaten man, "the audience may well have expected the third character in the story to be an Israelite layman, thereby giving an anti-clerical point to the story . . . Jesus, however, deliberately speaks of

---

37. Green, *Gospel of Luke*, 425.

a member of a community hated by the Jews."[38] Jesus' unexpected inclusion of a Samaritan in the story is a turn that surely would have shocked his listeners; however, "what distinguishes this traveler from the other two is not fundamentally that they are Jews and he is a Samaritan, nor is it that they had high status as religious functionaries and he does not. What individualizes him is his compassion, leading to action, in the face of their inaction . . . the parable of the compassionate Samaritan thus undermines the determination of status in the community of God's people on the basis of ascription, substituting in its place a concern with performance, the granting of status on the basis of one's actions."[39] Over against all the other social and cultural identifiers at work in this context, compassionate action is what differentiates the Samaritan and defines him as a good neighbor.

That a nameless Samaritan—perceived as less than fully human by many first century Jews—embodies a Christlike ethic of love and service to neighbor should call into question the cultural categories of race, class, and gender that accentuate the segregation of neighbors in the urban context. In an early 1990s Los Angeles contextualization of this parable, J. Timothy Kauffman illustrates the prophetic nature of being a good neighbor in a post-Rodney King riots era.

> Jesus said, "A certain young Anglo male stopped at a red light in his big-rig at Florence and Normandie. He was on his way to make a delivery. While he was sitting there, an angry crowd pulled him out of the truck and threw him to the ground. There in the middle of the street the mob attacked him, beat him, and left him to die. The first group that should have helped him were the enforcers of the law. They were conspicuously absent. The second group that could have helped him was the press in a helicopter overhead. They could have sounded their sirens immediately. Seeing a story, however, they just let their cameras roll until the man was almost dead. Then they hurriedly left the scene. About that time, a young African American male, watching this tragedy unfold on television in the safety of his home not far away, had compassion on the young white man. Risking his own life, he left his home, faced down the mob and helped the young man back into his truck. Emboldened by his courage, several others also came to his aid. Together, they drove the white man to the hospi-

38. Marshall, *Gospel of Luke*, 449.
39. Green, *Gospel of Luke*, 431.

tal where they were later told that if they had arrived one minute later, the young man would have died. Which was a neighbor to the man who fell into the hands of the angry crowd: the law, the media, or the African American?" Jesus asked.[40]

This retelling of a familiar parable in an urban context demonstrates a neighborly praxis of engaging those who are near, "other," and in need. Being a neighbor in the city is an active, intentional choice, and is perhaps best described as neighbor*ing*. Robert Lupton refers to the task of "reneighboring" our cities as the most constructive solution to combating issues of urban isolation and poverty.[41] Fragmented and ghettoized neighborhoods in larger segregated communities are in desperate need of many more good neighbors who are willing to "go and do likewise" in the city.

Neighbors and Race

No discussion of urban neighboring would be truly contextual without addressing how issues of diversity, ethnicity, and *race* shape the contemporary cultural landscape of the city. The fact that neighbors coexist in diverse but racially segregated communities is an urban reality that demands theological attention, if for no other reason than the demonstration of unjust correlations between density, diversity, and disparity. This discussion must go beyond the popular sentiments of multiculturalism[42] and the premodern concepts of ethnicity[43] depicted in the parable of the Good Samaritan. Both approaches stop short of engaging the particularly *modern* construction of race in the city, which is both social and theo-

40. Van Engen and Tiersma, *God So Loves the City*, 28.

41. Lupton, *Return Flight*.

42. I have previously referenced several pitfalls of the potential for a "politically correct" mentality to overrun multiculturalism's true agenda, which is to facilitate genuine equality, power sharing, and mutually transformative understanding between different cultural groups. Often, more popular understandings of multiculturalism (especially among evangelicals, who largely embrace a more individualistic perception of "color blindness" in American society) merely scratch the surface of those ideals and in fact work to reinforce existing structures with only slight modifications of diversity that fit an existing agenda, also known as tokenism. See Emerson and Smith, *Divided by Faith;* and Rah, *Next Evangelicalism*.

43. Ancient concepts of ethnicity (e.g., a Jew or Samaritan) must not be conflated with "race" in the modern sense of the word. The former has to do with a particular people group, while the latter carries a much more complex connotation of social construction in the modern world. See Gallagher, *Rethinking the Color Line*.

logical in nature.[44] Thus, an urban contextual theology of neighboring
that seeks to engage the segregation of the modern city must confront
the injustices of racial separatism and fragmentation with a distinctly
"audacious theological imagination."[45] This theological imagination
must be rooted in a vision of the equality and interdependence of *shalom* and committed to subverting the "racial imagination of modernity"[46]
that has segregated the world into whites, who are "civilized," and dark
bodies, who remain "primitive," particularly in the city.

Audacious theological imagination is the starting point because "the
virulence and all-pervasiveness of prejudice and racism in US society"[47]
is a fundamental social reality of racialization in America, especially
in the urban context. It will take more than a little creative thinking to
imagine that the oppressive structures of segregated public schools can
be dismantled by the theological convictions of good neighbors. In the
same way, changing the widespread discriminatory practices embraced
by much of the city's development industries will require neighbors with
a different theological vision of the status quo. Furthermore, altering
the stratified housing patterns that create ethnic ghettos and pockets of
harsh disparity along racial lines will only be possible when truly diverse
groups of neighbors choose to reject the racial expectations to cluster
and homogenize into ethnic-specific groups. All of this will require a
new and radical racial imagination that is alternative to the segregated
systems of the modern city.

Ultimately, this theological imagination has to be cultivated in the
church as a community of neighbors who reject the ideologies of urban
segregation. Becoming that truly diverse community in which all ethnicities are welcome at the table will be a difficult task for the church,
particularly one that is bound by "white, Western cultural captivity,"[48]
and conditioned by the separatism that plagues all American cities. But
all is not lost; some multicultural communities of faith on the margins

44. J. Kameron Carter's monumental new work, *Race: A Theological Account*, makes
the connections between theology, modernity, and race one of the central arguments
of his overarching thesis: that the concept of race in the modern world has distinctly
theological origins in both the vast colonial implications of the East-West divide and
the influence of supersessionism in the Christian church.

45. Carter, *Race*, 372.

46. Ibid., 4–6.

47. Claerbaut, *Urban Ministry in a New Millennium*, 161.

48. Rah, *Next Evangelicalism*.

are taking on the challenge in urban contexts by serving their neighbors in need, working through the difficult tensions of cultural assimilation and integration, and embracing the multiethnic character of the gospel.[49] These churches alone will not eradicate racism or turn the massive tide of racialization in modern society; however, their faithful presence in the urban context can effect genuine change in the city by intentionally cultivating this imagination, one neighborhood at a time.

Overall, putting this neighborly theological praxis in action means that an urban contextual theology of neighboring in the city must facilitate a *relational* understanding of density, diversity, and disparity. Relational knowledge of families and individuals who deal with physical overcrowding in housing projects provides a tangible context for understanding the real everyday issues. The pursuit of active relationships with those who are "other" establishes commonality in the shared challenges of being human, regardless of the diverse communities, stories, and identities that define us. A relational understanding of gentrification provides names and faces for those who are among the displaced, and looks beyond the appearances of economic status to evaluate the inherent worth of all people. Only when our knowledge of physical, social, and economic meaning in the urban context is both cognitive *and* relational can our advocacy for "the least of these" come from an authentic love of neighbor.

COMMUNITY IN THE CITY

Places and neighbors in the city exist in community. And though the physical community (as in the built environment) of the urban context may not always facilitate a social *sense* of community, an urban contextual theology of community in the city must seek to bridge the disparate contexts created by density, diversity, and disparity. In doing so, the physical dynamics of community require *proximity*, the social dynamics of community require *reconciliation*, and the economic dynamics of community require *redistribution*.[50] Each of these dynamics must also

49. DeYoung, *United by Faith*.

50. The marked similarity to the CCDA/Perkins model of the "3Rs" (Relocation, Reconciliation, Redistribution) is entirely intentional. As stated earlier, though not everyone may be "called" to Christian community development, I find the theological framework of the model to be much more widely applicable. See Perkins, *With Justice for All*.

be shaped by the prophetic vocation of the church in its pursuit of the Trinitarian model of community which exemplifies a submissive mutuality and a missional trajectory.

Community and Proximity

That community requires proximity should be no revelation to most of us. The difficulty of being "in community"—whether physically, relationally, or spiritually—across distance, boundaries, or obstacles is quite apparent when community, by definition, implies some form of "togetherness." Urban fragmentation and stratification work against this togetherness, even when density would seem to literally force people together. In the face of this urban reality, the church must become a distinct community of "place," where both geographic and spiritual neighbors can gather together in a spirit of unity and fellowship.

Community and proximity are particularly interdependent in the urban context because our sense of place has been dislocated by the size and complexity of urban life. Long commutes, suburban privatization, and consumer-driven individualism have put society's longing for "third places"[51] in the structures of corporately franchised cafés, instead of in the hands of community-based locales. Ironically, these corporate creations of place are actually just fabricated *imitations* of place because they design and mass produce a particular *space* to give the illusion of place. Thus this manufactured place is not tied to any particular geographic locale, and can in fact be recreated regardless of place.[52]

For churches to embody a countercultural critique of this commodification of place will require a distinctly "placed" community. A church that understands its place will be able to think contextually about the opportunities and challenges of its location, both in the immediate built environment and the surrounding neighborhood. Because

51. With the primary places in urban life of home (first) and work (second), café/coffeehouse culture has sought to become a societal "third place." Ironically, in urban sociology, third places are often described in contrast to the large structures of corporations. See Oldernburg, *Celebrating the Third Place*.

52. The easiest examples of this phenomenon are the consistent design cues that give an ordinary space a particular franchised feel. The intent is to create a sense of brand familiarity in a recognizable space; however, this is actually the opposite of place, which is always contextualized for a particular location and community. Starbucks CEO Howard Schultz unapologetically narrates his desire for the corporation to cultivate its status as a "third place" in *Pour Your Heart into It*.

the establishment of proximity lays the foundation for other aspects of community, an urban contextual theology of community must take into serious consideration the role of physical proximity in its communal life.

Community and Reconciliation

Secondly, in an urban contextual theology, the social dynamics of community in diversity require a commitment to reconciliation. The idea of reconciliation "has become a popular notion in our time, finding its way into the political rhetoric and public policy of many governments . . . interest in reconciliation in the academic world has increased. . . . Faith based and other NGOs in conflict areas around the world are working for reconciliation alongside Christian ministries that have adopted reconciliation as one of their goals."[53] However, this growth in the reconciliation "industry" has at times obscured the true meaning of the term. Amidst competing visions of reconciliation, Emmanuel Katongole and Chris Rice describe the process as the goal of God's story, a journey of lament, and a call to memory, hope, justice, imagination, and conversion.[54] Each of these aspects of reconciliation speak to the broad scope of God's reconciling work in the world, and call the church to engage in this redemptive mission in creation.

In the urban context, bridging the divides of race, class, and gender requires much more than a robust sense of place and a commitment to Christian neighboring, though being a community of good neighbors is certainly a helpful place to begin. But for churches to become actual *communities of reconciliation*—covenanted people known for their thorough and robust commitment to reconciling with others—will require a truly radical commitment to the prophetic nature of biblical reconciliation. That God has "given us the ministry of reconciliation"[55] in his declaration that in Christ there is no "Jew or Gentile, slave or free, male or female"[56] should saturate our praxis as peacemakers and bridge-builders

53. Katongole and Rice, *Reconciling All Things*, 25–26.

54. Ibid., 147–51.

55. 2 Cor 5:11–21 is a passage that situates the ministry of reconciliation in the divine initiative of conversion and new creation. Paul then commissions the church in Corinth as a reconciled community to be ambassadors of righteousness to the world, offering the message of the reconciling gospel to others.

56. Gal 3:26–29 is such a widely cited text that its full exegetical meaning cannot be exposited here. It is sufficient to say that Paul's "theology of the cross succinctly

in a context of communities that have been fractured by the racism and violence of class and gender hierarchies.

There is no simple solution to deepening the church's commitment to reconciliation, but becoming advocates for cities' "hard places" and engaging in authentic relationships with diverse neighbors is a starting point for moving from charity and tokenism to justice and empowerment. The city is a place where social fragmentation and segregation are often accepted as immutable, but reconciliation in the urban context that is rooted in a vision of communal shalom-bringing can slowly chip away at established structures by sowing seeds of peace and justice, block by block. The work of reconciliation is always a long, painstaking process—often marked more by laborious perseverance than successful arrival—but it is remains an essential task of the people of God in the city.

The patient pursuit of these ideals works to cultivate the people of God into becoming the kind of peculiar, alternative community that the church is called to be in the city. An urban contextual theology of community must shape people into agents of reconciliation as a "sign, foretaste, agent, and instrument"[57] of the kingdom of God, where an already but not yet reality of reconciliation is underway. The church can only model this radically inclusive ministry of reconciliation when its deep conversion to the way of the kingdom is unreserved.

Community and Redistribution

Lastly, in an urban contextual theology, the economic dynamics of community in contexts of disparity require a commitment to redistribution. Few economic ideas are as controversial and inflammatory as language of "redistribution" in a thoroughly capitalistic society. The mere suggestion that we should consider such "socialist" practices often raises suspicion about the "sinister agenda" of "Marxism" and "communism."[58]

---

proclaims that the Galatians should leave their present anxieties—contingently, about traditional Jewish practices—behind" (Gunton, *Theology of Reconciliation*, 62), and hence the traditional cultural boundaries that defined Jewish life had been redefined by the grace of baptism into Christ.

57. Guder and Barrett, *Missional Church*.

58. I've qualified these ideologies with quotation marks simply because the most common notions of these philosophies are often rife with mischaracterizations. As an economic principle, various forms of redistribution are common in most democratic societies. See Pafovano, *Politics and Economics of Regional Transfers*.

Must the church, in order to become a "contrast community," embrace the ideals of socialism?

Modern economic theory aside, if the church is going to be a community both *for* and *with* its neighbors in the urban context, then it must consider models of economic redistribution that work toward both love and service of neighbor, *and* care and concern for the poor. These dual commitments must be held together. Unless the church is able to truly see the poor as neighbors to whom we are accountable, the people of God will not understand the heart of the Prophets and the importance of economic justice for the marginalized[59] in the eyes of God. Until the church is willing to see "poverty as a scandalous condition,"[60] the people of God will not fully grasp the compassion of YHWH revealed in the righteous anger of Amos, the indignant admonitions of Isaiah, and the somber lament of Jeremiah.

To be a Christian community of redistribution is not to blindly adhere to human models of economics that preclude private ownership or wield an authoritarian rule. Rather, to be a Christian community of redistribution is to seek the heart of God in the fair and equitable treatment of the poor so that the whole people of God, and not just those with economic means, will be able to live under the gracious care of a generous, reconciling God. The church must model this kind of community, especially in the urban context, where the exploitative market forces of gentrification and unrestrained capitalism too often run rampant, trampling on the poor.

A steadfast devotion to radical economic justice is perhaps the most prophetic and countercultural commitment the church can make in an age of unbounded hyper-consumerism. Becoming a community of redistribution flies in the face of a society where cutthroat social Darwinism, left to its own devices, would have us all chasing after *The Wealth of Nations*[61] at any cost. Moreover, Christian redistribution is not

59. As the second chapter references, the Old Testament prophetic tradition is particularly interested in the "holy triad" of the "orphan, widow, and foreigner."

60. Gutiérrez, *Theology of Liberation*, 291

61. My rhetorical critique of Adam Smith's foundational treatise on free market economics is not intended to be a specific analysis of economic policy. Rather, I am attempting to offer an alternative view of the rarely-criticized principles of capitalism, which function so well at generating wealth primarily because they capitalize on the human capacity for greed in the face of manufactured perception of scarcity. Marx is merely one prominent example of such a critique; see Oakley, *Marx's Critique of Political Economy*.

simply about taking resources from the "hardworking haves" and giving them to the "nonworking have-nots;" quite to the contrary, it *is* about sharing what we have been entrusted as stewards and giving back "to God what is God's."[62]

Overall, an urban contextual theology's communal commitment to proximity, reconciliation, and redistribution shapes the Christian identity of the church in a way that gifts the urban context with transformed people who are instruments of healing and restoration in the city. By participating in God's redemptive narrative to call all of creation unto Himself, a church that is persistent and holistic in its dedication to these contextual theologies will fulfill its prophetic vocation by living into the task to "nurture, nourish, and evoke a consciousness and perception alternative to the consciousness and perception of the world around us."[63]

The city—as a particular place of density, diversity, and disparity—is in need of communities of faith that are willing to embrace this alternative vocation of the church in the world. It is a calling that must always resist the comfortable domestication of cultural accommodation in order to model in its life and witness a unique way of being a called and sent people. The urban church must remember that "Christianity entered history as a new social order, or rather a new social dimension. From the very beginning Christianity was not primarily a 'doctrine,' but exactly a 'community.' There was not only a 'Message' to be proclaimed and delivered, and 'Good News' to be declared. There was precisely a New Community, distinct and peculiar, in the process of growth and formation, to which members were called and recruited. Indeed, 'fellowship' was the basic category of Christian existence."[64] So it is to this fellowship of believers that the task of contextualization in the city is left. And if the congregation is truly a "hermeneutic of the gospel,"[65] then the power of this gospel should transform the church into a sign of the kingdom of God in the city.

---

62. Mark 12:13–17.

63. Brueggemann, *Prophetic Imagination*, 4.

64. Florovsky, *Christianity and Culture*, 19.

65. Newbigin, *Gospel in a Pluralist Society*.

THE VALLEY AND THE CORNER REVISITED

In order to construct an urban contextual theology that is committed to a critical understanding of the cultural and theological implications of the Valley and the Corner, it is necessary to examine the process of contextualization, both locally and universally. Based on a multifaceted understanding of culture, semiotic description of culture is an interdisciplinary method well suited to evaluating the meaning of the urban context. Balancing the systematic model of location, definition, interpretation, and categorization with the narrative and metaphorical approach of thick description provides a method of interpreting the many street signs in the city.

Applying this method of semiotic description to the urban context interprets the city as a place of density, diversity, and disparity, which function respectively as overlapping and interlocking semiotic domains of physical, social, and economic meaning. Through locating and defining cultural texts, and then interpreting their messages in context, the signs of the city work together to construct the complex meaning of the urban environment in all of its various settings.

Finally, by synthesizing the process of contextualization with semiotic description of the urban context, an urban contextual theology develops with an emphasis on the issues of place, neighboring, and community in the city. As these issues engage the harsh realities of physical density, social diversity, and economic disparity, the foundational components of an urban contextual theology are seeking to be faithful to both the lived experience of urban dwellers and the message of hope in the gospel.

Though the lens of contextual theology has focused primarily on the universality of the Corner, it has done so through the themes of locality in the Valley and both lenses are in turn connected to the first lens of cultural engagement. In this regard, the dialectical dependencies between the lenses are apparent. Understanding the Valley through urban exegesis illuminates the contextual theology of the Corner, and the urban contextual theology of the Corner mutually informs an urban exegesis of the Valley. Further, both the locality and the universality of the city are shaped by the missional theology of cultural engagement in the first lens, and the hermeneutic circle continues.

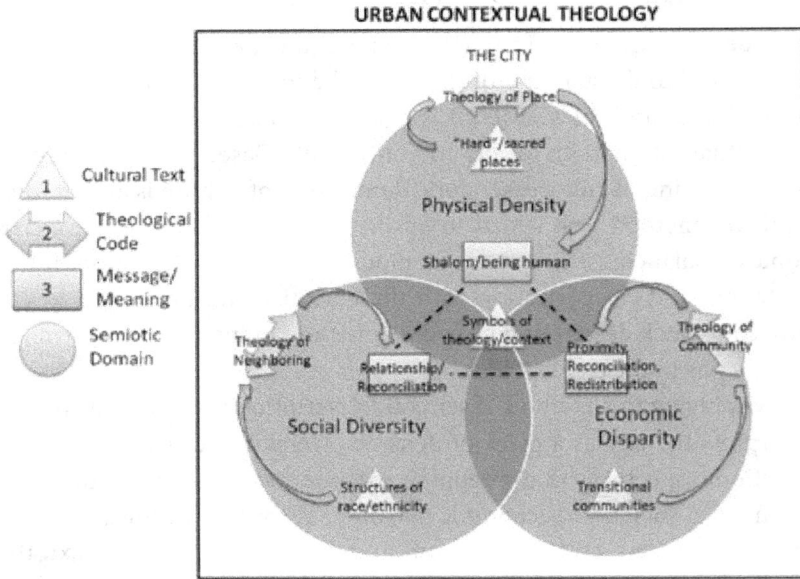

FIGURE 3: Urban Contextual Theology[66]

66. In moving from a semiotic model of the urban context to an urban contextual theology, the shift in this third diagram is that the regulatory codes become "theological codes," which produce different kinds of meaning in the city. Each of the three diagrams provides a different lens for observing and interpreting the urban context.

Conclusion

The Church Engaging the City

THE CHURCH, WHETHER EXPRESSED as the universal body of Christ or the particular urban congregation, consistently plays a central role in the praxis of this overall missional theology of urban cultural engagement. This research began by exploring some of the complexities between urbanism and contextualization, and though both the characteristics of the urban context and the various missiological challenges of contextualization have been examined to some degree of specificity, some questions remain. This conclusion will draw together the themes and findings of an urban exegesis of the Rainier Valley and an urban contextual theology, but it will do so with the aim of connecting the research to the life, witness, and community of the church as a tangible "hermeneutic of the gospel"[1] in the city.

THE VALLEY AND THE CORNER IN DIALOGUE

The various street signs present in the particular locality of the Valley and broad universality of the Corner have been contextual dialogue partners throughout this research. The recurring missional loci of incarnation, confrontation, and imagination infuse the practices of place-making, neighborly justice, and communal redistribution with a local theology that is contextual to the Valley, conversant with Christian tradition, and yet applicable and relevant far beyond the Valley's physical boundaries.

As a sign of the multivalent meaning in the urban context, the Corner continues to shape urban communities as a powerful symbol of life in the city. The Corner is a geographic but metaphysical space; simultaneously an ordinary object of the built environment and an abstract place of significance loaded with rich coded messages of cultural

---

1. Newbigin, *Gospel in a Pluralist Society*.

history and social identity. As a means to interpret this complex meaning theologically, the urban contextual theology developed here engages signs of density, diversity, and disparity in the city with urban theological reflections on place, neighboring, and community.

As the contextual transition is made from the particularity of the Rainier Valley's urban community to the broad urban setting of the city, the method of theological engagement shifts from urban exegesis, which develops a local, missional perspective on reading the urban neighborhood as a text, to a more universal urban contextual theology. This dynamic process of dialectical reflection between the neighborhood and the city is representative of the kind of contextual interaction that the Valley and the Corner typology is intended to signify.

As a thread that runs in and through this conversation, the presence of the church as a reconciled, covenant community in the city is a foundational component to ensuring that a missional theology of urban cultural engagement can actually become realized on the ground at the street level. The transition from theological conversation and ideology to missiological contextualization and praxis is always a difficult process, and as is so often the case, the viability of its success rests squarely on the life and witness of the church as a community of people "on the Way."

URBAN MISSIONAL ECCLESIOLOGY: A WAY FORWARD

Given this missional responsibility of embodying this theology of cultural engagement in the city, what does an urban, missional *ecclesiology* look like? Without entering into a robust, systematic discussion of the urban church's self-understanding, congregational polity, sacramental identity, and theological mission, as a starting point for reflection on a way forward into potential areas for further research, there are a few simple propositions that arise from the shape and character of this research.

First, a missional church in the city must think *incarnationally* about its place and presence in the community. A local neighborhood is both an asset to be organized and utilized, and a mission field to be loved and served in the process. This ideal is much easier said than done, and though helpful to some degree, innovative programs and well-funded community initiatives cannot replace the important role of deep, intentional reflection on the *theological* significance (and not just the logistical implications) of local parish models of ministry. How can a ministry of *presence* also inherently become a message of *proclamation*? To consider returning to a parish mentality in communal practice, leadership development, and resource allocation will require a radical reformulation of ecclesiological identity for those who have been indoctrinated with a "bigger is better" philosophy of attractional, institutional ecclesiologies that often tend to commodify and commercialize churches into "vendors of religious services and goods."[2] Instead of consumer-driven models of accumulation, an incarnational ecclesiology must take seriously the kenotic and downwardly mobile socioeconomic trajectory of the good news that the Word became flesh.

Rainier Avenue Church (RAC), an established congregation in the Rainier Valley, has—as its name suggests—taken this incarnational ethic to heart in its mission to "encourage everyone in the Rainier Valley to find wholeness in Jesus Christ."[3] With a long history in the neighborhood and more than three quarters of its congregation living in the Valley, the emphasis on embodying a strong local presence in the community has catalyzed a variety of urban partnerships, from the Coalition for Community Development and Renewal and the Rainier Chamber of Commerce to Urban Impact, RAC's own ministry of community development in the Valley that operates in partnership with another local church, Emerald City Bible Fellowship (ECBF). RAC's commitment to the neighborhood is also expressed in their desire to represent the vast cultural diversity of the Valley in all areas of the church. With an ongoing ministry of racial and ethnic reconciliation, RAC's diverse congregation is constantly working at developing its intercultural competencies as a welcoming, inclusive, multiethnic church. It is important to note that these incarnational considerations are rarely functions of a rigid, strategic program of "community outreach." Rather, they are birthed in

2. Guder and Barrett, *Missional Church*, 84. It should be stated that size and institutionalization are not inherently problematic categories of an established congregation's ecclesiology. Many mega-churches do remarkably genuine and generous work in the city, and their important contribution to the larger network of the body of Christ is significant and should continue. Nevertheless, size and institutionalization do have costs as they have the potential to pose a risk to the church's dynamic missionality in the urban context. Certainly not every church is "called" to embrace an exclusively rigid parish model of ministry, but a resurgence of interest in missional, incarnational ecclesiology must not ignore the subtle and often powerful influences of size and institutionalization on the church's vocation to mission, both broadly and in the urban context.

3. RAC is a Free Methodist church that was founded in 1904 on the corner of Rainier Avenue South and South Juneau Street.

relationship and grow organically out of RAC's fundamentally communal identity as a church that is *in, with,* and *for* the neighborhood.

Second, a missional church in the city must *act in prophetic confrontation* to embody a biblical, social justice that serves the fatherless, the single mother, and the immigrant. An urban congregation must have the ability to summon its theological and political will to act in continuity with the prophetic tradition that sought to care for the disenfranchised by bringing them from the margins to the center. This confrontational action is only truly prophetic when it holds criticizing and energizing in tension, a balancing act of dismantling the imperial consciousness while also nurturing an alternative vision of *shalom* in society.[4] Socially, the missional church in the city cannot accomplish this task or embody this ministry as a partial amalgamation of disjointed, autonomous individuals. Quite to the contrary, an urban church seeking to act in society with prophetic confrontation will by necessity have to embrace its collective identity as a *contrast community.* For the church, the power and efficacy of prophetic ministry is never isolated in the loud voice or strong convictions of a charismatic individual; rather, it is always rooted in the fellowship of believers who are empowered by the Spirit to proclaim an alternative reality in the kingdom of God. In all of its prophetic confrontation, this community is always a called and sent people. Simply stated, theologian Stanley Hauerwas reminds us that "Rauschenbusch rightly insisted that the Church does not exist for herself, but rather for the transformation of the world. To proclaim the kingdom of God therefore demands that Christians never forget we have been called from the world to be of service to the world."[5] As a believer in the importance of a social gospel,[6] Walter Rauschenbusch, along with the classic creed of

---

4. Brueggemann, *Prophetic Imagination.*

5. Rauschenbusch, *Christianity and the Social Crisis,* 175.

6. The Social Gospel Movement of the early twentieth century has too often been written off as a reaction of liberal Protestantism against the growing emphasis among fundamentalists on individual responsibility and personal salvation. "Conservative" theological traditions in general and evangelicalism in particular have frequently aligned themselves with the critics of the social gospel as a liberal distortion of Christianity. This polarization has been detrimental to the church's understanding of the holistic nature of the gospel itself, something that Rauschenbusch and Wesley understood quite well. See Sider, *Good News and Good Works;* and Rauschenbusch, *Christianity and the Social Crisis.*

John Wesley, affirms that "the Gospel of Christ knows of no religion, but social; no holiness but social holiness."[7]

Emerald City Bible Fellowship (ECBF), a church just down the road about a mile from RAC on Rainier Avenue South, is another urban congregation that is acting in prophetic engagement with its context in the Rainier Valley. As the other church partner in the collaborative ministry of Urban Impact, ECBF has always shared a sense of responsibility and accountability to its immediate neighborhood of Rainier Beach, a culturally and socioeconomically diverse community on the southern end of the Valley. Places like Rainier Beach need much more than charity and service; benevolence or magnanimity at a distance—no matter how "outward" its focus—is simply not missional. ECBF's concern for social justice and community development has been a part of its DNA from the beginning, and their ministries have always reflected these priorities. With a building that was designed for the church as a multipurpose community center, ECBF houses the staff of Urban Impact on a campus that serves as a hub for Christian community development in the neighborhood. Rainier Health & Fitness, a social venture project of Urban Impact, is an on-site gym that was started out of a desire to serve under-resourced neighbors with a high-quality, affordable fitness center that could also address holistic issues of health like diet, nutrition, and access to healthcare. The vision was "to start a gym with affordable rates that would encourage residents from different backgrounds to socialize and exercise regularly, combating obesity and diabetes—diseases that disproportionately afflict the poor and minorities."[8] In order to dismantle the structural inequities that perpetuate poor health in poor communities, ECBF and Urban Impact saw the opportunity to energize a neighborhood around an alternative vision of holistic well-being where the resources and burdens of some could be shared by all for the greater good.[9] These kinds of relationship-building efforts in the com-

---

7. Wesley, *Works of the John Wesley*, 593.

8. Bhatt, "Expanded Gym in Rainier Valley."

9. Rainier Health & Fitness subsidizes the sliding-scale rates of lower-income members with the fees of other members, and still manages to keep prices for all far below the membership costs of most other comparable facilities. Other innovative programs like "Ladies Night" allow gender-specific workout times that attract the many Muslim women in the community who cannot exercise in the presence of men. RHF is also currently in the process of starting a high-quality, full-service community health clinic alongside the gym, run by medical professionals affiliated with RAC and Urban Impact.

munity give ECBF and its faith-based partners a missional credibility in
a diverse neighborhood to facilitate further Christian community development, interfaith dialogue, and coalition building among the Valley's
many different people groups.

Third, a missional church in the city must live with an *imaginative
generosity* to mobilize and utilize its resources for the work of the kingdom in the community. If the life of the early church is any indication,
the apostolic witness to the risen Christ was made most evident in the
communal praxis of teaching, fellowship, sacrament, and prayer.

> Acts 2: Life among the Believers
>
> [42] They devoted themselves to the apostles' teaching and fellow-
> ship, to the breaking of bread and the prayers. [43] Awe came upon
> everyone, because many wonders and signs were being done by
> the apostles. [44] All who believed were together and had all things
> in common; [45] they would sell their possessions and goods and
> distribute the proceeds to all, as any had need. [46] Day by day, as
> they spent much time together in the temple, they broke bread at
> home and ate their food with glad and generous hearts, [47] prais-
> ing God and having the goodwill of all the people. And day by
> day the Lord added to their number those who were being saved.

The common familiarity of this text often masks its radical message
with a diluted ecclesiology that is fixated on what frequently amounts to
little more than parsing liturgical order or prioritizing church activities
structurally. But sandwiched in between the content and experience of
their worship commitments in verses 42–43 and the celebratory fellowship and evangelistic success of verses 46–47 is a fairly radical demonstration of their economic interdependence as a community in verses
44–45. Because of their common belief that they "were of one heart and
soul,"[10] "no one was claiming any exclusive right to whatever property
he or she had, and when need arose the early Christians readily liqui-
dated what assets they had to take care of fellow believers' needs."[11] In
a community with many needs, one can speculate that creativity was
regularly needed to ensure the just redistribution of resources. But
what is most striking about this practice among early believers is that it
was completely integrated with their life as a worshipping community.

---

10. This phrase comes from Acts 4:32, which further elucidates this common practice in the early church of sharing possessions among believers.

11. Witherington, *Acts of the Apostles*, 162.

Mobilizing resources for the poor was not a "good deed" for the well-to-do members of the church. Rather, it was a natural, reflexive outpouring of compassion and solidarity that was rooted in their understanding that they shared a singularly focused heart and soul that had been converted to the way of the kingdom. As the Spirit moved among them, a radical, contagious generosity enabled a mutual interdependency that resulted in many "glad and generous hearts" (v. 47) in the community of faith.

Bethany United Church of Christ (BUCC), "a Christian community growing in faith to seek justice, love kindness and walk humbly with God,"[12] is another multicultural, multigenerational congregation near Rainier Valley that has taken seriously its mission to love and serve the community through creative means of utilizing its resources for the neighborhood. With a corner property at the intersection of Beacon Avenue and Graham Street, BUCC has a number of community initiatives that range from partnerships with the Seattle Food Bank and the Refugee Women's Alliance to an on-site pre-school that houses a Head Start/ECEAP[13] program. In addition to sharing its property with these community organizations, BUCC also runs many of its own projects, which include an organic community garden and Bethany House, a transitional home for resettled refugees and recent immigrants in need of assistance. These local programs allow Bethany to live out its Micah 6:8 values of justice, kindness, and humility, while also reflecting a generous communal stewardship of the land and resources that this relatively small[14] congregation has been entrusted. That such a humble church of little means[15] can organize, facilitate, and sustain such a large number of relationships and initiatives in the neighborhood is a tribute to their imaginative generosity as a congregation that never turns away a person in need.

12. BUCC is on South Beacon Hill just west of Rainier Valley. Its congregation was part of a church revitalization effort led by Rev. Angela Ying, the first ordained Taiwanese-American minister in the U.S.

13. ECEAP is the Early Childhood Education and Assistance Program of the Washington State Department of Early Learning. ECEAP provides free educational support services and comprehensive pre-school programs for low-income children and families.

14. BUCC's weekly attendance ranges from 100 to 140 adults, not including the Samoan and African American congregations that share the facility.

15. This is a relative statement, but South Beacon Hill, along with the socioeconomic diversity in the church that is representative of the area, is far from wealthy.

These three markers of an urban, missional ecclesiology—incarnational presence in the neighborhood, prophetic action for justice as a community, and imaginative mobilization of resources for the kingdom—share much in common as the church seeks to live out its faith in the urban context. As a place of physical density, social diversity, and economic disparity, the city poses many challenges to the contextualization of the gospel. However, the good news of a missional theology of urban cultural engagement in the hands of a faithful congregation is that these structural divides can be reconciled in Christ by removing the boundaries we ourselves have constructed in the city. As we continue to read the street signs on the Corner and incarnate places like the Valley, may the church live into its calling as a people of embodied faith, prophetic hope, and subversive love.

Bibliography

ABT Associates, Linda Fosburg, Susan Popkin, and Gretchen Locke. "An Historical and Baseline Assessmentof Hope VI." Prepared for the U.S. Department of Housing and Urban Development, Office of Policy Development and Research. July 1996. Washington, DC: DHUD, 1996.

Adam, A. K. M. "New Horizons in Hermeneutics: The Theory and Practice of Transforming Biblical Reading." *Modern Theology* 10/4 (1994) 433–34.

Adelman, Larry, creator, executive producer. "Race—the Power of an Illusion." TV series. 3 episodes. California Newsreel, 2003.

Adeney, Miriam. *Kingdom without Borders: The Untold Story of Global Christianity.* Downers Grove, IL: InterVarsity, 2009.

Allen, Leslie C. *Jeremiah: A Commentary.* Old Testament Library. Louisville: Westminster John Knox, 2008.

Amara, Fadela, with Sylvia Zappi. *Breaking the Silence: French Women's Voices from the Ghetto.* Translated by Helen Harden Chenut. Berkeley: University of California Press, 2006.

Anderson, Elijah. *Code of the Street: Decency, Violence, and the Moral Life of the Inner City.* New York: Norton, 1999.

———. *A Place on the Corner.* Studies in Urban Society. Chicago: University of Chicago Press, 1978.

———. *Streetwise: Race, Class, and Change in an Urban Community.* Chicago: University of Chicago Press, 1990.

Athanasius, Saint. *On the Incarnation: The Treatise De Incarnatione Verbi Dei.* Translated and edited by Penelope Lawson. New York: Macmillan, 1946.

Atkinson, Rowland, and Gary Bridge, editors. *Gentrification in a Global Context: The New Urban Colonialism.* Housing and Society Series. New York: Routledge, 2005.

Augustine, Saint. *Concerning the City of God against the Pagans.* Translated by Henry Bettenson. New York: Penguin, 1984.

Baerny, Sharon. "From Blight to All Right." *Planning* 70/8 (2004) 24–27.

Bakke, Raymond J. *A Theology as Big as the City.* Downers Grove, IL: InterVarsity, 1997.

Bakke, Raymond J., and Jim Hart. *The Urban Christian: Effective Ministry in Today's Urban World.* Downers Grove, IL: InterVarsity, 1987.

Bakke, Raymond J., and Jon Sharpe. *Street Signs: A New Direction in Urban Ministry.* Birmingham, AL: New Hope, 2006.

Banks, Marcus. *Ethnicity: Anthropological Constructions.* New York: Routledge, 1996.

Baofu, Peter. *The Future of Post-Human Urban Planning: A Preface to a New Theory of Density, Void, and Sustainability.* Newcastle: Cambridge Scholars, 2009.

Bardhan, Pranab K. *Scarcity, Conflicts, and Cooperation: Essays in the Political and Institutional Economics of Development.* Cambridge, MA: MIT Press, 2005.

Barrera, Albino. *God and the Evil of Scarcity: Moral Foundations of Economic Agency.* Notre Dame, IN: University of Notre Dame Press, 2005.

Barrett, C. K. *The Gospel according to St. John: An Introduction with Commentary and Notes on the Greek Text.* 2nd ed. Philadelphia: Westminster, 1978.

Barth, Karl. *Church Dogmatics.* Vol. 4, *The Doctrine of Reconciliation.* Translated and edited by G. W. Bromiley. London: T. & T. Clark, 2004.

Barthes, Roland. "Semiology and the Urban." In *Rethinking Architecture: A Reader in Cultural Theory,* edited by Neil Leach, 165–72. New York: Routledge, 1997.

Beiser, Frederick C., editor. *The Cambridge Companion to Hegel.* New York: Cambridge University Press, 1993.

Benjamin, Rich. *Searching for Whitopia: An Improbable Journey to the Heart of White America.* New York: Hyperion, 2009.

Bennett, Larry, Janet L. Smith, and Patricia A. Wright, editors. *Where Are Poor People to Live?: Transforming Public Housing Communities.* Cities and Contemporary Society. Armonk, NY: M.E. Sharpe, 2006.

Berger, Peter L., and Thomas Luckmann. *The Social Construction of Reality: A Treatise in the Sociology of Knowledge.* Garden City, NY: Anchor, 1967.

Berkhof, Louis. *Systematic Theology.* 2nd ed. Grand Rapids: Eerdmans, 1941.

Berkovits, Eliezer. *Essential Essays on Judaism.* Edited by David Hazony. Jerusalem: Shalem, 2002.

Berry, Wendell. *Given: New Poems.* Washington, DC: Shoemaker & Hoard, 2005.

———. *Sex, Economy, Freedom, and Community: Eight Essays.* New York: Pantheon, 1993.

Bessenecker, Scott. *The New Friars: The Emerging Movement Serving the World's Poor.* Downers Grove, IL: InterVarsity, 2006.

Bevans, Stephen B. *Models of Contextual Theology.* Rev. ed. Faith and Cultures Series. Maryknoll, NY: Orbis, 2002.

Bhatt, Sanjay. "Expanded Gym in Rainier Valley Fulfills Big Dream." *Seattle Times,* March 4, 2007.

Birch, Eugenie Ladner, and Susan M. Wachter, editors. *Rebuilding Urban Places after Disaster: Lessons from Hurricane Katrina.* The City in the Twenty-First Century. Philadelphia: University of Pennsylvania Press, 2006.

Blakely, Edward James, and Mary Gail Snyder. *Fortress America: Gated Communities in the United States.* Washington, DC: Brookings Institution, 1997.

Blitz, Lisa V., and Greene Mary Pender, editors. *Racism and Racial Identity: Reflections on Urban Practice in Mental Health and Social Services.* New York: Haworth Maltreatment & Trauma Press, 2006.

Bonhoeffer, Dietrich. *The Cost of Discipleship.* Translated by R. H. Fuller. Rev. New York: Macmillan, 1959.

———. *A Testament to Freedom: The Essential Writings of Dietrich Bonhoeffer.* Edited by Geffrey B. Kelly and Nelson F. Burton. San Francisco: HarperSanFrancisco, 1990.

Boring, M. Eugene. *Mark: A Commentary.* New Testament Library. Louisville,: Westminster John Knox, 2006.

Bosch, David Jacobus. *Believing in the Future: Toward a Missiology of Western Culture.* Christian Mission and Modern Culture. Valley Forge, PA: Trinity, 1995.

———. *Transforming Mission: Paradigm Shifts in Theology of Mission.* AMSMS 16. Maryknoll, NY: Orbis, 1991.

———. *Witness to the World: The Christian Mission in Theological Perspective,* New Foundations Theological Library. Atlanta: John Knox, 1980.

Bouma-Prediger, Steven, and Brian J. Walsh. *Beyond Homelessness: Christian Faith in a Culture of Displacement*. Grand Rapids: Eerdmans, 2008.

Boyce, Ron. "A Note on How to Exegete Cities." Paper presented at Bakke Graduate University's Seattle Overture, 2008.

Boyd, Gregory A. *The Myth of a Christian Nation: How the Quest for Political Power Is Destroying the Church*. Grand Rapids: Zondervan, 2005.

Brueggemann, Walter. *The Church in Joyous Obedience: Biblical Expositions*. Laing Lectures 2008. Audio recording. Vancouver, BC: Regent College, 2008.

———. *A Commentary on Jeremiah: Exile and Homecoming*. Grand Rapid: Eerdmans, 1998.

———. *Hopeful Imagination: Prophetic Voices in Exile*. Philadelphia: Fortress, 1986.

———. *The Prophetic Imagination*. Philadelphia: Fortress, 1978.

———. *Theology of the Old Testament: Testimony, Dispute, Advocacy*. Minneapolis: Fortress, 1997.

Bryant, David J. *Faith and the Play of Imagination: On the Role of Imagination in Religion*. Studies in American Biblical Hermeneutics 5. Macon, GA: Mercer, 1989.

Byassee, Jason. "The New Monastics: Alternative Christian Communities." *Christian Century* 122/21 (2005) 38–47.

Carter, J. Kameron. *Race: A Theological Account*. New York: Oxford University Press, 2008.

Cashin, Sheryll. *The Failures of Integration: How Race and Class Are Undermining the American Dream*. New York: Public Affairs, 2004.

Chambers, Iain. *Migrancy, Culture, Identity*. London: Routledge, 1994.

Childs, Brevard S. *Isaiah*. Old Testament Library. Louisville: Westminster John Knox, 2001.

Chung, Paul S. *Karl Barth: God's Word in Action*. Eugene, OR: Cascade, 2008.

Claerbaut, David. *Urban Ministry in a New Millennium*. Rev. ed. Waynesboro, GA: Authentic Media; Federal Way, WA: World Vision, 2005.

Clapp, Rodney. *A Peculiar People: The Church as Culture in a Post-Christian Society*. Downers Grove, IL: InterVarsity, 1996.

Clay, Grady. *Close-Up. How to Read the American City*. New York: Praeger, 1974.

Cohen, Aubrey. "Columbia Plaza Plan Environmental Review Approved." *Seattle Post-Intelligencer*, June 29, 2009.

———. "Developer Buys Columbia City Plaza." *Seattle Post-Intelligencer*, June 19, 2007.

Cone, James H. *God of the Oppressed*. Rev. ed. Maryknoll, NY: Orbis, 1997.

Conn, Harvie M. *The American City and the Evangelical Church: A Historical Overview*. Grand Rapids: Baker, 1994.

Conn, Harvie M., and Manuel Ortiz. *Urban Ministry: The Kingdom, the City, & the People of God*. Downers Grove, IL: InterVarsity, 2001.

Cox, Harvey G. "The Secular City 25 Years Later." *Christian Century* 107/32 (1990) 1025–29.

Craigie, Peter C. *The Book of Deuteronomy*. New International Commentary on the Old Testament. Grand Rapids: Eerdmans, 1976.

Crowley, Walt. "Seattle Renton & Southern Railway: King County's First True Interurban." *History Link*, February 24, 1997. Online: http://www.historylink.org/_content/printer_friendly/pf_output.cfm?file_id=1756.

Cummings, Michael S. *Beyond Political Correctness: Social Transformation in the United States*. Transformation in Politics and Society. Boulder, CO: L. Rienner, 2001.

Davila, Florangela. "MLK Way." *Seattle Times*, July 29, 2005.

Davis, Ellen F. "The Holiness of Place." *Faith and Leadership: Leadership Education at Duke Divinity.* Online: http://www.faithandleadership.com/content/the-holiness-place.

Dawe, Donald G. *The Form of a Servant: A Historical Analysis of the Kenotic Motif.* Philadelphia: Westminster, 1963.

De Gruchy, John W. *Reconciliation: Restoring Justice.* Minneapolis: Fortress, 2002.

De Mesa, José M. *Why Theology Is Never Far from Home.* Manila, Philippines: De La Salle University Press, 2003.

De Souza Briggs, Xavier. *The Geography of Opportunity: Race and Housing Choice in Metropolitan America.* James A. Johnson Metro Series. Washington, DC: Brookings Institution, 2005.

Design Build-Network. "Beijing National Stadium: The Bird's Nest." *Design Build-Network Projects.* Online: http://www.designbuild-network.com/projects/national_stadium/.

DeYoung, Curtiss Paul. *United by Faith: The Multiracial Congregation as an Answer to the Problem of Race.* New York: Oxford University Press, 2003.

Diers, Jim. *Neighbor Power: Building Community the Seattle Way.* Seattle: University of Washington Press, 2004.

Dietterich, Inagrace Thoms. *Cultivating Missional Communities.* Eugene, OR: Wipf & Stock, 2006.

Driscoll, Mark. *On Church Leadership*, Wheaton, IL: Crossway, 2008.

Duany, Andres, Elizabeth Plater-Zyberk, and Jeff Speck. *Suburban Nation: The Rise of Sprawl and the Decline of the American Dream.* New York: North Point, 2000.

Dyrness, William A., and Veli-Matti Kärkkäinen. *Global Dictionary of Theology: A Resource for the Worldwide Church.* Downers Grove, IL: InterVarsity Academic, 2008.

Eco, Umberto. *Semiotics and the Philosophy of Language.* Advances in Semiotics. Bloomington: Indiana University Press, 1984.

———. *A Theory of Semiotics*, Advances in Semiotics. Bloomington: Indiana University Press, 1976.

Ehrenreich, Barbara. *This Land Is Their Land: Reports from a Divided Nation.* New York: Metropolitan, 2008.

Eichrodt, Walther, and J. A. Baker. *Theology of the Old Testament.* Old Testament Library. Philadelphia: Westminster, 1961.

Eliot, T. S. *Christianity and Culture: The Idea of a Christian Society and Notes Towards the Definition of Culture.* New York: Harcourt, Brace, 1960.

Ellis, Marc H. *A Year at the Catholic Worker: A Spiritual Journey among the Poor.* Waco, TX: Baylor University Press, 2000.

Ellul, Jacques. *The Meaning of the City.* Translated by Dennis Pardee. Grand Rapids: Eerdmans, 1970.

———. *The Subversion of Christianity.* Translated by G. W. Bromiley. Grand Rapids: Eerdmans, 1986.

Emerson, Michael O., and Christian Smith. *Divided by Faith: Evangelical Religion and the Problem of Race in America.* New York: Oxford University Press, 2000.

Evans, C. Stephen. *Exploring Kenotic Christology: The Self-Emptying of God.* New York: Oxford University Press, 2006.

Fan, C. Cindy. *China on the Move: Migration, the State, and the Household.* Routledge Studies in Human Geography 21. New York: Routledge, 2008.

Farmer, Paul. *Pathologies of Power: Health, Human Rights, and the New War on the Poor.* California Series in Public Anthropology 4. Berkeley: University of California Press, 2005.

Farr, Douglas. *Sustainable Urbanism: Urban Design with Nature.* Hoboken, NJ: Wiley, 2008.

Fee, Gordon D. *New Testament Exegesis: A Handbook for Students and Pastors.* Rev. ed. Louisville: Westminster John Knox, 1993.

Finger, Thomas N. *A Contemporary Anabaptist Theology: Biblical, Historical, Constructive.* Downers Grove, IL: InterVarsity, 2004.

Florovsky, Georges. *Christianity and Culture,* Collected Works of Georges Florovsky 2. Belmont: MA, Nordland, 1974.

Friedman, Avi. *Sustainable Residential Development: Planning and Design for Green Neighborhoods.* New York: McGraw-Hill, 2007.

Fukuyama, Francis. *America at the Crossroads: Democracy, Power, and the Neoconservative Legacy.* Castle Lectures in Ethics, Politics, and Economics. New Haven, CT: Yale University Press, 2006.

Gallagher, Charles A. *Rethinking the Color Line: Readings in Race and Ethnicity.* New York: McGraw-Hill, 2007.

Gates, E. Nathaniel. *Cultural and Literary Critiques of the Concepts of "Race."* Critical Race Theory 2. New York: Garland , 1997.

Geertz, Clifford. *The Interpretation of Cultures: Selected Essays.* New York: Basic, 1973.

———. "Thick Description: Towards an Interpretative Theory of Culture." *Enquête* 6/157 (1998) 73–105.

Gergen, Kenneth J. *An Invitation to Social Construction.* Thousand Oaks, CA: Sage, 1999.

Gerstenberger, Erhard. *Leviticus: A Commentary.* Old Testament Library. Louisville: Westminster John Knox, 1996.

Glasser, Arthur F., Charles Edward Van Engen, Dean S. Gilliland, and Shawn B. Redford. *Announcing the Kingdom: The Story of God's Mission in the Bible.* Grand Rapids: Baker Academic, 2003.

Goldsmith, Steven. "Mural's Beauty Is in Eyes of Beholders." *Seattle Post-Intelligencer,* August 30, 1994.

Gorman, Frank H. *Divine Presence and Community: A Commentary on the Book of Leviticus.* International Theological Commentary. Grand Rapids: Eerdmans, 1997.

Gorman, Michael J. *Inhabiting the Cruciform God: Kenosis, Justification, and Theosis in Paul's Narrative Soteriology.* Grand Rapids: Eerdmans, 2009.

Gornik, Mark R. *To Live in Peace: Biblical Faith and the Changing Inner City.* Grand Rapids: Eerdmans, 2002.

Gorringe, Timothy. *A Theology of the Built Environment: Justice, Empowerment, Redemption*: New York: Cambridge University Press, 2002.

Gottdiener, Mark, and Ray Hutchison. *The New Urban Sociology.* Boulder, CO: Westview, 2006.

Gottdiener, Mark, and Alexandros Ph Lagopoulos. *The City and the Sign: An Introduction to Urban Semiotics.* New York: Columbia University Press, 1986.

Gottdiener, Mark, and Budd Leslie. *Key Concepts in Urban Studies.* Thousand Oaks, CA: Sage, 2005.

Grange, Joseph. *The City: An Urban Cosmology.* Albany: State University of New York Press, 1999.

Green, Garrett. *Imagining God: Theology and the Religious Imagination*. San Francisco: Harper & Row, 1989.

Green, Joel B. *The Gospel of Luke*. New International Commentary on the New Testament. Grand Rapids: Eerdmans, 1997.

Greenway, Roger S., and Harvie M. Conn. *Discipling the City: Theological Reflections on Urban Mission*. Grand Rapids: Baker, 1979.

Greenway, Roger S., and Timothy M. Monsma. *Cities: Missions' New Frontier*. Grand Rapids: Baker, 1989.

Gries, Peter Hays. *China's New Nationalism: Pride, Politics, and Diplomacy*. Berkeley, CA: University of California Press, 2004.

Grusky, David B. *Social Stratification: Class, Race, and Gender in Sociological Perspective*. 2nd ed. Boulder, CO: Westview, 2001.

Guder, Darrell L. *The Continuing Conversion of the Church*. The Gospel and Our Culture Series. Grand Rapids: Eerdmans, 2000.

———. "God's Missionary People: Rethinking the Purpose of the Local Church." *International Bulletin of Missionary Research* 17/2 (1993) 80–80.

———. "Mission on the Way: Issues in Mission Theology." *International Bulletin of Missionary Research* 23/3 (1999) 136–37.

Guder, Darrell L., and Lois Barrett. *Missional Church: A Vision for the Sending of the Church in North America*. The Gospel and Our Culture Series. Grand Rapids: Eerdmans, 1998.

Gunton, Colin E., editor. *The Theology of Reconciliation*. London: T. & T. Clark, 2003.

Gutiérrez, Gustavo. *A Theology of Liberation: History, Politics, and Salvation. Translated and edited by Sister Caridad Inda and John Eagleson*. Maryknoll: NY, Orbis, 1973.

Hannerz, Ulf. *Exploring the City: Inquiries toward an Urban Anthropology*. New York: Columbia University Press, 1980.

Harvey, A. E., editor. *Theology in the City: A Theological Response to "Faith in the City"*. London: SPCK, 1989.

Hauerwas, Stanley, and William H. Willimon. *Resident Aliens: Life in the Christian Colony*. Nashville: Abingdon, 1989.

Hayden, Dolores. *The Power of Place: Urban Landscapes as Public History*. Cambridge, MA: MIT Press, 1995.

Hayes, John B., and Ashley Barker. *Sub-Merge: Living Deep in a Shallow World*. Ventura, CA: Regal, 2006.

Hedges, Chris. *American Fascists: The Christian Right and the War on America*: New York: Free Press, 2007.

Hellerman, Joseph H. *Reconstructing Honor in Roman Philippi: Carmen Christi as Cursus Pudorum*, Society for New Testament Studies Monograph Series 132. New York: Cambridge University Press, 2005.

Henry, Carl F. H., D. A. Carson, and John D. Woodbridge. *God and Culture: Essays in Honor of Carl F. H. Henry*. Grand Rapids: Eerdmans, 1993.

Herzfeld, Michael, editor. *Semiotic Theory and Practice: Proceedings of the Third International Congress of the IASS, Palermo, 1984*. Berlin: de Gruyter, 1988.

Hiebert, Paul G. *Anthropological Insights for Missionaries*. Grand Rapids: Baker, 1985.

———. *Anthropological Reflections on Missiological Issues*. Grand Rapids: Baker, 1994.

———. *Cultural Anthropology*. Philadelphia: Lippincott, 1976.

———. *Transforming Worldviews: An Anthropological Understanding of How People Change*. Grand Rapids: Baker Academic, 2008.

Higgins, John. *Raymond Williams: Literature, Marxism and Cultural Materialism*. Critics of the Twentieth Century. New York: Routledge, 1999.

Hirsch, Alan. "Defining Missional." *Leadership Journal* 29/4 (2008) n.p. Online: http://www.christianitytoday.com/le/2008/fall/17.20.html.

Hofstede, Geert H. *Cultures and Organizations: Software of the Mind*. Rev. ed. New York: McGraw-Hill, 2005.

Hoggart, Richard. *Contemporary Cultural Studies: An Approach to the Study of Literature and Society*. University Centre for Contemporary Cultural Studies, Occasional Paper 6. Birmingham, UK: University of Birmingham, 1969.

Hooker, Morna Dorothy. *The Gospel according to Saint Mark*, Black's New Testament Commentary. Peabody, MA: Hendrickson, 1991.

Hutchison, John Alexander. *Living Options in World Philosophy*. Honolulu: University Press of Hawaii, 1977.

Inge, John. *A Christian Theology of Place. Explorations in Practical, Pastoral, and Empirical Theology*. Burlington, VT: Ashgate, 2003.

Irarrázaval, Diego. *Inculturation: New Dawn of the Church in Latin America*. Faith and Cultures Series. Maryknoll, NY: Orbis, 2000.

Jacobs, Allan B. *Looking at Cities*. Cambridge, MA: Harvard University Press, 1985.

Jacobs, Jane. *The Death and Life of Great American Cities*. New York: Random House, 1961.

Jacobsen, Eric O. *Sidewalks in the Kingdom: New Urbanism and the Christian Faith*. The Christian Practice of Everyday Life. Grand Rapids: Brazos, 2003.

Jacoby, Tamar. *Reinventing the Melting Pot: The New Immigrants and What It Means to Be American*. New York: Basic, 2004.

Jamieson, Robert L. "A Violent Death in the Afternoon." *Seattle Post-Intelligencer*, April 6, 2007.

Jenkins, Philip. *The Next Christendom: The Coming of Global Christianity*. New York: Oxford University Press, 2002.

Jochnick, Chris, and Fraser A. Preston. *Sovereign Debt at the Crossroads: Challenges and Proposals for Resolving the Third World Debt Crisis*: New York: Oxford University Press, 2006.

Kahn, Charles H. *Plato and the Socratic Dialogue: The Philosophical Use of a Literary Form*. New York: Cambridge University Press, 1998.

Katongole, Emmanuel, and Chris Rice. *Reconciling All Things: A Christian Vision for Justice, Peace and Healing*. Downers Grove, IL: InterVarsity, 2008.

Kearney, Richard. *The Wake of Imagination: Ideas of Creativity in Western Culture*. London: Hutchinson, 1988.

Kraft, Charles H. *Anthropology for Christian Witness*. Maryknoll, NY: Orbis, 1996.

———. *Christianity in Culture: A Study in Dynamic Biblical Theologizing in Cross-Cultural Perspective*. Maryknoll, NY: Orbis, 1979.

———. *Culture, Communication, and Christianity: A Selection of Writings*. Pasadena, CA: William Carey Library, 2001.

———. *Worldview for Christian Witness*. Pasadena, CA: William Carey Library, 2008.

Kunstler, James Howard. *The Geography of Nowhere: The Rise and Decline of America's Man-Made Landscape*. New York: Simon & Schuster, 1993.

Langmead, Ross. *The Word Made Flesh: Towards an Incarnational Missiology*. Lanham, MD: University Press of America, 2004.

LaNoue, Deirdre. *The Spiritual Legacy of Henri Nouwen*. New York: Continuum, 2000.

Lawson, Tony, Ruth Moores, and Marsha Jones. *Advanced Sociology through Diagrams*. Oxford: Oxford University Press, 2000.

Lewis, Mike. "Angie's Keeps Columbia City's 'Essence' Alive as Area Changes." *Seattle Post-Intelligencer*, October 28, 2007.

Lienemann-Perrin, Christine, H. M. Vroom, and Michael Weinrich, editors. *Reformed and Ecumenical: On Being Reformed in Ecumenical Encounters*. Currents of Encounter 16. Amsterdam: Rodopi, 2000.

Lingenfelter, Sherwood G. *Transforming Culture: A Challenge for Christian Mission*. 2nd ed. Grand Rapids: Baker, 1998.

Linthicum, Robert C. *City of God, City of Satan: A Biblical Theology of the Urban Church*. Grand Rapids: Zondervan, 1991.

———. *Transforming Power: Biblical Strategies for Making a Difference in Your Community*. Downers Grove: InterVarsity, 2003.

Long, A. A. *Epictetus: A Stoic and Socratic Guide to Life*. New York: Oxford University Press, 2002.

Lovin, Robin W. *Reinhold Niebuhr and Christian Realism*. New York: Cambridge University Press, 1995.

Lupton, Robert. "Gentrification with Justice." *By Faith* 9 (June 2006) 19–24.

———. *Return Flight: Community Development through Reneighboring Our Cities*. Atlanta: FCS Urban Ministries, 1997.

———. "A Theology of Geography." *Urban Mission* 10/4 (1993) 60–61.

Luz, Ulrich. *The Theology of the Gospel of Matthew*. New Testament Theology. New York: Cambridge University Press, 1995.

Luzbetak, Louis J. *The Church and Cultures: An Applied Anthropology for the Religious Worker*. Techny: IL, Divine Word, 1963.

———. *The Church and Cultures: New Perspectives in Missiological Anthropology*. American Society of Missiology Series 12. Maryknoll, NY: Orbis, 1988.

Magesa, Laurenti. *Anatomy of Inculturation: Transforming the Church in Africa*. Maryknoll, NY: Orbis Books, 2004.

Markos, Louis A. "An Evening with Athanasius: Meditations on the Incarnation." *Theology Today* 62/2 (2005) 240–44.

Marquardt, Marie Friedmann. "Gods of the City: Religion and the American Urban Landscape." *Journal for the Scientific Study of Religion* 39/3 (2000) 391–92.

Marsden, George. *Reforming Fundamentalism: Fuller Seminary and the New Evangelicalism*. Grand Rapids: Eerdmans, 1987.

Marshall, I. Howard. *The Gospel of Luke: A Commentary on the Greek Text*. New International Greek Testament Commentary. Grand Rapids: Eerdmans, 1978.

Martin, Ralph P. *Carmen Christi: Philippians ii. 5–11 in Recent Interpretation and in the Setting of Early Christian Worship*. Society for New Testament Studies Monograph Series 4. London: Cambridge University Press, 1967.

Martin, William C. *With God on Our Side: The Rise of the Religious Right in America*. New York: Broadway, 1996.

Marty, Martin E. *The Christian World: A Global History*. Modern Library Chronicles 29. New York: Random House, 2007.

Massey, Douglas S., and Nancy A. Denton. *American Apartheid: Segregation and the Making of the Underclass*. Cambridge, MA: Harvard University Press, 1993.

Mata, Michael. "Entering the Community." In *Transforming the City: From Dream to Reality*, edited by International Urban Associates, 34–37. Chicago: Telchar Systems, 1994.

———. "Mailboxes, Stucco, and Graffiti." *Learning to Read and Assess the Story of an Urban Community*, 12–15. Claremont, CA: Claremont School of Theology, 1999.

Mayers, Marvin Keene. *Christianity Confronts Culture; a Strategy for Cross-Cultural Evangelism.* Contemporary Evangelical Perspectives. Grand Rapids: Zondervan, 1974.

McClure, Wendy R., and Tom J. Bartuska, editors. *The Built Environment: A Collaborative Inquiry into Design and Planning.* 2nd ed. Hoboken, NJ: Wiley & Sons, 2007.

McCurdy, David W., James P. Spradley, and Dianna J. Shandy. *The Cultural Experience: Ethnography in Complex Society.* Waveland, IN: Waveland, 2005.

McLuhan, Marshall. *Understanding Media: The Extensions of Man.* Edited by Gordon W. Terrence. Berkeley, CA: Gingko, 2003.

McNerthney, Casey. "City Targets South Seattle Bar for State Action." *Seattle Post-Intelligencer,* October 29, 2009.

Migliore, Daniel L. *Faith Seeking Understanding: An Introduction to Christian Theology.* Grand Rapids: Eerdmans, 1991.

Mitchell, Stacy. *Big-Box Swindle: The True Cost of Mega-Retailers and the Fight for America's Independent Businesses.* Boston: Beacon, 2006.

Moltmann, Jürgen. *The Church in the Power of the Spirit: A Contribution to Messianic Ecclesiology.* Translated by Margaret Kohl. New York: Harper, 1977.

Moore, William. *The Vertical Ghetto: Everyday Life in an Urban Project.* New York: Random House, 1969.

Moseley, James G. "Gods of the City: Religion and the American Urban Landscape." *Church History* 69/4 (2000) 943–44.

Murray, Harry. *Do Not Neglect Hospitality: The Catholic Worker and the Homeless.* Philadelphia: Temple University Press, 1990.

Neuhaus, Richard John, and Michael Cromartie, editors. *Piety and Politics: Evangelicals and Fundamentalists Confront the World.* Washington, DC: Ethics and Public Policy Center, 1987.

Newbigin, Lesslie. *Foolishness to the Greeks: The Gospel and Western Culture.* Grand Rapids: Eerdmans, 1986.

———. *The Gospel in a Pluralist Society.* Grand Rapids: Eerdmans; Geneva, WCC Publications, 1989.

———. *The Open Secret: An Introduction to the Theology of Mission.* Rev. ed. Grand Rapids: Eerdmans, 1995.

———. *The Other Side of 1984: Questions for the Churches.* The Risk Book Series 18. Geneva: World Council of Churches, 1983.

Niebuhr, H. Richard. *Christ and Culture.* New York: Harper, 1951.

Niebuhr, Reinhold. *Christian Realism and Political Problems.* New York: Scribner, 1953.

———. *Faith and Politics: A Commentary on Religious, Social, and Political Thought in a Technological Age.* Edited by Ronald H. Stone. New York: G. Braziller, 1968.

Noble, Trevor. *Social Theory and Social Change.* New York: St. Martin's, 2000.

Noll, Mark A. *The New Shape of World Christianity: How American Experience Reflects Global Faith.* Downers Grove, IL: InterVarsity, 2009.

Nöth, Winfried. *Handbook of Semiotics.* Advances in Semiotics. Bloomington: Indiana University Press, 1990.

Oakley, Allen. *Marx's Critique of Political Economy: Intellectual Sources and Evolution.* 2 vols. International Library of Economics. London: Law Book Co. of Australasia, 1984.

Oldenburg, Ray, editor. *Celebrating the Third Place: Inspiring Stories about the "Great Good Places" at the Heart of Our Communities.* New York: Marlowe, 2001.

Orsi, Robert A., editor. *Gods of the City: Religion and the American Urban Landscape.* Religion in North America. Bloomington: Indiana University Press, 1999.

Ouroussoff, Nicolai. "Olympic Stadium with a Design to Remember." *New York Times,* August 5, 2008.

Padovano, Fabio. *The Politics and Economics of Regional Transfers: Decentralization, Interregional Redistribution and Income Convergence.* Studies in Fiscal Federalism and State-Local Finance. Northampton, MA: E. Elgar, 2007.

Palen, J. John, and Bruce London, editors. *Gentrification, Displacement, and Neighborhood Revitalization.* Suny Series in Urban Public Policy. Albany: State University of New York Press, 1984.

Parker, T. H. L. *Calvin: An Introduction to His Thought.* Louisville: Westminster John Knox, 1995.

Parsons, Talcott. *The Social System.* Glencoe: IL, Free Press, 1951.

———, editor. *Theories of Society; Foundations of Modern Sociological Theory.* 2 vols. New York: Free Press of Glencoe, 1961.

Perkins, John. *Beyond Charity: The Call to Christian Community Development.* Grand Rapids: Baker, 1993.

———. *Restoring at-Risk Communities: Doing It Together and Doing It Right.* Grand Rapids: Baker, 1995.

———. *With Justice for All.* Ventura, CA: Regal, 2007.

Perlman, Janice E. *The Myth of Marginality: Urban Poverty and Politics in Rio De Janeiro.* Berkeley: University of California Press, 1976.

Petersen, David L. *Haggai and Zechariah 1–8: A Commentary.* Old Testament Library. Philadelphia: Westminster , 1984.

Pew Forum on Religion & Public Life. "U.S. Religious Landscape Survey: Religious Affiliation: Diverse and Dynamic." February 2008. Washington, DC: Pew Research Center, 2008.

Philip, T. V. *Edinburgh to Salvador: Twentieth Century Ecumenical Missiology: A Historical Study of the Ecumenical Discussions on Mission.* Delhi: CSS & ISPCK, 1999.

Phillips, Tom. Ethnographic Interview with Rainier Vista Multicultural Committee. Field notes edited by David Leong. Seattle, 2009.

Pipkin, John, Mark La Gory, and Judith R. Blau, editors. *Remaking the City: Social Science Perspectives on Urban Design.* Albany: State University of New York Press, 1983.

Postman, Neil. *Amusing Ourselves to Death: Public Discourse in the Age of Show Business.* New York: Penguin, 1986.

Poythress, Vern S. "New Horizons in Hermeneutics: The Theory and Practice of Transforming Biblical Reading." *Westminster Theological Journal* 55/2 (1993) 343–46.

Punter, John. *Design Guidelines in American Cities: A Review of Design Policies and Guidance in Five West Coast Cities.* Town Planning Review Special Studies 2. Liverpool: Liverpool University Press, 1999.

Rad, Gerhard von. *The Message of the Prophets.* Translated by D. M G. Stalker. New York: Harper, 1972.

Rah, Soong-Chan. *The Next Evangelicalism: Freeing the Church from Western Cultural Captivity*. Downers Grove, IL: InterVarsity, 2009.

Rauschenbusch, Walter, and Paul B. Raushenbush. *Christianity and the Social Crisis in the 21st Century: The Classic That Woke Up the Church*. New York: HarperOne, 2007.

Reist, John S., Jr. "New Horizons in Hermeneutics: The Theory and Practice of Transforming Biblical Reading." *Journal of the Evangelical Theological Society* 38/3 (1995) 457–59.

Relph, E. C. *Rational Landscapes and Humanistic Geography*. Totowa, NJ: Barnes & Noble, 1981.

Romanowski, William D. *Eyes Wide Open: Looking for God in Popular Culture*. Grand Rapids: Brazos, 2001.

Roseland, Mark, editor. *Eco-City Dimensions: Healthy Communities, Healthy Planet*. Gabriola Island, BC: New Society, 1997.

Rosenblum, Karen Elaine, and Toni-Michelle Travis, editors. *The Meaning of Difference: American Constructions of Race, Sex and Gender, Social Class, Sexual Orientation, and Disability*. 5th ed. New York: McGraw-Hill, 2008.

Rosin, H. H. "*Missio Dei*": *An Examination of the Origin, Contents and Function of the Term in Protestant Missiological Discussion*. Leiden: Interuniversity Institute for Missiological and Ecumenical Research, 1972.

Roy, Arundhati. *Public Power in the Age of Empire*. New York: Seven Stories, 2004.

Rutba-House. *School(s) for Conversion: 12 Marks of a New Monasticism*. Eugene, OR: Cascade, 2005.

Ryle, Gilbert. *Collected Papers*. 2 vols. New York: Barnes & Noble, 1971.

Saussure, Ferdinand de. *Course in General Linguistics*. Translated by Wade Baskin, edited by Charles Bally and Albert Reidlinger. New York: Philosophical Library, 1959.

Savage, Michael, Alan Warde, and Kevin Ward. *Urban Sociology, Capitalism and Modernity*. 2nd ed. Sociology for a Changing World. New York: Palgrave Macmillan, 2003.

Schaeffer, Francis A. *A Christian Manifesto*. Westchester, IL: Crossway, 1981.

———. *How Should We Then Live?: The Rise and Decline of Western Thought and Culture*. Old Tappan, NJ: Revell, 1976.

Schreiter, Robert J. *Constructing Local Theologies*. Maryknoll, NY: Orbis, 1985.

———, editor. *Faces of Jesus in Africa*. Faith and Cultures Series. Maryknoll, NY: Orbis, 1991.

Schultz, Howard, and Dori Jones Yang. *Pour Your Heart into It: How Starbucks Built a Company One Cup at a Time*. New York: Hyperion, 1997.

Sebeok, Thomas A. *Signs: An Introduction to Semiotics*. Toronto Studies in Semiotics. Toronto: University of Toronto Press, 1994.

Sedmak, Clemens. *Doing Local Theology: A Guide for Artisans of a New Humanity*. Faith and Cultures Series. Maryknoll, NY: Orbis, 2002.

Segundo, Juan Luis. *Liberation of Theology*. Translated by John Drury. Maryknoll, NY: Orbis, 1976.

Shachtman, Tom. *Rumspringa: To Be or Not to Be Amish*. New York: North Point, 2006.

Sharkey, Patrick. "*Neighborhoods and the Black-White Mobility Gap*." Report for the Economic Mobility Project. New York: Pew Charitable Trusts, 2009.

Shaw, Linda. "The Resegregation of Seattle's Schools." *Seattle Times*, June 1, 2008.

Sherman, Robert J. *King, Prophet, and Priest: A Trinitarian Theology of Atonement*. Theology for the Twenty-First Century. New York: T. & T. Clark, 2004.

Sider, Ronald J. *Good News and Good Works: A Theology for the Whole Gospel.* Grand Rapids: Baker, 1999.

Simon, David, and Ed Burns. *The Corner: A Year in the Life of an Inner-City Neighborhood.* New York: Broadway, 1997.

Simpson, Gerry. "From Horror to Hopelessness: Kenya's Forgotten Somali Refugee Crisis," Human Rights Watch Short Reports. New York: Human Rights Watch, 2009.

Smith, Glenn. "Exegesis of a City." *Lausanne World Pulse,* September 2006, 44–46.

———. "Towards the Transformation of Our Cities/Regions." Lausanne Occasional Paper 37. *2004 Forum for World Evangelization, Pattaya, Thailand.*

Snyder, Howard A. "God's Missionary People: Rethinking the Purpose of the Local Church." *Missiology* 21/3 (1993) 353–54.

Speidel, William C. *Sons of the Profits; or, There's No Business Like Grow Business: The Seattle Story, 1851–1901.* Seattle: Nettle Creek, 1967.

Stackhouse, John G., Jr. *Making the Best of It: Following Christ in the Real World.* New York: Oxford University Press, 2008.

Stapel, Diederik A., and Jerry Suls, editors. *Assimilation and Contrast in Social Psychology.* New York: Psychology Press, 2007.

Storey, John. *Cultural Studies and the Study of Popular Culture.* 2nd ed. Athens: University of Georgia Press, 2003.

Strasser, Hermann, and Susan C. Randall. *An Introduction to Theories of Social Change.* International Library of Sociology. London: Boston Press, 1981.

Sullivan, Shannon. *Living Across and Through Skins: Transactional Bodies, Pragmatism, and Feminism.* Bloomington: Indiana University Press, 2001.

Sztompka, Piotr. *The Sociology of Social Change.* Cambridge, MA: Blackwell, 1994.

Tennent, Timothy C. *Invitation to World Missions: A Trinitarian Missiology for the Twenty-First Century.* Invitation to Theological Studies Series. Grand Rapids: Kregel, 2010.

Thiselton, Anthony C. *New Horizons in Hermeneutics: The Theory and Practice of Transforming Biblical Reading.* Grand Rapids: Zondervan, 1992.

Tiénou, Tite, and Paul G. Hiebert. "Missional Theology." *Missiology* 34/2 (2006) 219–38.

Tillich, Paul. *Theology of Culture.* Edited by Robert C. Kimball. New York: Oxford University Press, 1959.

Tuan, Yi-fu. *Space and Place: The Perspective of Experience.* Minneapolis: University of Minnesota Press, 1977.

Tylor, Edward Burnett. *Anthropology: An Introduction to the Study of Man and Civilization.* New York: D. Appleton, 1881.

Ujvarosy, Steve, editor. *Transforming the City: From Dream to Reality.* International Urban Associates. Chicago: Telchar, 1999.

U.N. Population Fund. "State of World Population 2007: Unleashing the Potential of Urban Growth." New York: UNFPA, 2007.

U.S. General Accounting Office. "HUD's Oversight of Hope VI Sites Needs to Be More Consistent." Report to the ranking minority member, Subcommittee on Housing and Transportation; Committee on Banking, Housing, and Urban Affairs, U.S. Senate. May 2003. GAO-03-555. Washington, DC: GAO, 2003.

U.S. General Accounting Office. "Status of the Hope VI Demonstration Program." Report to the Subcommittee on VA, HUD, and Independent Agencies, Committee on Appropriations, House of Representatives." February 1997. GAO/RCED-97-44. Washington, DC: GAO, 1997.

Van Engen, Charles Edward. "Biblical Perspectives on the Role of Immigrants in God's Mission." *Journal of Latin American Theology* 3/2 (2008) 15–38.

———. *God's Missionary People: Rethinking the Purpose of the Local Church.* Grand Rapids: Baker, 1991.

———. "Mission Defined and Described." Unpublished paper. Pasadena, CA, 2010.

———. *Mission on the Way: Issues in Mission Theology.* Grand Rapids: Baker, 1996.

———. "Mission Theology in the Light of Postmodern Critique." *International Review of Mission* 86/343 (1997) 437–61.

———. "What Is Mission?: Theological Explorations." *International Bulletin of Missionary Research* 25/2 (2001) 91–91.

Van Engen, Charles Edward, and Jude Tiersma. *God So Loves the City: Seeking a Theology for Urban Mission.* Monrovia, CA: MARC, 1994.

Van Gelder, Craig. *Confident Witness—Changing World: Rediscovering the Gospel in North America.* The Gospel and Our Culture Series. Grand Rapids: Eerdmans, 1999.

Van Rheenen, Gailyn. *Contextualization and Syncretism: Navigating Cultural Currents.* Evangelical Missiological Society Series 13. Pasadena, CA: William Carey Library, 2006.

Vanhoozer, Kevin J., Charles A. Anderson, and Michael J. Sleasman, editors. *Everyday Theology: How to Read Cultural Texts and Interpret Trends.* Cultural Exegesis. Grand Rapids: Baker, 2007.

Van Steenwyk, Mark. "Christian Radicalism" community discussion, Mustard Seed Associates, Seattle, 2009.

Vicedom, Georg F. *The Mission of God: An Introduction to a Theology of Mission.* Translated by Gilbert A. Thiele and Dennis Hilgendorf. The Witnessing Church Series. St. Louis: Concordia, 1965.

Volf, Miroslav. *After Our Likeness: The Church as the Image of the Trinity.* Sacra Doctrina. Grand Rapids: Eerdmans, 1998.

Waite, Richard. "Beijing 'Bird's Nest' Stadium Wins Coveted Lubetkin Prize." *The Architect's Journal,* July 15, 2009. Online: http://www.architectsjournal.co.uk/beijing-birds-nest-stadium-wins-coveted-lubetkin-prize/5205134.article.

Walsh, Brian J., and Sylvia C. Keesmaat. *Colossians Remixed: Subverting the Empire.* Downers Grove, IL: InterVarsity, 2004.

Webber, Robert. *The Younger Evangelicals: Facing the Challenges of the New World.* Grand Rapids: Baker, 2002.

Wells, Richard. "Parnells Mini-Mart Parking Lot." *Central District News,* February 20, 2008.

Wenham, Gordon J. *The Book of Leviticus.* New International Commentary on the Old Testament. Grand Rapids: Eerdmans, 1994.

Wentz, Richard E. "Religion in the Secular City: Toward a Post-Modern Theology." *Christian Century* 101/15 (1984) 468–69.

Wesley, John. *The Works of the Reverend John Wesley, A.M.* Edited by John Emory. 7 vols. New York: B. Waugh and T. Mason, 1835.

Wesley, John. *John Wesley's Sermons: An Anthology.* Edited by Albert C. Outler and Richard P. Heitzenrater. Nashville: Abingdon, 1991.

Wessler, Seth. "Race and Recession: How Inequity Rigged the Economy and How to Change the Rules." New York: Applied Research Center, 2009.

Whiteman, Darrell. "Contextualization: The Theory, the Gap, the Challenge." *International Bulletin of Missionary Research* 21/1 (1997) 2–7.

Williams, Raymond. *Culture and Society, 1780–1950.* New York: Columbia University Press, 1958.

———. *Keywords: A Vocabulary of Culture and Society.* New York: Oxford University Press, 1976.

Wilma, David. "Columbia Branch, the Seattle Public Library." *History Link*, September 12, 2008. Online: http://www.historylink.org/_content/printer_friendly/pf_output. cfm?file_id=4057.

Wilson-Hartgrove, Jonathan. *New Monasticism: What It Has to Say to Today's Church.* Grand Rapids: Brazos, 2008.

Wirth-Nesher, Hana. *City Codes: Reading the Modern Urban Novel.* Cambridge: Cambridge University Press, 1996.

Witherington, Ben. *The Acts of the Apostles: A Socio-Rhetorical Commentary.* Grand Rapids: Eerdmans, 1998.

———. *The Gospel of Mark: A Socio-Rhetorical Commentary.* Grand Rapids: Eerdmans, 2001.

———. *The Letters to Philemon, the Colossians, and the Ephesians: A Socio-Rhetorical Commentary on the Captivity Epistles.* Grand Rapids: Eerdmans, 2007.

Wolterstorff, Nicholas. *Until Justice and Peace Embrace: The Kuyper Lectures for 1981 Delivered at the Free University of Amsterdam.* Grand Rapids: Eerdmans, 1983.

Woodward, Mikala. *The Rainier Valley Food Stories Cookbook: A Culinary History of the Rainier Valley Going Back 100 Years with Recipes and Stories from Our Multicultural Community.* Seattle: Rainier Valley Historical Society, 2003.

World Council of Churches. "History of World Mission and Evangelism." Online: http:// www.oikoumene.org/en/who-are-we/organization-structure/consultative-bodies/ world-mission-and-evangelism/history.html.

Wright, Christopher J. H. *The Mission of God: Unlocking the Bible's Grand Narrative.* Downers Grove, IL: InterVarsity, 2006.

Wright, N. T. *Simply Christian: Why Christianity Makes Sense.* San Francisco: HarperSanFrancisco, 2006.

Yinger, John. *Closed Doors, Opportunities Lost: The Continuing Costs of Housing Discrimination.* New York: Russell Sage Foundation, 1995.

Yoder, John Howard. *The Politics of Jesus: Vicit Agnus Noster.* Grand Rapids: Eerdmans, 1972.

Yunus, Muhammad, and Alan Jolis. *Banker to the Poor: Micro-Lending and the Battle against World Poverty.* Rev. ed. New York: PublicAffairs, 2007.

Zhang, Mei. *China's Poor Regions: Rural-Urban Migration, Poverty, Economic Reform, and Urbanisation.* Routledge Curzon Studies on the Chinese Economy. New York: Routledge, 2003.

Zinn, Howard. *A People's History of the United States.* New York: Harper, 1980.

Author Index

Subject Index

adaptation, 158–60
anthropology, 15, 26–27, 96, 110,
  156–58, 160–63, 175

Catholicism, 28, 61, 87, 135, 159
Christendom, 43–44, 57, 64, 79–81,
  85, 87, 93
Christian Realism, 53, 55–61, 79
Civil Rights, 13, 103, 186, 188–91
civilization, 26, 153, 160–62, 168
Columbia City, 13–14, 121, 126–30,
  142
commodities, 17, 51, 90–91, 145
community development, 103, 117–
  18, 205, 213, 223, 225–26
creation, 35–38, 42, 51, 53, 71, 87,
  92, 112, 135, 140, 181, 203,
  206

dialectical, 6, 32, 148, 157, 159, 219,
  222
downward mobility, 47, 50–51, 89,
  136, 148, 196
dwell, 37, 77, 93, 95, 133, 136–37,
  140, 208

ecclesiology, 40–44, 93, 222–23,
  226, 228
education, 1–2, 18, 88, 227
embodiment, 32–38, 53, 58–59, 72,
  83, 87, 148, 156, 172, 214,
  222–24
empire, 48, 49, 53, 65–67, 71,
  79–88, 91–94, 147, 198, 204

ethnography, 6, 16, 99, 102–3, 109,
  122, 162–63, 169, 175

foreigners, 69, 75–76, 139, 145, 206

generosity, 91–94, 145–46, 226–27
gentrification, 19–20, 124–30,
  141–47, 194–96, 213, 217
geography, 13, 29, 45, 97, 101–6,
  180, 184, 190–91, 206

hermeneutics, 27, 97, 110–13, 172
hesed, 71

immigrant, 17, 18, 20, 116, 139,
  143, 185, 224
indigenization, 158–60

Jubilee, 144–48

liberation, 6, 55, 65, 80, 141, 151,
  217

methodology, 5–6, 106, 157, 177
mishpat, 69–71, 26
mobility, 3, 13, 47, 50–52, 81, 89,
  136, 148, 184, 195–96, 204
monasticism, 79, 84–89, 94

orphans, 69–71, 76, 77, 137, 139,
  206

pluralism, 2, 36, 66, 157, 184, 203
postmodernism, 26, 64, 106

Scripture Index

www.ingramcontent.com/pod-product-compliance
Lightning Source LLC
Chambersburg PA
CBHW071849270326
41929CB00013B/2157